MW00474312

MAJOR FIGURES IN SPANISH AND LATIN AMERICAN LITERATURE AND THE ARTS

Major Figures in Spanish and Latin American Literature and the Arts will publish comprehensive books on canonical authors and artists from any period, adhering to a variety of approaches, but generally following the form of a literary biography. Grounded in thorough and original scholarship, and written in a jargon-free style, the books should be accessible to the educated nonspecialist.

DELMIRA AGUSTINI, SEXUAL SEDUCTION, AND VAMPIRIC CONQUEST

Cathy L. Jrade

Yale

UNIVERSITY

PRESS

New Haven and London

Published with assistance from the
Mary Cady Tew Memorial Fund.

Yale University Press books may be purchased in
quantity for educational, business, or promotional use.
For information, please e-mail sales.press@yale.edu
(U.S. office) or sales@yaleup.co.uk (U.K. office).

Set in Baskerville and Bulmer type by
Tseng Information Systems, Inc.
Printed in the United States of America.

Library of Congress Cataloging-in-Publication Data
Jrade, Cathy Login.
Delmira Agustini, sexual seduction, and vampiric conquest /
Cathy L. Jrade.
p.   cm. — (Major figures in Spanish and Latin American
literature and the arts)
Includes bibliographical references and index.
ISBN 978-0-300-16774-0 (cloth : alk. paper) 1. Agustini, Delmira,
1886–1914 — Criticism and interpretation. I. Title.
PQ8519.A5Z67 2012
861'.62 — dc23   2011040636

A catalogue record for this book is available from the British Library.

This paper meets the requirements of
ANSI/NISO z39.48-1992 (Permanence of Paper).

10 9 8 7 6 5 4 3 2 1

For Ramón, Rachel, and Jonathann

CONTENTS

PREFACE

When I was teaching Delmira Agustini's "Las alas" (The wings) several years ago, I tried to impress upon my class the shattering devastation of the poem's final stanzas. The fall to earth and the melting of the wings seemed to me overwhelmingly heart-wrenching, but these events seemed to hardly have an impact upon my undergraduates. It was not simply that the poet, who had flown so high, who had soared with hope, confidence, and vision, was rendered impotent. The tragedy was the prosaic ordinariness with which Agustini portrays the descent and the acceptance of its apparent inevitability. To make my point I had the students turn to Rubén Darío's "Sonatina," which we had studied earlier. The comparison was striking. The wings in Darío's poem announced the certainty that his poet's voice would be heard, that he would achieve greatness, and that woman would silently facilitate his empowerment. We began to explore why the same image was linked to two such different outcomes. From that moment I became convinced that Agustini's verse concealed a broader, more complex story that I had to pursue.

In the course of my research I came to understand Agustini's profound emotional and artistic attachment to Darío, a creative genius whose work has been the object of my own professional attention for years. I also came to recognize that Agustini is a much more accomplished and dynamic poet than has traditionally been recognized. Critics have acknowledged her daring eroticism, her inventive appropriation of vampirism, her morbid embrace of death and pain, and her startling use of dualities and opposites. But what they have overlooked is how her poetry reflects a search for an alternate language, an imaginative dialogue with Darío's magnificent recourse to literary paternity, and a thoughtful and audacious rejection of social and poetic conventions.

Like all her contemporaries Agustini understood that Darío was the supreme poet of the day. It would be difficult to exaggerate Darío's preeminence among writers. He has been acclaimed as the innovative and revolutionary poet who, through *modernismo,* the movement he named, defined, and headed, changed the course of Spanish poetry. But his work extends beyond modernismo. He is one of the great modern poets in any language and certainly the most important poet of the Spanish language since the seventeenth century.

Agustini sets for herself a daunting task. She takes Darío as her poetic other to seduce, to conquer, and, with him, to produce creative offspring. The story of her endeavor appears in her four volumes of verse and is presented in this book. Its protagonist is the most unlikely of young women in the most surprising of contexts. Protected and prodded, infantilized and thrust into the adult world of publications, Agustini is a bundle of contradictions, one which is not easily untangled in her poetry. Yet the previously unrecognized breadth of her aspiration is truly remarkable. She sets out to rewrite the language of male authority and female passivity, and her achievements are unparalleled. Her verse becomes a model of artistic reimagining and provides a glimpse into the creative shifts that energize poetic production. These groundbreaking endeavors are the focus of my book.

No scholarly work comes into existence without the assistance and support of many individuals and organizations. I am particularly grateful to Roberto González Echevarría, who encouraged me to submit my manuscript to Yale University Press. His scholarship has been a constant source of inspiration, and his confidence in my research and its worth has been a motivational force throughout my career. I am deeply honored that my book is the first in the series that he envisioned.

Roberto, together with my esteemed colleague Enrique Pupo-Walker and the much-missed Andrew Debicki, supported my early research on this topic and my successful application to the National Endowment for the Humanities Fellowship Program. The NEH fellowship allowed me to spend a year researching, writing, and developing the germ of an idea that, as mentioned above, emerged in one of those magical moments that occasionally occur in undergraduate classes. Vanderbilt University has provided not only those opportunities but also the indispensable support of research funds and leaves. Accordingly, I would like to thank Chancellors Gordon Gee and Nick Zeppos, Provost Richard McCarty, and Dean Carolyn Dever for their generous support.

As the project came closer to its final form, other colleagues magnanimously offered to read the manuscript. I welcomed Andrés Zamora's feedback on the first chapter, where I explore some of the same issues related to literary paternity that he had pursued in his book on Clarín. I accepted a greater commitment of time and energy from Christina Karageorgou, my partner in poetry at Vanderbilt. Christina's encouragement and perceptive insights kept me moving forward. My most enthusiastic reader to date is Ana Eire, who, many years ago, happily chose me to direct her dissertation and who has since become both a valued friend and respected scholar. Her generous and enthusiastic reports on the entire manuscript were a tonic to my soul.

The renewal of my contact with Alejandro Cáceres was a fortunate coincidence. Alejandro was a graduate student at Indiana University when I was a young professor there. When I started working on Agustini, I came across his articles and his editions of her poetry in both Spanish and English. I contacted him, and he immediately volunteered to help me in any way possible. His assistance has been immeasurable. He sent me his microfilm of the Agustini collection, and he put me in contact with individuals who have provided me with materials that appear in this book. María Teresa Silva, an independent scholar on Agustini, Virginia Friedman of the Biblioteca Nacional de Uruguay, and its director general, Carlos Liscano, have all facilitated my access to the documents and photographs published here, materials that add a revealing dimension to this study.

Because I believe that the issues of artistic appropriation and poetic re-castings I explore through Agustini's poetry are relevant to scholars in many other fields, I opted to include English translations of the poems I discuss. Since Cáceres's bilingual edition offers only a selection of her work, I undertook the challenging task of translating all the poems discussed and of rendering Agustini's poetically idiosyncratic Spanish into the most direct prose versions possible. I asked Camille Sutton, a graduate student in my department, to review my work, and I am grateful for the extraordinary care and attention to detail with which she carried out her task.

I end with my greatest debt of gratitude and with the hope that I can express the ways that my husband, Ramón, and our daughter, Rachel, have made this study possible. Rachel is an unfailing source of pride and delight. The love, good humor, and emotional support she and her husband, Jonathann, constantly provide keep my priorities clear and my thoughts unencumbered. Ramón is my caring companion and my devoted friend. His reading of my work is driven by the singular goal that it say what it aspires to say with grace and clarity. He honors my efforts, invites me to take challenges, and encourages me to soar.

CHAPTER ONE

AGUSTINI AND HER WORLD

In an outburst of enthusiasm Luisa Luisi called Delmira Agustini (1886–
1914) "the first woman poet of America" (169). Taken with Agustini's imaginative power and groundbreaking alterations to *modernista* discourse, Luisi,
like many of her contemporaries, was ready to overlook earlier women
writers of world-class stature like Sor Juana Inés de la Cruz and Gertrudis
de Avellaneda and to declare the Uruguayan poet the first of her kind in
Spanish America. This type of sweeping response to Agustini's poetry was
not untypical, for Agustini combined a creative rewriting of modernista
tropes with an aggressively sexualized perspective never before found in
texts written by Spanish American women. The eroticism of her verse
enhanced and fed into the speculation that swirled around her tragically
premature demise at the hands of her ex-husband, whom she had taken as
a secret lover. Yet all the while she maintained the incongruous representation of herself as "la Nena" (the little girl).

On the public level Agustini played the part of the dutiful, infantilized
young woman who abided by the staunchly paternalistic, conservative expectations of her class and gender. She acted out the role common among
her contemporaries, who, according to José Pedro Barrán, understood

their femininity to be "a mixture of equal doses of childishness, virtue, and romanticism" (*Historia de la sensibilidad* 153).[1] On the private level and in her writing, however, she decided to take full advantage of the liberties that were being heralded by diverse advocates of a more open and liberal society. She attempted to operate on an equal footing with the men around her who were freeing themselves and their writings from traditional sexual limitations and, even more daringly, to respond to their language with her own, feminized discourse.[2] By boldly assuming she could claim the same rights and freedoms as a man in her behavior and in her writing, she broke expectations, pushed aside barriers, and, whether she intended to or not, staked out a linguistic and imaginative space for women and women poets. The internal contradictions that appear throughout her poetry as well as the paradoxical way in which she chose to live reflect the multifaceted dynamics that were at work in the Uruguay of the end of the nineteenth century. For those with a more traditional point of view unwilling or unable to recognize the complexity of her endeavor, she became "the most problematic figure of Uruguayan literature . . . and probably of Spanish American poetry" (Silva, *Pasión* 7).[3]

The divergent forces that came to play a central role in the shocking originality of Agustini's verse, her deliberate proliferation of masks, and her scandalous life and death (all of which have fascinated casual readers, serious scholars, and creative writers alike) were part and parcel of her immediate milieu.[4] Though often contradictory, if not restrictive and punishing, in nature, these forces had a direct impact on the way she came to formulate the language of desire from a woman's point of view. Understanding the often subtle but far-reaching implications of the dominant patriarchal and modernista rhetoric of the day, Agustini developed an original way of expressing her own conflicted attitudes toward sexual and artistic equality—an elusive option which appeared to be promised by contemporary debates.[5] To this end she reconfigured from a woman's standpoint the male language of literary paternity through which she was able to assert her personal and poetic passions.

In broad terms the focus of my book is this hitherto unobserved rebellious and imaginative contribution to Spanish American poetry. I will show that poems that have often been read as presenting an intrepidly erotic stance are laced with innovative declarations of poetic goals. More specifically, I will map out how Agustini at first reenvisions the linguistic models she finds in the poetry of *modernismo*'s principal figure, namely, Rubén Darío, converting him in the process into her poetic foil and the male other of her verse. Darío becomes, in this manner, both person and poetry; he becomes the one to seduce, to conquer, and the one with whom she will "breed" the new race of poets to which she refers in her later collections.

In truth, the entire Uruguayan Generation of 1900, of which Agustini was a younger member, was influenced by Darío's writings and the vision he presented for Spanish American literature. In his early study of this group of writers, Emir Rodríguez Monegal clarifies the numerous social and literary factors that gave it its cohesion. Above all else, however, he emphasizes the impact of Darío's work. He links the consistency of concerns, language, and style among this community of writers to Darío's writings and iconic presence. Under "Experiences of the Generation," he states, "For this group the fundamental experience was *Modernismo*. The change in sensibility to life . . . was explicitly indicated by the content of [Darío's] *Prosas profanas* and *Los raros* (both from 1896). The young writers of the Generation of 1900 captured this change and noted in their first works their desire for new formulas, for new routes, for new teachers" (48–49).[6] Under "Leadership," he writes, "In the strictest sense there is no leader in the group, which on the flip side is perfectly in accord with the cult of personality, with the anarchic individualism, of *Modernismo*. There is, on the other hand, a model or paradigm for which the writers of the group oscillated between complete acceptance and conscious distancing: Rubén Darío" (52).[7]

Agustini's poetry includes both acceptance and rejection. She patterns much of her early work on key texts that had already become canonical by the time she began to write. Yet even in *El libro blanco (Frágil)* (The white book [fragile]), her first collection, one senses a struggle with Darío's power, the patriarchal perspective implicit in all his work, and his narrowly defined view of woman. As a result, the other that I identify with Darío is an ensemble. He is this imposing figure, this erotically charged image of artistic supremacy and sexual discourse, and the human face given to the modernista movement. As Agustini's work matures (toward the end of the tragically short seven-year period in which she wrote her best work), Darío recedes and turns into a vague, ghostlike figure who haunts her poetic imagination. At times she relegates him to the past, to winter, and to a rigid iciness, converting her early, timid allusions to usurpation into dramatic and organic metaphors in which she becomes the new source of fruitful reproduction. At other times, her struggle with his imposing presence turns into a sadomasochistic vision of erotic entanglement in which she alternately injures or is injured.[8]

These images startled her contemporaries, who for the most part maintained the strongly traditional and conservative perspective common to turn-of-the-century Spanish America. Quite surprisingly, however, Agustini's family and her immediate social circumstances provided the support that made her impressive breakthroughs possible.[9]

Delmira was born on October 24, 1886, to Santiago Agustini and María Murtfeldt in Montevideo, Uruguay. Agustini's father, a young, prosperous merchant, had inherited a sizeable fortune from his parents, who were French immigrants. Agustini's mother was an Argentinian of German descent known for her strong will and domineering personality. This financially comfortable family provided a propitious setting for the precocious, beautiful young poet. Their affluence is displayed in the two photographs of Agustini as well as the one of her wedding included here (see figs. 1–3). The family lived in the heart of the newly planned and constructed downtown section of town, still called La Ciudad Nueva (The new city). They were surrounded by daily reminders of Uruguay's considerable wealth and sense of well-being as buildings and plazas in the grand style of European capitals appeared around them.[10] This optimism about the future was translated into a heady willingness to break with the past and to chart new social and cultural territory.

Agustini reaped the benefits of these exciting times. In an unpublished letter, she claims to have learned to read, write, and even compose verses by the age of three and to have published her first poems at twelve (qtd. in Larre Borges 19). These endeavors were encouraged by her parents, who supplied her with a private room as well as the uninterrupted time she needed for her literary pursuits. Her father is known to have recopied her poetry, which she often set down at night and with considerable disorder and abandon (see figs. 7–10).[11] Though they indulged Agustini's independent stance with regard to goals and undertakings, they maintained a conventional lifestyle and controlled, or thought they controlled, her interaction with the outside world. While a few young women of Montevideo had begun to study at the university after attending high school and receiving diplomas, all of Agustini's education was home based. As noted by Clara Silva, her primary teacher was her mother, from whom she received all basic instruction. She also took classes in piano, painting, and French.[12]

Though one might assume that home schooling was unique to Agustini, it was actually common among the Generation of 1900. Both Rodríguez Monegal and Carlos Real de Azúa emphasize the degree to which this group of authors was self-taught. Rodríguez Monegal finds this point worthy of elaboration: "A strongly characteristic trait of this group is that (with the exception of Vaz Ferreira) its participants did not belong to the university community. On another occasion, I have underscored this divorce, indicating that the members' links with the University were weak and uncertain. In effect, the majority of them never earned a university degree. . . . At the end of the century there flourished a culture that was distinct from the university culture and that was acquired patiently and laboriously by reading, with enthusiasm and distractions at the table of a café, and in the exalted atmosphere of literary circles. The writers of the Generation of 1900 were in reality self-taught" (45).[13]

By 1902 Agustini had begun to publish in *La Alborada* (Daybreak), a local magazine, and by 1903 she had been placed in charge of its society pages, a task she executed under the fashionable pseudonym Joujou. Because of her youth and her gender, she attracted a fair amount of attention and celebrity. In 1907, at the age of twenty-one, she published her first book of verse, *El libro blanco (Frágil)*. Three years later *Cantos de la mañana* (Songs of the morning) appeared. From this point forward, she gained ever-greater prestige even as the tensions between her image as la Nena and her increasingly more sexual poetry drew commentary, if not notoriety.

During her late teens and early twenties Agustini developed deep friendships with a number of renowned artists of the day.[14] Those who played a prominent role in her life were Manuel Medina Betancort, Alberto Zum Felde, André Giot de Badet, Ángel Falco, Roberto de las Carreras, and, perhaps most significantly, Manuel Ugarte, who, according to Rodríguez Monegal, was the real-life object of desire in much of her erotic poetry.

Combining good looks, wealth, and literary talent, Ugarte was, according to Rodríguez Monegal, "the closest thing that Delmira had to a model of an authentic and exotic prince of poetry. Her imagination soon weaves around him a fabric of passions" (*Sexo* 60).[15]

Some epistolary remnants of these friendships are extremely revealing. Larre Borges refers to a letter that de las Carreras wrote to Agustini as evidence of her need to communicate with those she believed shared her affinities and were in essence kindred spirits (24). Agustini's daring and her desire to find support and companionship among those who made up the predominantly male artistic circles of the day is further demonstrated by the letter she wrote to Darío shortly after meeting him in Montevideo in July of 1912. Because of the multiple implications of what she tells him, I quote the letter in its entirety:

> Forgive me if I bother you one more time. Today I have achieved a moment of calm in my eternal and painful state of excitation. And these are my saddest times. During them I arrive at an awareness of my insensibility. I do not know if your neurasthenia has ever reached the level of mine. I do not know if you have ever looked insanity in the face and have fought with it within the anguished solitude of a hermetic soul. There is no, there cannot be any, more horrible sensation. And the yearning, the immense yearning to ask for help against all—against my very self above all else—from another martyred soul suffering the same martyrdom. Perhaps your will, of necessity stronger than mine, will not allow you ever to understand the distress caused by my weakness in struggle with so much horror. In such a case, if you were to live one hundred years, life would not give you enough time to laugh at me—if, that is, Darío can laugh at anyone. But if by some morbid affinity you are able to perceive my spirit, in the whirlwind of my insanity, you will have my most profound and affectionate compassion that you could ever feel.
>
> Think that I no longer have the hope of death, because I imagine it full of horrible lives. And the right to dream has been denied me almost since birth. And the first time my insanity floods out of control it is before you. Why? No one could be more imposing upon my shyness. How can I make you believe in it, you who only know the valor of my thoughtlessness? Perhaps because I recognized in you more divine essence than in all the human beings I have dealt with until now. And therefore more tolerance. At times my daring scares me; at time (why deny it?) I reproach the disaster of my

pride. It is like a beautiful statue broken into pieces at your feet. I know that such a tribute is worthless to you, but I cannot make it greater. In the middle of October I plan to get admitted into a sanatorium for my neurosis; from there, for good or ill, I will leave in November or December in order to marry. I am resolved to throw myself into the cowardly abyss of marriage. I do not know: perhaps happiness waits for me at the end. Life is so strange! Do you wish to let fall upon a soul that perhaps recedes forever a single fatherly word? Do you want to write me one more time, even though it may be last, only to tell me that you do not despise me? (*Correspondencia íntima* 43)[16]

While this piece of correspondence has been offered as proof that Agustini's marriage was doomed even before it began, it also underscores the special bond she had created, at least in her own mind, with Darío. She sees them sharing the same attitudes, demons, and suffering. They are united in their struggle with the torment of poetic obligations, martyrs to a higher calling. She appeals to him in an ambivalent declaration of timidity and pride, insecurity and boldness, and she presents herself as an uncertain reflection of his "divine" spirit, a quality that she objectifies in her poetry. Equally important, however, is how the letter reveals the different levels on which Agustini operated. She was a proud, audacious poet writing to the most important poet of the day; she was a child asking for advice; she was also a disaffected woman profoundly unhappy with the script she had resigned herself to follow.

Assuming the role of a rebellious intellectual reluctant to limit her options to the conventional and bourgeois alternative of marriage, she presents the decision to marry Enrique Job Reyes more as a product of social expectations than as a response to personal desire, and she encourages Darío to save her from the "abyss of marriage." In short, one finds here the contradictory elements that were shaping the identity of women in Uruguay at the beginning of the twentieth century. Despite their newly won freedoms, one finds the ongoing and unrelenting pressure for young women to marry, pressure Agustini was likely to have felt, pressure that was captured by her friend and fellow modernista Julio Herrera y Reissig in his ribald *El pudor. La cachondez* (Modesty. Sexual arousal):

When some young woman because of fickleness rejects a boyfriend (which happens very infrequently) alleging that she does not love him, the mother

with the help of the married women in the family, all come together to per-
suade her that she should accept. Speaking with the strongest of conviction
she tells her: "You do not have experience; you do not know; love comes
later. . . ." Horniness at this point is not misdirected. The young women are
grateful. . . . When they taste that candy, they idolize their husbands. "The
same thing happened to us who advise you," they say. "Recently married
we have learned what love is. Get married, get married as quickly as you
can, my dear! (138)[17]

One might further see in Agustini's inappropriate confession to Darío her
willingness to circumvent the limitations imposed by traditional arrangements. Indeed, the relationship she establishes with Reyes after dissolv-
ing their marriage is testament to Agustini's disinclination to abide by the
social constraints imposed on women of the period.

Agustini ends the letter with a flirtatious flourish, even though she calls
Darío's possible advice paternal. Throughout the letter, but particularly
in this fusion of father and lover, Agustini exposes the tortured tensions
of creative women writing at the end of the nineteenth century. This apprehension does not simply reflect what Harold Bloom has identified as
the "anxiety of influence" that poets feel when dealing with powerful predecessors. Neither is it simply related to the "anxiety of authorship" that
Sandra Gilbert and Susan Gubar have traced in the works of many women
writers. Her language reveals the complexity of her confrontation with the
social and poetic realities that surrounded her.

Just six months after writing her letter to Darío, in February of 1913
Agustini published her third volume of poetry, *Los cálices vacíos* (The empty
chalices). The volume opens with Darío's words of praise, in which he
states, "Of all the women writing poetry today, none has impressed my
spirit as has Delmira Agustini, for her soul without veils and her heart of
flowers" (qtd. in Agustini, *Poesías completas* 223).[18] As much as he might have
wanted to laud Agustini's work, his tribute is unquestionably mitigated by
his language, by his comparing her only to women writers, and by his referring to her as "esta niña bella" (this beautiful girl). In this volume Agustini announced the forthcoming "Los astros del abismo" (The stars of the
abyss), a collection that was eventually published in 1924, ten years after
her death, as *El rosario de Eros* (Eros's rosary).

Despite her success, her independent nature, and the strains that her literary life may have provoked within the context of her more mundane activities, Agustini married Enrique Job Reyes on August 14, 1913, after a five-year engagement (see fig. 3). Reyes, an auctioneer by trade, was completely removed from the intellectual circles she liked to travel in. He is considered by most to have been a respectful, if uninspiring, suitor who held to traditional beliefs about gender roles and honor. In the notes Agustini wrote to Reyes before their wedding, two of which are included here (see figs. 4–5), she too observes the trappings of conventional courtship. Even her childlike pose can be attributed to the sexual stereotypes prevalent at the time. An additional question surrounding the marriage is the issue of whether Reyes was initially well received by the family or if, as indicated by García Pinto, Agustini's mother opposed the relationship from the start (21). Whatever the case, a bitter antagonism developed between Reyes and his mother-in-law after Delmira's departure from their conjugal home on October 6, 1913, one month and twenty-two days after their wedding, because he blamed her mother for her decision to end their marriage. Delmira, with the help of the radically new law underwritten by the liberal regime of President José Batlle y Ordóñez, filed for divorce a few weeks after her return to her parents' residence. Speculation regarding the reasons for the separation and divorce ranges from Agustini's continuing attraction to Ugarte to the "vulgarity" she encountered when living with Reyes.[19]

On July 6, 1914, in a house in which he had rented a room and where, after their divorce, Reyes and Agustini had repeatedly met as lovers, Reyes shot Agustini and then turned the pistol on himself. The murder/suicide has continued to fascinate readers and critics. Most observers hold this turn of events to reflect Reyes's desperation as he faced what might have been Agustini's intention to end their relationship once and for all. What is known with certainty is that she died immediately and Reyes died later in the Hospital Maciel. She was not yet twenty-eight.

It would be difficult to exaggerate how unusual the course of action taken by Agustini was. Divorcing her husband shortly after their wedding constituted a dramatic break with normative behavior, but her decision to take him as a lover afterward can be understood only as a rebellious assertion of independence and entitlement. Though this choice might have remained a secret known only by the family that facilitated their encounters, the tragic conclusion to their liaison exposes the clash of divergent expectations, desires, and values in circulation in the Montevideo of the beginning of the twentieth century. Many of these disparate concepts arrived at Agustini's doorstep in an unusual configuration of national and international forces.

The writers of this period belonged to an intellectual elite that looked beyond regional borders and embraced cultural and literary trends from across the hemisphere and from the other side of the Atlantic. The breadth of these influences is examined by Real de Azúa in his article "Ambiente espiritual del 900" (The spiritual atmosphere of the 1900s), in which he argues that new ideas imported from Europe held the greatest sway. According to him, "European domination was absolute" (20), especially when it came to innovative positions such as those presented by Friedrich Nietzsche, Gustave Le Bon, Peter Kropotkin, Anatole France, Leo Tolstoy, Max Stirner, Arthur Schopenhauer, Enrico Ferri, Ernest Renan, Jean-Marie Guyau, Alfred Jules Émile Fouillée, Charles Darwin, Thomas Huxley, Ludwig Büchner, Ernst Haeckel, Hyppolite Taine, and Émile Zola. These and other international influences appeared most clearly in politics, journalism, and literature, areas that had a direct impact upon each other and upon developments in nineteenth-century Spanish America. A figure like Juana Manuela Gorriti (1818–92), perhaps the most famous woman writer in the Southern Cone of Spanish America during the nineteenth century, epitomizes this phenomenon. Her life and career underscore the international breadth of the intellectuals who would have an impact on younger authors like Agustini. Born in northern Argentina, Gorriti was forced into exile in Bolivia, where she met the man who would become her husband and later the president of that country. After his assassination she moved between Peru and Bolivia, opened schools, taught, and began to publish in newspapers, periodicals, and journals. These activities reflected her two primary concerns, namely, the role and status of the intellectual in the newly independent countries of Spanish America and the participation of women in the emerging national cultures (Masiello, "Introduction" xxvi). She returned to Buenos Aires in 1875, having published in *La Nación*, the most influential Argentinian newspaper of the day. Two years later she started a new cultural review entitled *La Alborada del Plata* (The dawn of the River Plate).

Gorriti gathered around her a wide circle of influential Argentinian women writers, many of whom had traveled extensively in the Western Hemisphere and in Europe. In 1880 she founded *La Alborada Literaria del Plata* (The literary dawn of the River Plate), a second journal with a focus on transnational cultural developments and educational concerns. Francine Masiello has correctly noted that in addressing progress, modernity, and cosmopolitanism Gorriti anticipates key features of the modernista literary movement, the movement to which Agustini belonged. Equally significant is the way her work sought to feminize the move toward modernity (ibid. xxxii–xxxiii). Gorriti represents the broad cultural and specifically feminist influences that would have had an impact on Agustini, and her successes reveal the evolving possibilities that appeared on the horizon for women.[20]

Yet it was another world traveler who had the greatest influence on Agustini's writings. As noted, Rubén Darío (1867–1916), the head of the modernista movement, became the role model not only for Agustini but also for the entire Generation of 1900. Darío traveled extensively throughout the Spanish-speaking world and lived in the major urban centers of Spanish America and in Paris and Madrid. He incorporated in his work the latest tendencies of the French Parnassians and symbolists as well as a love for traditional Spanish verse. Equally significant was his embrace of the great art and literature from across the centuries and from every corner of the globe. Both Gorriti and Darío demonstrate what Roberto González Echevarría has asserted with regard to Latin American literature in general, namely, that its great writers have considered themselves citizens of Western culture and literature, limited neither by their nationality nor by the specifics of their immediate circumstances ("Oye mi son" 10). Even in the somewhat provincial environment of Montevideo, Agustini's perspective was international. The poetry she was reading, the performances she attended, the buildings that were being designed, and the urban development that was under way all reflected what was going on in the great capitals of the world, from Buenos Aires to Paris, Rome, London, New York, and Madrid. Similarly, the sociocultural factors that had the greatest impact upon her were a product of global trends that affected, among other things, long-standing, widely held gender arrangements and patriarchal assumptions.

With these shifts, what were once considered immutable structures within an enduring and divinely ordained social order came under scrutiny. Patriarchy came to be understood as a set of beliefs embedded in a language propagated by men for the benefit of men. Gerda Lerner, in her extensive study, traces the formation of Western patriarchal thought to principal founding texts. She shows how, on the one hand, the Hebrew Bible presented the symbolic devaluing of women in relation to the male divinity, and how, on the other, the works of Aristotle defined women as incomplete and damaged human beings entirely different from men. Through these two central and enduring metaphorical constructs, the subordination of women, according to her, became natural, normal, and invisible in Western civilization (*Patriarchy* 10). By being defined as part of the natural order of existence, patriarchy for the most part escaped both critical examination and censure.[21]

While Lerner's work traces the earliest development of patriarchal domination in the West, Stephanie Merrim shows how these patriarchal paradigms shaped the thinking and discourse of the culture that arrived in Spanish America at the beginning of the colonial period. The response to prevailing beliefs generated by Sor Juana Inés de la Cruz and her female contemporaries in Spain, France, and North America reveals the way in which women over the course of centuries have attempted to find a place for themselves in the inhospitable terrain of patriarchal scorn. In addition, because of their lack of formal schooling and limited knowledge of their own history, these early modern women writers found themselves individually inventing ways of confronting and responding to the "pan-Christian imaginary" of Western culture. These efforts gave rise, as Merrim notes, "to an unceasing, unwitting, almost inevitable, textual sorority between early modern feminists who were unaware of one another" (xxiii). Her metaphor of a "textual sorority" helps explain a phenomenon I will discuss shortly, namely, Agustini's repeated but coincidental recourse to images that occur in the works of earlier and contemporaneous women writers from other parts of the world.

Despite the entrenched nature of patriarchal attitudes, women thinkers like Gorriti were, by the time Agustini came of age, finding ways to alter the social and political landscape of nineteenth-century Spanish America. Since Agustini lived in Montevideo, a city that was simultaneously more socially provincial and more politically liberal than Buenos

Aires, its so-called big sister across the river, she too was affected by the far-reaching shifts that were taking place. As Buenos Aires (and to a lesser extent Montevideo) became an imposing capital of international trade and culture, everyday life began to change. For some, the benefits were evident and immediate. Others, however, were thrown into a harsh new world of capitalist production, commodification, and exploitation.[22] The wealthy and powerful spoke of these transformations in terms of progress, modernization, and the abandonment of outdated and backward ways that plagued the region. Diverse segments of society jockeying for the most advantageous ideological positions led to the erosion of the conservative, hegemonic, and patriarchal premises that had dominated Spanish America for centuries. Along with the arrival of wealth, science, and technology came new ideas about education, trade, language, and women. Along with the steamship, the railroad, the trolley, the dirigible, immunology, analytic chemistry, the telephone, the telegraph, the phonograph, and numerous other scientific and technological advances came progressive beliefs with regard to the nature and role of women. In addition to countless pronouncements about the advantages of educating and employing women, there even appeared the option, as indicated in the study by Real de Azúa, of the elimination of the double standard and the possibilities of free love.

Clear fractures in the dominant beliefs of the day began to appear in articles as early as 1875.[23] For example, the new rational, analytic approach to female sexuality opened possibilities that had never received serious consideration and that remained subversive well into the twentieth century. Writing in 1908, Santiago Locascio states,

> Admitting, as we admit, the equality of the sexes, we cannot deny women the same feelings as men. Once this premise, so important for us, is established, I ask myself: can we deny women the same freedom to multiply their sexual feelings by cohabitating with two or more men? Today don't we, the emanicipators, feel driven by necessity to possess two or more women? Thus, if we admit this, let us also accept as the logic of identical desire that woman can feel.
>
> To contradict this reasoning means that the subject that discusses is still saturated with the old doctrine of the superiority of the male over the unfortunate female.[24]

For many, the model for social change was the United States, which, depending on the perspective taken, was either the enlightened guide or the inspired devil. One of the strong supporters of the ideas coming from the United States was the Peruvian Clorinda Matto de Turner, who raised another strong voice for women's rights in various parts of Spanish America. Perhaps best known as the author of *Aves sin nido* (Birds without a nest), she established several journals throughout her homeland. In Buenos Aires she founded *Búcaro Americano* (American vase) and became the director of the Escuela Comercial de Mujeres, which was created during the last decade of the nineteenth century by the Ministro de Instrucción Pública de la Argentina (Glickman, *Fin del siglo* 26). In *Búcaro Americano* Matto de Turner published articles, some of them her own and some of them written by others, in which the United States is portrayed as a paradigm for the changes that could eventually reach the Southern Hemisphere. One of her pieces honoring women writers from various regions of Spanish America identifies women as "verdaderas heroínas" (true heroines) and describes the progress made in the United States as the raising of "the drawbridge" of opportunities.[25] Another article from 1896, written by Zoila Aurora Cáceres under the pseudonym Eva Angelina, links the United States with the pragmatic and rationalist treatment of women: "The day that the male convinces himself that the enlightened woman, far from being useless for the home, not only elevates it but also extends her advantage to those who surround her, we will have laws that protect us like those of the United States of America."[26]

Besides receiving news of the progress made by women in the United States, writers like Agustini were exposed to ideas that were taking root within Uruguay. In particular, political, social, and economic changes initiated under the presidency of Batlle y Ordóñez (1903–7 and 1911–15) were fertile ground for the development of feminist tendencies. Pablo Rocca underscores the unusual nature of the Uruguayan situation. Comparing Montevideo with the more conservative Buenos Aires, he refers to the Batlle government, especially during its second term, as a natural ally of feminism. Batlle took this stance despite resistance from conservatives and from the Catholic Church. His disregard for the Catholic position on women reflected in part that the Church had been greatly weakened by decades of underground opposition (162). Russell H. Fitzgibbon cites three factors that contributed to the diminished presence of the Catholic Church in Uruguay:

> In the first place, effective Spanish colonization did not begin until the eighteenth century, by which time the religious fervor of the earlier generations and centuries had in considerable measure atrophied. . . . In the second place, the revolutionary period was characterized by a large influx of foreigners, especially English and French, who were either non-Catholic or only nominally Catholic. Third, the large immigration beginning late in the nineteenth century, while it came in great part from Catholic countries, represented social and economic strata which were often of less than fervent attachment to the Church. (231)

Uruguayan anticlericalism was long-standing among the bourgeois, petty bourgeois, and university classes, and it found additional support around 1890 in labor, union, anarchist, and socialist movements (Rocca 163). In addition, as Fitzgibbon explains, Batlle himself contributed to these tendencies, for early on he developed a skeptical attitude toward the Church and its beliefs (213–15). He was, therefore, open to feminist ideas such as those expressed by the influential Domingo Arena, one of the president's closest supporters. Arena became a strong defender of the emancipation of women, who, according to him, had been condemned to marry the first serious suitor to enter their home (Rocca 164). These liberal views were reinforced by other segments of society. Christine Ehrick, who has studied the workers' movement in Montevideo, emphasizes how it produced an anarchist press which sought to address the oppressive situation of women and their need to subvert the bourgeois structure of the family. In response to the limitations imposed on women by traditional marriages, these writers proposed the options of free love and the right of sexual gratification (231).

The Catholic Church did not sit quietly by as these liberal ideas started to take hold. Gerardo Caetano and Roger Geymonat, in the first volume of *La secularización uruguaya (1859–1919)*, show that in an attempt to revitalize its old strengths the Church turned to women, who had traditionally been pillars of support. It did not, however, provide them with new and enabling options. Instead, it reverted to traditional language and reasserted attitudes that reach back to the origins of patriarchy. Women were linked to weakness, frivolity, and emotionality, and they were asked to fulfill the role of loyal wife and mother that has remained virtually unchanged since the publication of Fray Luis de León's *La perfecta casada* (The perfect wife) in 1583. As was the case during the Renaissance, the works that repeated the premises stated by Fray Luis offered a way to incorporate women into the architecture of society and into its male-dominated vision of harmony and order. This harmony and order meant limiting women's options. They were sent into internal exile in the home, their only education was that which would enhance their virtue, and their goodness and sweetness were linked to blind obedience to men, who were given full authority to rule over them (see Merrim xxviii–xxix).

Whether they were the priest, the father, or the husband, these "directors of conscience" had to take charge of women and correct their inherent feminine "defects." Women were to be made acceptable through their subservience to men and by having them control their supposedly natural flaws of impressionability, excessive imagination, and hypersensitivity. They were encouraged to emulate the superior masculine trait of rational thought. *La caridad sacerdotal o Lecciones Elementales de Teología Pastoral* (Priestly benevolence or elementary lessons of pastoral theology) stated, "The virility of a woman is in controlling emotion with reason and giving to her will the nobility that belongs to it. Excessive impressionability and imagination together with an overly developed sensitivity and inferiority relative to mental faculties is the nature of woman. It is wise, therefore, to train her to moderate excess and correct failings" (262–63, qtd. in Caetano 266).[27]

Regardless of how successfully women were able to control their womanly weaknesses, they could never overcome their inherent inferiority and therefore were relegated to positions of subordination, locked within the only proper, presumed natural role for all women who did not embrace a religious vocation, that of obedient wife and mother. A guidebook for religious life published in Montevideo in 1901 demonstrates how little the Church's attitudes regarding proper behavior for a married woman had changed over the centuries:

> Consider if she cares for her family well. If she treats her husband with love and humility. If she loves her children with excessive affection, letting them live according to their whims, excusing them or defending them when their father wants to punish them justly. . . . If she has unjustly resisted her hus-

band and has argued obstinately with him. If she has misspent money on foolishnesses, finery, and impulses. . . . If in her dress, her way of speaking, and acting she has maintained appropriate caution and modesty. If she has wasted time with visits, frivolous conversations, and gossip.[28]

While this restrictive view of women arose, at least in part, as a response to the liberal ideas that emerged toward the end of the nineteenth century (including debates about a woman's right to vote and to seek a divorce), the Church did not oppose other alterations to secular society. On the contrary and somewhat surprisingly, during the second half of the nineteenth and beginning of the twentieth century, the Church supported many of the political and materialistic goals of the ruling and the nascent bourgeois classes. Though there was substantial room for divergent opinions about specific issues, the complex move away from "barbarism" and "disorder" toward "civilization" and "order" (echoing Renaissance goals of establishing a place and purpose for everyone) created a certain degree of overlap between civic and religious ideology and discourse. As Barrán makes clear,

> "Disorder," the essence of sin for Catholics, was, in brief, disobedience against the Father, against God and his rules; "barbarism," the essence of Uruguayan ills for the anticlerical liberals, was, also in brief, disobedience, namely, that of the "savage" to the dictates of "civilization." Church and Bourgeoisie were in agreement about imposing on everyone, including their own constituents, the regulation of their drives and desires, in other words, about creating a type of individual determined by culture and this type of individual ended up tied, in some way, to the mode of production and the dominant sector of society, for which reason the bourgeois imprint was stronger than the ecclesiastical. (23)[29]

Civilization was linked to modernity and, in turn, modernity to science. Though on one level scientific knowledge and discourse challenged the authority of religion, on another they reinforced the traditional social structures and patriarchal designs the Church had supported for centuries. The connection between conventional social structures and scientific innovation translated into a philosophy of order, progress, and free enterprise. In this way, science became, in large part, an ideological tool of the entrenched and fundamentally conservative, self-serving establishment that spoke, somewhat contradictorily, in terms of change and advancement.

The expectation that science would produce modern, civilized societies was a dominant feature of Spanish American political thought during the second half of the nineteenth century and resulted from the impact of ideas, events, and inventions that transcended national boundaries. As Spanish America entered the world economy, members of the ruling classes allied themselves with foreign financiers and investors and sought to modernize their countries through the importation of foreign technology and manufactured goods. In urban centers there developed a perceptible Europeanization of life as the powerful turned their attention to the accumulation of wealth and to the consumption of imported items. Positivism supplied the political ideology that facilitated and justified this trend. While Auguste Comte had developed the foundations of this philosophical system in the hope of reforming society and of improving conditions for all citizens through the positive sciences, in Spanish America it furnished the ruling elites with a new vocabulary to legitimate whatever evils arose as a by-product of national development. It provided a way of accounting for and eliminating undesirable behavior and of imposing order and peace in the pursuit of stability and prosperity. At the same time, it offered the rationale for the ruthless disavowal of those members of society who failed, through no fault of their own, to fit in and to partake of the benefits and wealth of their increasingly modernized economies.

As cracks began to appear on the shining surface of scientific advancement, as the sweeping promises of a brighter future for all began to tarnish, and as the growing prosperity of some brought unruly social dislocations and strife, a sense of crisis developed among both the established authorities and the intellectual elite. The ruling authorities led a push to control acceptability and participation in society. Models were set up to limit behavior deemed injurious to the national good (or at least to the hegemonic powers). Rationality, pragmatism, utilitarianism, progress, and virility were exalted to the detriment of femininity and the multiple qualities linked to it, such as intuition, spirituality, sensitivity, and otherworldliness, which in turn became tied to an array of ills, including effeminacy, weakness, disease, and decay.[30]

For the many disenfranchised, including women, the national goal of advancing from barbarism to civilization had mixed repercussions. While liberal forces struggled to advance the cause of workers, women, and children, much of the debate was couched in the dominant language of order, control, hard work, and moral moderation (Barrán 28–33). Taken to its extreme, this discourse opened the way for constraint and suppression, an outcome that Masiello discusses in *Between Civilization and Barbarism*.[31] As pressures from anarchist and socialist workers and demands by middle- and upper-class women for rights of suffrage and divorce grew, activist women became associated with subversion (7). Even more damaging was the way in which ruling elites, in their attempt to control and channel all divergent forces, identified women and other marginalized factions as morally defective, ill, or mad: "Women were situated in the realm of the irrational, outside the sphere of official discourse, while the state became synonymous with reason and progress" (89).[32]

These conflicting models for women regarding behavior, rights, and language directly influenced Agustini, her life choices, the image she projected in society, and her writing.[33] Her immediate intellectual context, however, was conditioned by the general reaction to the overall crisis of change among Spanish American writers of the second half of the nineteenth century, most of whom joined the ranks of the modernista movement, the title of which underscored their sense of having entered a dramatically new era. They developed a unique language and worldview that reflected the profound tensions they experienced every day.[34] The modernistas accepted the benefits and possibilities modernity provided at the same time that they refused to acknowledge scientific empiricism as the absolute measure of all things, insisting on truths that lay beyond the material realities of existence. They supported progress but abhorred the sociopolitical and cultural problems it engendered. They criticized the mores of the bourgeoisie and ruling classes that encouraged blind acquisition and excess at the same time that they aspired to become fully incorporated into the ranks of the privileged. They voiced, from the vantage point of the great urban centers of Spanish America and Europe, modern dilemmas and angst while they maintained an awareness that, in most cases, the vast majority of their compatriots continued to lead premodern lives. Torn between the reigning faith in science and an enduring fascination with intangible realities, modernistas, like their European, British, and Anglo-American contemporaries, often sought answers that went beyond secular realities. By the same token, however, most were incapable of returning to the unquestioning faith of their ancestors. Their art revealed their ambivalent longing for the ease, elegance, and increasing European-ization of the bourgeoisie and ruling elites at the same time that they, for the most part, cast themselves in the tradition of the great romantic poets, who saw themselves as outsiders and social critics. For all these reasons, failure to recognize the contestatory nature of modernista texts offers a distorted reading of the movement.

Using an artistic and cosmopolitan language that was subsequently at-tacked as elitist, modernistas protested the technological, materialistic, and ideological impact of positivism. They sought to challenge the hege-mony of the economic in modern life and to offer an alternative view of existence that would be more inclusive. Their aim was to produce a uniquely Spanish American literature in which the goals of language were dual, that of revealing profound realities concealed by the inflexibilities of scientific methods and the stultification of everyday life and that of provid-ing insights into politics, power, and national identity. Writing in opposi-tion to the dominant bourgeois perspective, these authors actively sought to open the door to the possibilities of the irrational and the spiritual as well as the beautiful, the artistic, and the antiutilitarian. Recourse to the stories and language of erotic desire became an essential feature of this tendency. It served to challenge traditional discursive, conceptual, and moral limits, it offered a defiant view of personal freedom, it provided a critique of civilization, most specifically, the imposition of set rules of order, rationality, and practicality, and it even promised access to a divine transcendence.[35] The fact that modernismo arose as a confrontation with and response to modernizing forces that swept across Spanish America as it entered the world economy is central to untangling the vibrancy and complexity of Agustini's verse. It is modernismo's own sexually charged, contestatory discourse that afforded the means by which Agustini set out to explore, alter, and undermine some of its essential features.

Carla Giaudrone, in her "Deseo y modernización: el modernismo ca-nónico esteticista en el fin de siglo uruguayo" (Desire and modernization: Canonical aesthetic modernismo in the Uruguayan fin de siècle), focuses on the role of sexual desire and language in modernismo's—especially Uruguayan modernismo's—ability to open cultural spaces for those ex-cluded from social involvement. She writes,

The other, perceived as a threat to hegemonic power, should by necessity be controlled, nullified. With that goal, starting in the second half of the nineteenth century, cultural models for women and citizens are created with the aid of science and religion. . . . The ensemble of these marginal identities [women, immigrants, homosexuals] led to the weakening of masculine supremacy within the apparatus of power and of virility as one of the essential causes for its domination. The "modern" state was not willing to leave room for any desire other than the masculine.

Modernismo, on the other hand, from a position that is expressed in opposition to the bourgeois Philistinism ensconced in power, makes the other visible again, offers him a space, even if it is conditional. . . . Similarly, the sexualized nature of modernista writing, especially in Uruguay, invites everyone equally to look at and participate in such attractive margins. Against the tide of existing prejudices in a society that denies sexuality, a writing of intense erotic content emerges and opens for women and homosexuals, two "peripheral sexualities," a means of artistic expression. (260)[36]

As much as this struggle over the language of personal and national self-representation resulted from the disruptive inroads of modern life, recourse to the stories and imagery of sexual desire to challenge or affirm social conventions was not new. As Octavio Paz observes in *Los hijos del limo* (The children of the mire), the exaltation of what they held to be the natural, unaltered order of things, especially sexuality, became for many romantics a means by which they formulated a moral and political critique of civilization (56–60). Similarly, modernismo's adaptation and incorporation of erotic tales and sexually charged language provide insight into its contestatory positions. The problem, however, is that the supposedly natural order of things is not always natural. As much as modernismo as a movement welcomed openness and inclusiveness and was disposed to reject rigid limitations and exclusionary perspectives, the majority of its practitioners were men, and its overall tenor was overtly male and solidly patriarchal. This perspective, which had been embedded in daily life, social arrangements, language, art, and even the concept of artistic production, is a social construct that operated as a natural, immutable, invisible force for centuries. As a result, despite the movement's rebellious spirit, modernista views on women and on the privileges of men tend to fall squarely within established, traditional patterns.

In their groundbreaking study *The Madwoman in the Attic,* Sandra M. Gilbert and Susan Gubar trace the roots of the patriarchal construction of authorship back to the origins of Western literary civilization, beginning with the notion that the writer "fathers" his text just as God fathered the world.[37] Since "God the Father" both engenders the cosmos and writes the Book of Nature, both tropes are united by a single act of creation. More specifically, the text's author is a father whose pen is an instrument of generative power like his penis; his pen's power, like that of his penis, is also capable of creating a posterity to which he lays claim (4–6). After examining this thesis in detail, Gilbert and Gubar turn their attention to English-language writers of the nineteenth century, that is, to those writers who are most immediately contemporaneous to Agustini and the other major modernista authors.

Sexual metaphors are a constant of Hispanic texts as well. Andrés Zamora Juárez has shown how these images infiltrated the literary discourse of Spain during the same period and how they came to structure realist fiction. The following passage highlights how he extends the arguments made by Gilbert and Gubar regarding literary paternity. Not only is the author always male, his imposition of authority also includes the feminization of characters: "Sexual metaphors that shape the poetics of the realist novel contain all the elements needed for the commission of incest: the author is seen in the figure of the authoritarian and all-powerful father; the character appears as a child of flesh and blood; virility is conceived as one of the essential features in the execution of authorship; writing is equated with coitus; finally, the character, man or woman, is unfailingly feminized" (55).[38]

Within this metaphorical universe the creative force is consistently male, and women are relegated to a passive receptivity. In other words, if the dominant Western tradition envisions man to be the active, inseminating force, it similarly holds woman to be the submissive object of his attention and energies or, as Gubar notes in a separate study, man holds the pen-penis that writes on the virgin page. As a result, woman in this worldview is always a "secondary object lacking autonomy, endowed with often contradictory meaning but denied intentionality" ("The Blank Page" 77). The figures that emerge from these conventions (Eve, Minerva, Sophia, Galatea, and all their descendants) are crafted by, from, and for men and expose their desires, aspirations, fears, and insecurities regarding their abilities to control both their own creations and women as well (Gilbert and Gubar 12). These patterns are embedded in modernista texts—as best represented by Darío's writing—and underscore the conceptions of woman, and therefore of herself, that Agustini, like many other women authors throughout the nineteenth and twentieth centuries, had to confront in order to write herself into modernista discourse.[39]

What might surprise the newcomer to modernista discourse is just how consistently Darío and his male colleagues turned to these gender-based metaphors to express their literary goals and to assert their natural authorial authority. For Darío this identification starts with the search for the soul of language and its musical nature. As he states in "Palabras liminares" (Opening words) of *Prosas profanas,* "Since each word has a soul, in each verse there is, in addition to verbal harmony, an ideal melody. Many times the music comes only from the idea" (180).[40] The reference to the soul of language implies a body, which, in Darío's poetry, is female. For language to become poetry it must be impregnated with ideas that are in essence "an ideal melody." This image of poetic creation permeates the views of woman and sexuality expressed throughout *Prosas profanas* and is nowhere clearer than in "Sonatina" (187–88), a poem that epitomizes the entrenched male-centered perspective against which Agustini wrote.

At the end of "Sonatina" the sad princess is given hope that she will attain happiness, love, life, and salvation with the impending arrival of a special beloved. She is told this important information by her fairy godmother, who begins her announcement of "good news" with the telling words "—Calla, calla, princesa" (Hush, hush, princess). The princess is told not to speak as she waits for her gentleman suitor to arrive. The knight who arrives on his winged steed, victor of Death, is more than the proverbial Prince Charming who appears in time to revive the lovesick princess. The linking of the hero/savior with Pegasus, the horse of the Muses, identifies the hero as an artist. His ability to lead his love, and his readers, out of the imperfect present into a paradisiacal future recalls the messiah-like attributes that become a recurrent feature of Darío's poetry about poetic responsibility.[41]

The poet/hero's attributes also affirm long-established sexual divisions. The male hero/poet/savior that arrives at the end of "Sonatina" has all the power. The female consort of the male creator, poetic language, must sit and wait. Love and union with woman allow the poet to carry out his supreme destiny. She offers; he executes. The princess serves as a female other, a type of *muse,* who makes possible the creative eloquence of the male voice. She allows him to fulfill his role as savior by turning language into *music*.[42]

Though the princess's role is crucial, she is above all else weak and passive, unable to achieve her goals without her male savior. Her spiritual longing is noble and praiseworthy, yet, without the aggressive male, she is doomed to languish with unfulfilled desires. Thus, reasserting traditional sex roles, Darío's female can achieve nothing without her male poet/savior, who sets forth to conquer the world as assertively as any warrior.

Darío constantly returns to the image of the sexual partner with or through whom he is able to create, for Darío is constantly writing about writing. This simple but powerful observation is essential to understanding not only modernismo but also Agustini's response to the dominant modernista discourse. Agustini also constantly writes about writing, even when she appears to be writing about other topics, for, as noted by González Echevarría with regard to José Martí's "Amor de ciudad grande" (Love of the big city), each modern work reflects upon itself and embodies its own goals and standards: "Each book of modern poetry, each modern poem, formulates its own poetics, precisely because Modernity has abandoned poetics as an autonomous category that delineates a language and dictates its rules" ("Martí" 27).[43] Indeed, as will become clear throughout this book, Agustini's erotic language addresses her passion for poetry as much as or more than it speaks to her sexual desire. It becomes a poetics in which she answers the language of male authority and literary paternity and in which she forges metaphors of insight. Through her writing she fights what might have been her natural inclination to defer to Darío's imposing vision of male superiority and female passivity. At the same time, these very acts of willful violation of discursive norms may have stirred those hungers deep within her that patriarchal dictates would have sought to suppress. The intensity of the passions aroused has tended to hold the critics' attention, leading them to define Agustini's verse in terms of erotic experiences or sexual politics.

That Agustini strives to find a way to be a modernista without relinquishing herself to a type of secondariness—either as a disciple or as a poet writing in the role of a subservient female—is consistent with the goals of modern authors in general. Scholars as diverse as Paz and Bloom have emphasized the modern writer's constant struggle to be original, that is, to break away from models, patterns, and traditions. As a woman writer, however, Agustini must battle not only against the power of strong, influential predecessors but also against the inhibiting visions of female inferiority, docility, and purity. The similarity of concerns that Agustini shared with other women is evident in the degree of overlap between her work and that of others, including those from other cultures. In their response to the sexualized language of domination one finds the type of coincidence that developed among early modern feminists and is studied by Merrim (xxiii). As much as they sought to reimagine the erotic discourse of authorial authority, these women struggled against the patriarchal tradition that would stifle women and limit their options. They fought for self-assertion in the face of an overwhelming tradition in which they were the pure, selfless, empty ciphers of male authorial desire, a tradition that doomed them to silence, to death, and, if they were good enough, to heaven. They felt compelled to address the discursive conventions that made a woman's choice to write, live, and love freely a presumptuous, castrating, even monstrous act. Women writers felt so straitjacketed that any move away caused pain and injury. They were so muzzled that any effort to speak turned their mouths into hideous wounds (see Gilbert and Gubar 43–44). For this reason, Agustini, like her contemporaries, imagines writing as violent and injurious. She sees herself bleeding and staining the white page of creative production. The alternative is to become a monster of disobedience, like the many female freaks who stare back at women artists from the pages of patriarchal writings. From the traditional male point of view, if they dare to break free from the conventional range of options to which they have been relegated, they become some sort of terrifying creature that embodies male fears of female dissipation and autonomy (see Gilbert and Gubar 25–27 and Dijkstra).

According to Gilbert and Gubar, women writers, in order to enter the literary arena, first had to confront these portrayals of who they are. Drawing upon the language of the texts they study, Gilbert and Gubar contend that, before the writer can journey through the looking glass toward literary autonomy, she must come to terms with the images on the surface of the glass, with, that is, those mythic masks of angel or monster that male artists have fastened over her human face both to lessen their dread of her supposed inconstancy and to control her more thoroughly.

This begins to explain why reflections and reflective surfaces appear throughout Agustini's work. She is reflected in lakes, mirrors, and eyes, for she too strains to see herself in the looking glass of male discourse. These reflections are about the way she seeks to come to know and define herself. Looking into the mirror/page, she attempts to make sense of the interplay of her desires, her outside self, and the world around her.[44] In the process, she takes control over the monstrous representations of women by converting them into a tool of her own imaginative power. The vampires, serpents, and free-floating heads of her poetry are assertive appropriations of and reinventions of antifemale attacks. Though she boldly takes possession of her own image, converting the negative into a sign of independence and power, she still suffers severe aftereffects. As she tears herself away from the limitations that had been set for her, she imagines herself fragmented and torn to pieces by the pursuit of independence and vitality. At the same time, however, she speaks up and declares her sense of self and voice by rewriting Darío, appropriating the iconic swan of modernismo, and activating, energizing, and sexualizing the passive, domesticated, subservient female figures of his poetry.[45] The erotic force and overtones of literary disobedience extend into other areas of life, generating the language of lust and longing tinged with despair and pain that made her poetry so revolutionary.

The question that emerges from Agustini's poetry is whether one can define the source of her torment. Are her anguish, suffering, and injuries the consequence of her confrontation with and separation from the dominant modernista other (specifically Darío)? Do they result from her fight against the implicit and explicit beliefs that women have no right to create, and any attempt to do so is monstrous? Or are they the product of her struggle, common to writers of both sexes, to find the right words, given the rigidity and the inflexible physicality of language? In their effort to respond to these types of questions, Gilbert and Gubar pitted themselves against Bloom and his imposing theory regarding the "anxiety of influence." They set out to correct Bloom's heavy emphasis on the relationship of fathers and sons, which they believe does not apply equally to women:

> On the one hand . . . the woman writer's male precursors symbolize authority; on the other hand, despite their authority, they fail to define the ways in which she experiences her own identity as a writer. More, the masculine authority with which they construct their literary personae, as well as the fierce power struggles in which they engage in their efforts of self-creation, seem to the woman writer directly to contradict the terms of her own gender definition. Thus the "anxiety of influence" that a male poet experiences is felt by a female poet as an even more primary "anxiety of authorship"—a radical fear that she cannot create, that because she can never become a "precursor" the act of writing will isolate or destroy her. (48–49)

While their work provided a productive groundwork for later studies, Bloom's "anxiety of influence" and Gilbert and Gubar's "anxiety of authorship" leave some patterns unexplained, especially in those cases, like that of Agustini, in which a central metaphor is the sexual seduction of an older man by a younger woman. In the recent *Lot's Daughters*, Robert M. Polhemus explores the depths of signification attached to this scenario.

Polhemus, like the authors of *The Madwoman in the Attic*, considers the father–son patterns represented by the Oedipal theories of Sigmund Freud and Bloom to be of limited use in elucidating the development of father–daughter and older men–younger women relations in modern culture. He proposes instead that the story that structures "the high drama of the change in the status of women and the liberation of female aspirations" beginning in the nineteenth century is that of Lot and his daughters (4). The myth emphasizes the transfer of authority from the corrupt established order to a new generation led by women, who must "give up the past with its memories to which [they are] wed . . . and make [themselves] ready, under any circumstances, to give birth to the future" (5). While, for the most part, the shocking tale of survival through incest between father and daughter has been driven underground, the need to liberate oneself from the failings and constraints of the past is evident in the much-recalled figure of Lot's unfortunate and foolish wife, who is turned into a pillar of salt for looking back.[46]

Both aspects of the story come into play in the struggle by women to find a voice in patriarchal society. Because the Lot story addresses the conflicts, transgressions, and sexual longings related to the control of culture, it is a useful backdrop to exploring the works of major women writers of the nineteenth and twentieth centuries and the way they address the anxiety-laden relationship between fathers and daughters and between older men and younger women. It offers, above all else, a model of sexual conquest, however transgressive that vision may be, through which women might hope to take up the reins of culture and successfully move toward the future.[47] It does so, according to Polhemus, by presenting a more accurate image of the power structure between the sexes than the skewed Oedipal emphasis on the primacy of sons and mothers (9). Moreover, Polhemus suggests that, through different variations of the Lot story, authors like Jane Austen, Mary Wollstonecraft Shelley, and the Brontë sisters were able to alter the way people talk, think, see, and feel, especially about the role of women (113).

The intricate and multivalent pattern that Polhemus relates to the story of Lot and his daughters shares features with many other stories he does not mention about young women seducing older men for noble purposes and future redemption. Scheherazade, for example, uses her sexuality as well as her extraordinary storytelling abilities to battle the abuse of women.[48] Esther relies on her beauty and daring to seduce her husband, King Ahasuerus, into hearing her plea for her people. While not involving the seduction of an older male, the myth of Electra portrays the aggressive actions by a daughter who wanted her brother to avenge the death of their father, Agamemnon, by killing their mother, Clytemnestra. Perhaps more significantly, it became the basis of Carl Jung's response to Freud's Oedipal complex, countering Freud's emphasis on male psychosexual development. By the twentieth century, Electra, as myth and complex, afforded artists a new way of imagining the world. In her study of the subject, Jill Scott shows how Electra, in the hands of male writers, became emblematic of their fears, their misogyny, and, somewhat contradictorily, their hidden desires. In the hands of women writers like H.D. and Sylvia Plath, the figure of Electra opens a path from trauma to healing and renewal.[49]

What is significant about Lot's daughters and these other stories is that in all cases women rewrite male dominance, breaking the silence of subservience. All the stories are laden with sexuality and desire that either subtly or aggressively reformulate authority. The two aspects Polhemus underscores in the tale of Lot's daughters that make it particularly paradigmatic of women's writing in the nineteenth and twentieth centuries is the daughters' assertive break with the past (and with all memories of the past) and the incestuous, eroticized representation of the birth of a new cultural reality. This last feature of the biblical story is crucial because the sexual language of literary paternity that had come to dominate Western literature demanded an erotic response. Women writers had to appropriate the language of sexual procreation that had been the domain of men and that had, in effect, made the pen a metaphorical penis. It should, for this reason, not be surprising that the disturbing Lot family narrative with its radical departure from normative sexual behavior and the morally conflicted drive by young women to adapt and to expropriate male (paternal) power in order to save the world for the future finds parallels within Agustini's life and works. Moreover, it reveals a mythic dimension to Agustini's struggles with memory and death and her anguished pursuit of redemption.[50]

All these models and theories shed light on the emotional turmoil Agustini felt as she confronted Darío and his imposing poetry. Unique among her predecessors, he becomes the one she aspires to engage, equal, and eventually master. She fights for the access to literary privileges that he, consciously or not, would have denied her. Despite the words of the fairy godmother in Darío's "Sonatina," Agustini is not silenced. On the contrary, she creates a poetic vocabulary that screams with sexuality, violence, and a disruptive authority that granted her unusual prestige and power. Her accomplishments were met with an unusual and unexpected degree of support, both from her family and from the literary circles of Montevideo. Acknowledged as a skilled and talented poet, Agustini may even have had a sense—alluded to with regard to the general condition of women by Gilbert and Gubar—that she was forging a tradition of her own (50), a situation that was affirmed by the acclaim showered on her by the next generation of women writers, including Alfonsina Storni, Gabriela Mistral, and Juana de Ibarbourou.[51] Her influence goes even further. It reaches the poetry of Olga Orozco and the women poets of the generation of the 1980s in Argentina that counts among its members Irene Gruss, Tamara Kamenszain, Diana Bellessi, María del Carmen Colombo, and Mirta Rosenberg.[52]

Regardless of how she read her own situation, Agustini leaves ample evidence that she considered the act of creation to be an anguish-ridden endeavor, one in which, as I will show, she often, though implicitly, compares her achievements with Darío's. Neither specifically an anxiety of influence nor an anxiety of authorship, her creative anxiety is evident in the wide-ranging artistic tensions and contestatory positions in her work. It also appears in her apprehension as she surveys the great distance between herself and her male precursors, a distance that appears so enormous as to be unbridgeable in her early work. The young, inexperienced poet adopts male masks that allow her to write like a modernista but not like a woman. Not until she is able to forge an erotic language that is different from that of the accomplished males around her is she able to write like a modernista who is also a woman.

Even after the assertive reinvention of male discourse, women writers had to remain vigilant against the threat of being silenced, which operated on a practical and commercial plane as much as it did on a metaphoric one. Women were consistently excluded from the opportunities open to men. They were generally made to feel unwelcome in literary circles, publishing houses, and journals controlled by men. Bonnie Frederick in *Wily Modesty: Argentine Women Writers, 1860–1910* uses Darío as an example of male hostility toward women writers, indicating that he helped create a productive environment for men in Buenos Aires after his arrival there in 1893 but failed to do the same for women writers (30). And even when given the chance to write and publish, many women were ultimately silenced through a systematic omission from literary histories. They have regularly been left out of the literary canon, often because their works do not fit into the neat categories organized around the genres, styles, and perspectives of male authors or because their works are undervalued for the same reasons. Such was the case with Agustini, who only recently has become firmly established as a central figure of modernismo. As Frederick points out (5–7), giving women their due is complicated by the fact that "restoring women writers to their place in literary history cannot be accomplished simply by inserting their names into chapters already written, since they represent a literature that is often at odds with that of their male colleagues" (7).

In addition to struggling with exclusion, women had to worry about abandoning the safe, conventional, protected role of wife and mother (49). Concerned about their status in society and about their economic well-being, women writers were put in extremely conflicted situations. These tensions certainly must have had an impact on Agustini, who ultimately opted to marry Reyes despite her serious reservations.

While these details of Agustini's life as well as her murder continue to hold the attention of readers, it is her poetry that resonates and that provides insights into the troubled relationship between older male poets and younger women writers. Agustini responds to her sociocultural context, turning to and altering from a woman's perspective the sexually charged, contestatory discourse of earlier modernista writers. She is guided in this move, as I have indicated, by the modernismo practiced in Uruguay, which, at the turn of the century, is unique in the way it situates the body at the center of its poetics, sexualizing writing (Giaudrone 262).[53] The erotic language associated with Agustini's writings does not, however, appear in her poetry from the beginning. Quite the contrary, critics such as Jacqueline Girón Alvarado have long acknowledged that Agustini struggles to find a place for herself, to find a "poetic voice," in the no-[wo]man's land between the assimilated patriarchal discourse of the day and her own sense of entitlement as a woman and poet (3). Critics have also recognized the growing sexualization of her language as a revolutionary development not only for Hispanic poetry but also for women writers. I believe, however, that an important feature of her work has been overlooked. More than simply coming to affirm in her poetry her desirous nature and rejecting the limitations placed upon her by traditional views of women, Agustini sets up a powerful conceit to deal with her personal creative anxieties. She chooses a sexual model to combat the sense of weakness and ineffectuality suggested by imitation. She makes this bold and innovative move in order to respond to Darío's male-centered discourse and, at the same time, to claim for herself full and equal status in the modernista movement. She turns herself into a seductress and an aggressive partner and in this way rewrites from a woman's perspective many of the erotic images that run throughout Darío's work.

This poetic maneuver must be clearly distinguished from issues of biography; indeed, it must be distinguished from the expression of personal desire. As mentioned earlier, Rodríguez Monegal identifies the dominant

male in Agustini's erotic imagination as Manuel Ugarte. Though Rodríguez Monegal acknowledges Darío's role in Agustini's creative formation,
he shifts focus away from Darío, who, at forty-five, Rodríguez Monegal
insists, is already an old man, and he turns his attention instead to the
dapper Argentine Ugarte (60). While Ugarte may have aroused Agustini's
sexual longings, the language in her poetry grows out of her literary exchange with Darío—not as an object of erotic attraction but as the most
powerful poetic force of the day, that is, as an incomparable foil to her
own poetic aspirations. It might well be assumed even that Agustini would
settle for no lesser other than Darío as she set out to write herself into
modernista discourse. The most audacious, dramatic, and ultimately productive feature of this maneuver is Agustini's attempts to wrestle control of
the images of creativity away from Darío.[54] Needless to say, however, this
struggle, though it is about literary control and authority, has a physically
erotic dimension. The passion Agustini evokes most certainly portrays and
invites physical arousal, whether through the contemplation of literary
or real-life behavior. For many readers the eroticism is redoubled by the
knowledge that the author is a woman who, by using sexually charged language to claim literary primacy and generative power, has crossed the line
into forbidden territory.

It is not by chance that Agustini's creative conceit, her imaginative leap,
parallels, in an unconnected but contemporaneous coincidence, the recourse by the Brazilian modernist Oswald de Andrade to the language of
cannibalism to conceive a striking new metaphor for countering European
cultural hegemony in Brazil. The Brazilian modernists, who were actually
closer to the Spanish American *vanguardistas* than to the modernistas in
style and form, redefined themselves through the central metaphor of devouring assimilation through which the new body of "native originality"
came into existence. Through this powerful turn of phrase, they were no
longer dependent imitators but resourcefully aggressive creators; they
vitiated the language of insult, claiming cannibalism as a label of pride
and purging it of all negativity. While this feature of Brazilian modernism
has long received critical discussion, Agustini's attempts to find an assertive way of addressing the crushing power of established arrangements
have tended to be interpreted through her biography. Agustini, in a move
not unlike Andrade's, turns the attack against monstrous, blood-sucking

women on its head; claims pride in her new powers; and goes so far as to draw the blood, eat the wounds, and drink the tears of the dominant other in an effort to take what she needs and make it hers.[55] She writes in "El vampiro,"

> ¿Por qué fui tu vampiro de amargura?
> ¿Soy flor o estirpe de una especie oscura
> Que come llagas y que bebe el llanto? (186)[56]

[Why was I your vampire of bitterness? / Am I a flower or the stock of a dark species / that eats wounds and that drinks tears?]

In this poem Agustini turns the tables on the oppressor; she resists the subservience that might have been expected of her as a woman and as a disciple. She seeks to overcome whatever creative anxieties she may have had by incorporating in her poetic perspective the privileges revealed by the sociopolitical and cultural debates of the day. Yet she goes even further; she is defiantly shocking in her fusion of sexual and poetic images, and her language evokes a sadomasochistic delight in the exploration of pain. She asserts the dark pleasure of her involvement with the other against whom she struggles. She digs into his soul and flesh in the hope of achieving both poetic and sexual heights. The painful poetic enterprise arouses a sexual passion, and erotic arousal produces poetic insight. As a result, the "tú" of this and other poems functions on many levels. He is both her lover and the poet against whom she writes. While this poetic partner is not always clearly identifiable as Darío (or as his discourse), Darío's presence is a constant. He is, at the least, the modernista other created under Darío's immediate and direct influence. This revelation is the central structuring device of this book, and through it I will explore the dynamic breadth and creative complexity of Agustini's work.

I will also explore the powerful implications that Agustini's appropriation of modernismo's main tenets and poetic language have for the movement. By looking at Darío and, by extension, at modernismo through the prism of Agustini's daring endeavors, I expose previously unobserved aspects of his language, assumptions, and poetic stances as well as her creative reinvention of the movement's most basic and generally acknowledged features. Indeed, Agustini's confrontation with the taken-for-granted and hence invisible nature of male-dominated modernista discourse underscores what has tended to remain unnoticed. Once altered, embedded beliefs, cultural values, and linguistic patterns yield up their hidden qualities. Within the modernista idiom, images like the statue, the chrysalis, the swan, the nights of insomnia, and the figures of Orpheus, Pygmalion, and Prometheus all resonate differently in Agustini's work and call attention to different issues. Equally significant, however, is the process of change itself, which for Agustini depends on her creative and imaginative relationship with Darío, whom she envisions as her significant other, the sexual partner of her erotically charged poems. It is through the careful examination of this process of rewriting and reinventing that I add to the growing criticism on woman writers and their literary responses to patriarchal discourse.[57]

In order to elucidate the course and nature of this poetic evolution, the chapters of this book proceed chronologically, taking up each volume of Agustini's verse as a unit. Even within the chapters, I have chosen to follow, wherever a coherent analysis allows, the order laid out by Agustini within her collections, for there too the flow of thoughts and the interrelationship of poems appear crucial. The story of Agustini's literary journey, like that of her life, confounds expectations, contains revelations, and is simultaneously uplifting and tragic. The story starts with chapter 2, "The Dialogue Begins," which explores how Agustini rather timidly takes up the pen and begins to write like a modernista in her first volume of verse, *El libro blanco (Frágil)* (1907). It reveals how she cleverly establishes an implicit give and take with Darío's poetry, developing a personal response to his masculine perspective. By the end of the collection, Agustini finds her voice and begins to formulate a way to move out from under Darío's imposing presence. This formulation becomes increasingly defiant, erotic, and violent in *Cantos de la mañana* (1910), the focus of chapter 3, "Drinking from the Fountain of the Other." As she progresses to greater artistic independence and leaves the specifics of Darío's verse behind, she starts the process of defining herself as sexually and poetically aggressive, a process that leads to the metaphorical dismemberment and killing of the other. This attempt at separation from the inhibiting perspective of the past first appeared with the subtlest of veiled allusions in *El libro blanco (Frágil)*, evolves in *Cantos de la mañana*, and becomes a dramatically emphatic element in her next collection, *Los cálices vacíos* (1913). Chapter 4, "Turning Loss into Empowerment," reveals how, in her third volume of poetry, Agustini rethinks the nature of art, language's ability to control and limit, and the artist's struggle against intractable structures and binding recollections as well as the contradictory desire to embrace and destroy her lover. All the while, she continues her inventive reworking of the patterns of literary paternity and traditional patriarchal images. By the time Agustini writes "Los astros del abismo," the collection that was published posthumously under the title *El rosario de Eros* (1924), she comes to realize that all verse, including her own, regardless of how vibrant and dynamic, recedes into memory. In chapter 5, "Aspirations and Abiding Disappointments," I explore the vision of death that begins to overtake the lyric voice. While these allusions have been attributed to a prophetic intuition, it is actually the natural evolution of a way of thinking that began with her first volume, progressed steadily throughout her career, and reflects her take on the brutal struggles of personal and literary survival in the context of punishingly restrictive impulses. As a result, these final poems offer an appropriate point of departure for my conclusions.

CHAPTER TWO

THE DIALOGUE BEGINS

El libro blanco (Frágil)

Like many of the contemporaneous Anglo-American women writers mentioned in chapter 1, Agustini fashions a language of artistic creation reflective of erotic arousal linked to the seduction of an older male counterpart. She pushes herself "not to look back," to break out of the old, constraining patterns, and she begins to distance herself from the linguistic and moral traditions dominated by men. She begins to alter modernismo's sexual metaphors for literary paternity and to formulate an innovative language for her carnal and poetic passions. She looks for a way to produce poetic offspring that is not limited by convention. These desires fuse around the figure of Rubén Darío and his work. He is the poet of the day and the other that must be conquered. She responds to the power of his verse and his image of women, and, by addressing his male-centered vision of writing, she explores modernismo's fundamental linguistic, aesthetic, and philosophic issues. Just as Darío constantly writes about his struggle to find the right word and the right form (which is often identified with a beautifully alluring but passive female), Agustini constantly explores the nature of writing and her place in the artistic landscape that she surveys and alters.

Most of the fifty-two poems of *El libro blanco (Frágil)* (1907), Agustini's first published collection, deal directly with the question of artistic style and goals.[1] To overlook the artistic objectives that she spells out in these texts diminishes her as a poet, that is, it minimizes how seriously engaged she was with the enterprise of writing. To translate the trajectory of her work, which becomes progressively more erotic, into a history of personal obsessions or as a declaration of goals tied exclusively to the sexual politics of the day is to fail to recognize her sophisticated participation in the literary debates about Spanish America's search for a modern poetics. Agustini often portrays these erotic encounters as a struggle between young and old, rejuvenation and decay, the future and the past, thereby asserting her combined passions for life, love, and art. The resulting poetry startled her compatriots, set a path for future generations of women writers, and earned her a singular place in the history of Spanish American literature.

Agustini starts modestly, almost apologetically, but quickly becomes more assertive.[2] In the process she creates images of the seduction of a powerful male. In other words, the story of *El libro blanco (Frágil)* is of how Agustini's determination to write gradually fuses with her growing sexual awareness and desires. The other that must be conquered in order to move poetry toward a new vitality increasingly becomes the other of erotic dreams and desires. That Darío is the poetic other in Agustini's rapidly maturing outlook becomes evident through the poetry itself—though her letters to him also amply support this conclusion. The poetic clues to this rather one-sided exchange are many, and they start with *El libro blanco (Frágil)*. It cannot, of course, be determined whether Agustini turns to Darío's verse consciously for textual guidance or whether his poems are so powerful as to take hold in her poetic imagination, becoming a type of embedded lyric mother lode that she unwittingly mines. What is clear, however, is that in her first collection Darío's language and images reside just beneath the surface. Agustini's recognition of this latent relationship is suggested by the title of the volume, in which, like Darío in *Prosas profanas*, she plays with the multiple associations of its words. Her book is both white and blank. The title, therefore, speaks to her sense of innocence and fragility, if not her feelings of inadequacy and limitation. If it is still blank, she must discover a way to fill its pages; she must attempt to find her voice and to speak for herself.

The first poem of *El libro blanco (Frágil)*, a sonnet known both as "Levando el ancla" (Weighing anchor) and as "El poeta leva el ancla" (The poet weighs anchor) (95), is about a male poet who is about to set out on a journey with his female muse on a ship with blue sails.[3] This early reluctance to break away from gender-defined roles has been thoroughly examined by Jacqueline Girón Alvarado (72). Less well studied is the fact that Agustini begins to write by relying on and distancing herself from Darío's vision for the poet and poetry. To this end, the poem begins with a dual orientation of escape and ascent:

> El ancla de oro canta . . . la vela azul asciende
> Como el ala de un sueño abierta al nuevo día.
> Partamos, musa mía!
> Ante la prora alegre un bello mar se extiende. (95)

[The golden anchor sings . . . the blue sail ascends / like the wing of a dream open to the new day. / Let us depart, my dear muse! / A beautiful sea stretches out before the happy prow.]

The music that accompanies the raising of the anchor, the liberating conversion of sail into wing capable of lifting the poet up toward the dreams of a new day, and the beautiful expanse of the sea before him all combine to assert the optimism of the lyric voice. They reflect the promise of success and of the ability to capture the musicality and vitality of existence, so essential to modernista verse. The stylized and archaic "prora" of the last line of this first quatrain catches the reader's attention with its studied artifice, seemingly underscoring that this sonnet is about language and beauty, not life and its mundane concerns. The outdated "prora" also appears in Darío's "La hoja de oro" (The golden leaf) (237) and seems to signal this poem as its antecedent, for both sonnets address artistic aspiration, desire, and doubt and contain references to a ship's bow, laurel wreaths, and Jason's quest for the Golden Fleece. Similarly, the rich imagery that appears in Agustini's second quatrain is consistent with Darío's elaborate descriptions.

The masculine poet of Agustini's title invites his muse to leave with him, to undertake the adventure of sailing toward the dawn, and of witnessing "Fantasy" dressed in bejeweled adornment as she travels toward unknown worlds. In short, he invites the muse on a modernista voyage in which imagination is adorned with rare gems as it wanders in search of inspiration:

> En el oriente claro como un cristal, esplende
> El fanal sonrosado de Aurora. Fantasía
> Estrena un raro traje lleno de pedrería
> para vagar brillante por las olas.

> Ya tiende
> La vela azul a Eolo su oriflama de raso . . .
> ¡El momento supremo! . . . Yo me estremezco; ¿acaso
> Sueño lo que me aguarda en los mundos no vistos! [*sic*]

> ¿Acaso un fresco ramo de laureles fragantes,
> El toison [*sic*] reluciente, el cetro de diamantes,
> El naufragio o la eterna corona de los Cristos? . . . (95)

[In the East, clear as crystal, the lantern shines rosy with the Dawn. / Fantasy tries on a strange outfit full of precious stones / to roam brilliant over the waves.

The blue sail now offers its satin banner to Aeolus, the wind . . . / The supreme moment! . . . I shudder; do I perhaps / dream what awaits me in the worlds not seen?

Perhaps a fresh bouquet of fragrant laurels, / the shining Golden Fleece, the diamond scepter, / the shipwreck or the eternal crown of Christs? . . .]

Doubts about the poet's destiny are held in abeyance until mention of the journey's uncertain conclusion. Will it end, the lyric voice asks, with a mark of honor, with the supreme reward, with disaster, or with salvation? The poem's title together with the title of the collection that it opens, its subject, its blue sails, the appearance of a female muse, and its reference to Christ in the plural all recall Darío's poetry, especially "La página blanca" (The white page) (213–14), which was published in *Prosas profanas* (Profane proses) in 1896.[4] In that poem Darío makes specific reference to Christs, emphasizing the sacrifices and saviorlike qualities he attributes to poets.[5] The journey Darío presents is not across a vibrant and vital sea but to a type of Bethlehem by way of a caravan of camels and dromedaries across the frightening wasteland of the white page. Though Darío's poem ends with the hint of a possible salvation, the passage across the inhospitable terrain communicates the anguish he feels as he confronts both creative sterility and physical mortality. The suffering of life's voyage and its end in death as well as the constant fear of artistic failure and desolation are captured in the desert setting and in the troubling visions that parade across the poetic landscape. In contrast, Agustini's marine imagery and its affirmation of movement, creation, and rebirth declare her youthful optimism about the adventure that lies before her. They draw upon associations with the successful maritime quests undertaken by classical figures like Ulysses and Jason. More subtly, they underscore the feminine side of creation, often represented in paintings and poetry by the birth of Venus.

Though the vision of Venus's emergence in full form from the foam of the sea, simultaneously sexually receptive yet pristinely virgin, is nowhere to be seen in this poem, the erotic nature of poetic production appears in the shudder that accompanies "the supreme moment" of initiation into "worlds not seen." Could Agustini, as she has her lyric voice survey the waters before her, be thinking about Darío's statement regarding the poetic implications of the birth of Venus in his masterly "Coloquio de los centauros" (Colloquy of the centaurs), also published in *Prosas profanas* in 1896? The frisson of this key moment goes to the core of Agustini's artistry. It speaks to the arousal that, in the transgressive process of entering worlds that have been prohibited to her in the past, is simultaneously poetic and erotic. The tremulous thrill she feels as she begins to write hints at the sexuality that will take center stage in her later work. At this point, however, her declaration of pleasure is subtle but strong enough to overcome her fears of failure. She limits her expression of her anxieties to a reference to a possible shipwreck, which she juxtaposes to the equally possible realization of salvation and messianic ascent.[6]

It is not until the seventh poem of *El libro blanco (Frágil)*, namely, "La estatua" (The statue) (101) that Agustini directly confronts the worries that are the primary focus of "La página blanca." She does so by rewriting the first vision Darío presents in this quintessentially metapoetic poem, namely, the parade of fantastical women with statuelike faces.[7] This somewhat enigmatic passage expresses Darío's fear of creating something of great beauty that is both physically and spiritually dead, a fear that grows out of his move away from Parnassian models of poetic creation to more symbolist goals.[8] Agustini's poem similarly addresses the inadequacy of form without spirit, beauty without vitality, craft without passion and feeling.[9] In its final section the majesty of the eponymous sculpture is humbled—turned into something less than a worm, as the last line specifies—by its artificiality and its false tranquility. At the same time, however, this strangely rhymed sonnet suggests the artistic potential Agustini hopes to develop. Turning to her readers, the poet asks that they contemplate the art before them:

> Miradla, así, sobre el follaje oscuro
> Recortar la silueta soberana . . .
> ¿No parece el retoño prematuro . . .
> De una gran raza que será mañana?
>
> Así una raza inconmovible, sana,
> Tallada a golpes sobre mármol duro,
> De las vastas campañas del futuro[10]
> Desalojara a la familia humana!
>
> Miradla así —de hinojos!— en augusta
> Calma imponer la desnudez que asusta! . . .
> Dios! . . . Moved ese cuerpo, dadle un alma!
> Ved la grandeza que en su forma duerme . . .
> ¡Vedlo allá arriba, miserable, inerme,
> Más pobre que un gusano, siempre en calma! (101)

[Look at it, thus, above the dark foliage / outlining its unrivaled silhouette . . . / Does it not seem to be the unseasonable sprouting / of a great race that will exist tomorrow?

In this manner an unshakable, wholesome race / sculpted by blows upon hard marble, / from the vast campaigns of the future / might dislodge the human family!

Look at it thus —on its knees!— impose with magnificent calm the nakedness that frightens! . . . / God! . . . Move that body, give it a soul! / See the greatness that sleeps in its form . . . / See it there on high, miserable, defenseless, / More unfortunate than a worm, always calm!]

Art, achieved through hard work and enormous effort ("tallada a golpes sobre mármol duro"), produces a superior race. Although this alternative scion fails here, a similar image, that of "la estirpe sobrehumana" (the superhuman race), in "Supremo idilio" (Supreme idyll) of *Cantos de la mañana,* eventually comes to represent both poetic success and one of Agustini's answers to Darío's metaphors of literary paternity.[11] In her later poetry her lyric voice becomes the active and assertive breeder of a new superhuman race, and woman is no longer limited to being the passive recipient of male creative power. At this point, however, the statue's failure is, at least in part, tied to the limitations of a poetic discourse that remains locked within stony confines. The poem thereby offers a critique not only of artistic shortcomings but also of a perspective anchored in the past — as opposed to the forward-moving campaigns of the future. The grammatically feminine statue is humbled both by the great art that preceded it and by the rules of representation, which are doubly restrictive, having been dictated until this time by men. These rules interfere with the expression of her/its true being, the nakedness of her/its soul, which frightens as much as it is desired. For these reasons, the lyric voice pleads for the readers and possible future poets to see beyond the surface and to awaken the grandeur that sleeps within the rigid female form.

Agustini knows that the artist must respond to the potential of the raw materials before her and that she must release the life force within the stone in order to achieve her artistic goals. While these goals are similar to Darío's, they also hint at differences rooted in gender. She turns to metaphors that appear in Darío's "Coloquio de los centauros," the consummate expression of his worldview, and affirms the priority of life over formal beauty evident in Darío's "Yo soy aquel que ayer no más decía . . ." (I am the one who only yesterday recited . . .), the autobiographical poem that opens *Cantos de vida y esperanza* (Songs of life and hope), published in 1905, two years before *El libro blanco (Frágil).*[12] Nevertheless, Agustini recognizes that unlocking the inner grandeur within the stone is difficult. Her plaintive tone reflects what she judged to be the inadequacy of her efforts. She laments her inability to expose the inherent poetry and vitality of language and to create a personal perspective within the rigidity of social and poetic conventions. Despite her disappointment, she continues these efforts, most notably in later elaborations upon the figures of the statue, "the superhuman race," and Pygmalion.[13]

"Por campos de ensueño" (Through fields of reverie) (96), the second poem of *El libro blanco (Frágil)* reverberates, as does "La estatua," with strong echoes of the majestic "Coloquio de los centauros" (200–207). By reworking Darío's alexandrine lines, strong rhyme scheme, and brilliantly original and moving descriptions, Agustini acknowledges both her debt to his work and her attempts to move away from him. She converts his strong, assertive, masculine images into a figurative language she begins to tame.[14] The two quatrains of her sonnet read as follows:

> Pasó humeante el tropel de los potros salvajes!
> Feroces los hocicos, hirsutos los pelajes,
> Las crines extendidas, bravías, tal bordones,
> Pasaron como pasan los fieros aquilones!
>
> Y luego fueron águilas de sombríos plumajes
> Trayendo de sus cumbres magníficas visiones
> Con el sereno vuelo de las inspiraciones
> Augustas, con soberbias de olímpicos linajes. (96)

[The rush of wild colts passed by steaming! / Their nostrils ferocious, their coats hairy, / their manes extended, spirited, like staffs, / they passed by the way the savage north winds pass by!

And then they were eagles of somber plumage / bringing magnificent visions from their peaks / with the serene flight of imposing inspiration, / with the arrogance of Olympic lineages.]

Through simile and association she links the ferocious colts of the poem with the savage gusts of the northerly wind and with eagles, their visions, their inspirational flight, and an Olympian heritage. In short, she converts the young steeds into symbols of male poetic power and imaginative energy. Following behind, through the celestial clarity, is the essence of purity, innocence, and fragility in the form of a white dove, a provocative visual metaphor of what Agustini must have felt as she followed in Darío's wake and that of other contemporaneous poets, for she was not only a woman but also one of the youngest members of her literary cohort:

> Cruzaron hacia Oriente la limpidez del cielo;
> Tras ellas como cándida hostia que alzara el vuelo,
> Una paloma blanca como la nieve asoma,

Yo olvido el ave egregia y el bruto que foguea
Pensando que en los cielos solemnes de la Idea
A veces es muy bella, muy bella una paloma! (96)

[They crossed the transparency of the sky toward the East; / behind them,
like the white wafer of the Eucharist that their flight might elevate, / a dove
as white as snow appears, / I forget the illustrious bird and the beast that is
baptized by fire / thinking that in the solemn heavens of the Idea / at times
a dove is very beautiful, very beautiful!]

She follows but ultimately sets her own path, separating herself from the
pack by deliberately choosing to forget. With this declaration, Agustini
turns her back on the past and asserts her rights to agency and rational
action in the creation of the future (cf. Polhemus, especially 10–11, 113–15).
At the same time, she is able to affirm a special sense of belonging within
the solemn heavens of the "Idea."

Agustini rejects the brute strength of the wild colts and the dark eagles,
for she cannot find herself among them. Instead she allies herself with
the gentle, softly feminine dove. By comparing the dove to the Eucharist
she reinforces the divine nature of her mission and recalls the traditional
Catholic imagery of the Annunciation. The arrival of the white dove in
the solemn heaven of the "Idea" suggests her openness to inspiration and
a type of virginal impregnation that would allow her to offer, like her
modernista colleagues, a type of salvation. If the concept of impregnation
seeps into this image, it is veiled in a modesty that Agustini quickly spurns.
Because the Eucharist is described as "cándida," that is, simultaneously
white and guileless, it evokes the multiple associations present in the title
of the collection. Yet Agustini's stance in the poem is far from ingenuous.
While the initial metaphors pay homage to Darío and acknowledge the
male-centered discourse of modernismo, the movement away from them
reveals Agustini's aspirations. Throughout her career she struggles to alter
modernismo in such a way that she can feel entitled to write and to express
her unique desires. These three early poems, "Levando el ancla," "La estatua," and "Por campos de ensueño," reveal how she begins to rewrite the
language of authorial authority, believed at that time to be the exclusive
privilege of men.

Agustini's poetic dialogue with Darío continues in the fourth poem of *El libro blanco (Frágil)*, "La sed" (Thirst) (98), which responds to his statement of modernista ideals contained in "La fuente" (The spring), a sonnet written in 1899 and published in the 1901 edition of *Prosas profanas*. The first quatrain of Darío's poem reads,

> Joven, te ofrezco el don de esta copa de plata
> para que un día puedas calmar esta sed ardiente,
> la sed que con su fuego más que la muerte mata.
> Mas debes abrevarte tan sólo en una fuente. (235)

[Young man, I offer you the gift of this silver goblet / so that one day you can calm this burning thirst, / the thirst that with its fire kills more than death. / But you should drink from only one spring.]

Poetry is the silver goblet that the young man will use to calm his burning passion to create.[15] As in "La estatua," in "La fuente" the central tension is between the immutable beauty of the artistic form and the vitality it seeks to capture and convey. For Darío the goblet must be filled with the water that flows within the poet in rhythmic accord with the pulse of existence. The music of the spring is muted in the goblet, but, if properly contained, it can still quiet the poet's thirst.[16]

The lyric voice of Darío's "La fuente" is that of an undefined master who offers advice to an aspirant. In Agustini's poem the lyric voice is of the sexually undefined poet who speaks to "la maga" (the magus), the female supplier of inspiration and knowledge. The poet demands relief from the all-consuming thirst that plagues her, and the female sage responds by offering her nectars, which are immediately rejected as too sweet and overwhelming. What follows is an experiment in tastes and a refinement of style:

> Tengo sed, sed ardiente! —dije a la maga, y ella
> Me ofreció de sus néctares. —Eso no, me empalaga!—
> Luego, una rara fruta, con sus dedos de maga,
> Exprimió en una copa clara como una estrella;
>
> Y un brillo de rubíes hubo en la copa bella.
> Yo probé. —Es dulce, dulce. Hay días que me halaga
> Tanta miel, pero hoy me repugna, me estraga!—
> Vi pasar por los ojos del hada una centella.

Y por un verde valle perfumado y brillante,
Llevóme hasta una clara corriente de diamante.
—Bebe! —dijo. Yo ardía, mi pecho era una fragua.
Bebí, bebí, bebí la linfa cristalina . . .
¡Oh frescura! ¡oh pureza! ¡oh sensación divina!
—Gracias, maga, y bendita la limpidez del agua! (98)

[I have a thirst, a burning thirst! —I said to the magus, and she / offered me her nectars. —Not that, it sickens me with its sweetness!— / Then, she squeezed a rare fruit with her magician's fingers / into a goblet as luminous as a star;

And there was a splendor of rubies in the beautiful goblet. / I tried it. —It is sweet, sweet. There are days that so much honey pleases me, / but today it disgusts me, it corrupts me! / I saw a spark pass through the eyes of the fairy.

And she led me through a perfumed and shining green valley / toward a clear, diamond spring. / —Drink! —she said. I was burning, my chest was a forge. / I drank, I drank, I drank the crystalline liquid . . . / Oh what freshness! Oh what purity! Oh what divine sensation! / —Thank you, dear magus, and blessed be the transparency of the water!]

"La sed" echoes "La fuente," but it also builds upon its central metaphor to evoke an erotic excitation that goes beyond thirst and points to broader, more sensual desires. These allusions are reinforced by the rejection of the sweet drinks of childhood. Though the lyric voice of the poem confesses to being tempted by the juice of "a rare fruit" which is squeezed into a crystalline goblet that shines like a star, she admits that "today" she finds this liquid unpalatable and unacceptable.[17] She refuses the goblet and the drink it contains, preferring the waters of the clear, uncontaminated stream. The purity of the water cools her burning chest, her passion for art and life. She comes to realize that the only way she can achieve her personal and poetic ambitions is by refusing what others provide, even if that means rebuffing the crystalline goblet of modernista verse or the essence of the rare fruit of earlier inspiration. She must, like Darío and other modernistas before her, find her own way, her own direct contact with the profound truths embodied in the harmonious unity of undefiled nature. She must drink from a source that is pure, the only source that will satisfy her longings. In this way she accepts Darío's directive, pursuing a poetry that is true to who she is, free from the imposition of limiting patterns and molds.

Later in the collection, in "El poeta y la diosa" (The poet and the goddess) (130–31), Agustini reconfigures the image of a female source of inspiration (diosa/hada/maga) who fills a sculpted goblet with desired drink. In
this poem, however, the lyric voice does not reject the "rare wines" that are
poured "in the shadow of a lyre." Since they are all different but all equally
satisfying, the poet chooses to take a little of each, that is, to create a unique
mixture from the wide selection of possible thirst-quenching possibilities,
including the demonic, the noble, the pure, the past, and the future. Agustini thereby embraces the modernista enthusiasm for the modern fusion of
all times and all styles evident, though through a different central metaphor, in Darío's "Divagación" (183–87) (Wandering) from *Prosas profanas.*[18]

These echoes of Darío are not the only ones heard in "El poeta y la
diosa." The poem's fearsome beginning recounts the aspirant's frightening journey into the grotto of creativity and reverberates with the images
and worries expressed at the end of Darío's "La fuente" and "Alma mía"
(My soul), both of which outline the obstacles that block the road to artistic success. "La fuente" concludes with the following injunctions:

> Guíete el misterioso eco de su murmullo;
> asciende por los riscos ásperos del orgullo,
> baja por la constancia y desciende al abismo
> cuya entrada sombría guardan siete panteras;
> son los Siete Pecados, las siete bestias fieras.
> Llena la copa y bebe: la fuente está en ti mismo. (235)

[Let the mysterious echo of its murmur guide you; / climb up over the
rough cliffs of pride, / descend through steadfastness and go down to the
abyss / the dark entrance to which seven panthers guard; / the seven wild
beasts are the Seven Sins. / Fill the goblet and drink: the spring is within
you.]

The final command in "Alma mía" urges the poet forward through the forest of evils: "atraviesa impertérrita por el bosque de males / sin temer las
serpientes; y sigue, como un dios . . ." (240) (go through the forest of evils
intrepid / without fearing the serpents; and continue on, like a god . . .).
Similar frightening features populate the first half of Agustini's poem:

> Entré temblando a la gruta
> Misteriosa cuya puerta

Cubre una mampara hirsuta
De cardos y de cicuta, [*sic*]
Crucé temblando la incierta

Sombra de una galería
En que acechar parecía
La guadaña de la muerte.
—El Miedo erguido blandía
Como un triunfo mi alma fuerte—.

Un roce de terciopelo
Siento en el rostro, en la mano.
—Arañas tendiendo un velo—
¡A cada paso en el suelo
Siento que aplasto un gusano!

A una vaga luz de plata,
En cámara misteriosa,
Mi fiera boca escarlata
Besó la olímpica nata
Del albo pie de la diosa!
—Brillante como una estrella,
La diosa nubla su rara
Faz enigmática y bella,
Con densa gasa: sin ella
Dicen que el verla cegara—. (130)

[Trembling I entered the mysterious grotto / the opening to which is covered by a screen hairy with thistles and hemlock. / Trembling I crossed the uncertain

Shadow of a passageway / in which the scythe of death / seemed to lie in ambush. / —Fear swollen with pride brandished / Like a victory my strong soul—.

I feel a rub of velvet / on my face, on my hand. / —Spiders extending a veil— / With each step on the ground / I feel that I am squashing a worm!

In the vague silver light, / In a mysterious chamber, / My fierce scarlet mouth / Kissed the Olympic cream of the snow white foot of the goddess! / —Brilliant as a star, / The goddess clouds her strange / enigmatic

and beautiful face / With dense gauze: without it / They say that seeing her
would blind—.]

As much as the poem points to the sacrifice and suffering that Darío describes as part of his quest for poetic insight, the subtleties of the specific
metaphors are even more revealing. Whereas Darío presents his efforts in
broadly masculine terms that evoke the athleticism of conquering heroes,
Agustini's initiation reverberates with sexual innuendo. She has the trembling poet enter the "hairy" grotto, brushed by hymenlike spider webs and
smashing "worms" as she proceeds. With this language she conflates her
anxieties about the dangers of sexual and poetic activity. Despite the risks
she refuses to allow gender-based assumptions about privilege, prowess,
and power to condemn her to exclusion. She accepts the perils she describes because, as the allusions to biblical and mythic injunctions against
seeing the face of God (here made female) underscore, the knowledge she
pursues is divine.

Even more directly than in "La sed" and "El poeta y la diosa," poetic
discourse is the subject of "Rebelión" (Rebellion) and "El arte" (Art),
both of which follow "La sed" in this collection. "Rebelión" (99) focuses
on freedom and rejects the stifling rhyme schemes that impede the flow
of ideas, enslave thought, and hide, as stated in the second stanza, the
"divine essence, music, light, color, strength, and beauty" that exist in
poetry before it is put into words and given form. Agustini thus elaborates
upon Darío's much-quoted dictum from "Palabras liminares" (Opening
words): "And the question of metrics? And rhythm? Since each word has
a soul, in each line of verse there is, in addition to verbal harmony, an
ideal melody. Often the music is only from the idea" (180).[19] Darío com-
plements this opening statement with "Yo persigo una forma . . ." (I pursue a form . . .) (240–41), the poem that closes *Prosas profanas* and elaborates upon his struggle to find a style that would develop naturally, like the
blooming of a rose or the music flowing from a flute. While following the
broad outlines of Darío's lead, Agustini forges her own dynamic images,
images that reappear in her later poems.

In the first section of the freely structured "Rebelión," Agustini vaguely
invokes Pegasus as she presents poetry as being tied both to divinity and to
flight. While it would be impossible to assert with any certainty that Agus-

tini had Darío's "Pegaso" (Pegasus) (254–55) in mind, echoes of Darío's allusions to "cimas" (peaks), "cascos" (hoofs), and "gran volar" (great flight) reverberate strongly throughout the poem. What stands out, however, is that Agustini goes beyond the common recourse to the adjective "divine" and compares poetic thought to a god:

> La rima es el tirano empurpurado,
> Es el estigma del esclavo, el grillo
> Que acongoja la marcha de la Idea.
> No aleguéis que es de oro! El Pensamiento
> No se esclaviza a un vil cascabeleo!
> Ha de ser libre de escalar las cumbres
> Entero como un dios, la crin revuelta,
> La frente al sol, al viento. ¿Acaso importa
> Que adorne el ala lo que oprime el vuelo? (99)

[Rhyme is the ennobled tyrant, / It is the stigma of the slave, the cricket / that oppresses the march of the Idea. / Do not allege that it is golden! Thought / does not enslave itself to a vile jingle! / It has to be free to scale the mountaintops / Undiminished like a god, its mane disheveled, / Its forehead facing the sun, facing the wind. Could what / adorns the wing possibly be important if it weighs down flight?]

By asserting that poetic thought must be free to scale the heights of achievement, that it must soar above the mundane and the material, and that it must be robust and honest like a god, Agustini fuses Pegasus, Bellerophon, and artistic impetus into an anthropomorphized divinity whose free flight should not be inhibited by adornment. Frivolous embellishment is described as an impediment to serious endeavors, and, as if primping and preening were exclusive to women, this statement begins a series of metaphors that not only recalls Darío's language regarding poetry but also underscores how gender-specific preoccupations have hindered women in their pursuit of art. Agustini's recourse to Darío's "teclado" (keyboard) and "estrellas" (stars) becomes tied not only to musicality and a refusal to accept limits but also to a denunciation of the restrictions of bourgeois behavior, especially those associated with feminine domesticity. It is almost as if Agustini were angrily responding to Darío's emphatically male assertion "¡Yo soy el caballero del la humana energía, / yo soy el que presenta su cabeza triunfante / coronada con el laurel del Rey del día" (I am the knight of human energy, / I am the one who presents his triumphant head / crowned with the laurel of the King of day) (255). She asks,

> ¿Por qué ceñir sus manos enguantadas
> A herir teclados y brindar bombones
> Si libres pueden cosechar estrellas,
> Desviar montañas, empuñar los rayos? (99)

[Why gird its gloved hands / to injure keyboards and offer chocolates / if free they can harvest stars, / divert mountains, clutch lightning bolts?]

The question implies that the "gloved hands," freed from playing the household piano out of obligation and without passion (thus "injuring" the keyboard) or released from offering sweets at afternoon tea, can reach for the stars, move mountains, and catch thunderbolts. The poem thus subtly progresses from a discussion of the restrictions that impede artistic inspiration to an indictment of the social expectations that limit women. The poem contrasts the triviality of tasks demanded of bourgeois women with the glory of artistic creation. It juxtaposes the superficiality of being an "ángel del hogar" (angel of the home) to the transcendence of being a poet. The resulting frustration with stultifying domesticity recalls the tensions within other modernista poems, such as Julián del Casal's famous "Neurosis" (1: 231). With the same mixture of defiance and sexuality, Agustini's images turn traditional sexual roles on their heads.

The subversion of gender-related conventions continues in the next four lines: beauty becomes rebellious, the god of the poem becomes a goddess, and the symbol of formal perfection becomes male, specifically, Apollo's divine torso:

> Y la Belleza sufre y se subleva . . .
> ¡Si es herir a la diosa en pleno pecho
> Mermar el torso divinal de Apolo
> Para ajustarlo a ínfima librea! (99)

[And Beauty suffers and rebels . . . / if to diminish the divine torso of Apollo / to make it fit a lowly uniform / is to injure the goddess in the middle of her chest!]

In another metaphor tied to domesticity, Agustini asserts that artificially imposed limitations are as damaging to beauty as the altering of Apollo's torso to fit the unworthy uniform of a servant, thereby presenting poetic constraints as the artistic equivalent of mutilation.[20] This sadistically evocative reference serves to critique not only the inflexibility of poetic rules but also the distortive masks that Agustini may have felt compelled to assume in her daily life. With these clever elaborations upon prevailing associations, her choice of title becomes multivalent. Her rebellion is against personal and artistic constraints. The freedom she seeks is as natural as Apollo's naked torso and as open as the unencumbered sea or the Uruguayan pampa of the poem's final stanza, upon which the linguistically feminine "Idea" seeks to emerge:

> Para morir como su ley impone
> El mar no quiere diques, quiere playas!
> Así la Idea cuando surca el verso
> Quiere al final de la ardua galería,
> Más que una puerta de cristal o de oro,
> La pampa abierta que le grita «¡Libre!» (99)

[To die as its law demands / the sea does not want dikes, it wants beaches! / Thus the Idea when it plows poetry / wants at the end of the arduous passageway, / more than a door of crystal or gold, / the open pampa which shouts "Free!"]

In short, "Rebelión" defines the manifold struggles of the woman poet to break free of inhibiting rules and to become an individual and an artist.[21]

The next poem, "El arte" (100), continues this anguished sense of struggle and further develops the figure of the poet/god. Its central metaphor, however, is the unmentioned—except for the title—"tree of art" that comes to literally overshadow the "tree of life" and emphasizes the vitality and immortality of art. The blessed, golden tree of art survives in the face of unnamed foes through the combined efforts of the larks that fill its boughs and, most intriguingly, a mysterious bird that nests within its foliage:

> Rara simiente de color de fuego
> Germinó en una hora bendecida

A la sombra del árbol de la vida . . .
Nació trémulo y triste como un ruego.

Como oriflama victorioso luego
Yergue triunfal la pompa florecida,
Y se puebla de alondra. —Un día anida
Entre sus frondas, misterioso y ciego,

Un pájaro que canta como un dios
Y arrastra la miseria en su plumaje—.
Con las alondras viene a su follaje
De alimañas sin fin la acometida,
Y él vence y sigue de la Estrella en pos . . .
Hoy es sombra del árbol de la Vida! (100)

[A strange fire-colored seed / germinated at a blessed time / in the shadow of the tree of life . . . / It was born tremulous and sad like a prayer.

Like a victorious banner / the triumphant blooming ostentation then rises up straight, / and it is inhabited by a lark. —One day / a mysterious and blind / bird that sings like a god /

and drags misery in its plumage / nests among its leaves—. / With the larks comes the endless attack / of pests to the foliage, / and it is victorious and it continues in pursuit of the Star . . . / Today it is the tree of Life's shade.]

This blind, mysterious bird "sings like a god" and drags along a wretchedness that is only vaguely defined by the forces of prey that attack it "endless[ly]." Yet this unhappiness also seems to be an inherent part of its being, locked within its plumage, an allusion to those parts of its being that cannot be altered: perhaps its gender and sexuality, perhaps the unrelenting burden of poetic responsibility and the fear of artistic failure. These concerns appear subtly in the description of the birth of the sheltering tree in the first quatrain: "It was born tremulous and sad like a prayer."[22] The reader is, nevertheless, left to speculate who this poet/god of art might be. While to suggest that it is Darío might appear audacious, Agustini does not hesitate to draw this connection in the two letters she sent to the poet himself in August of 1912. In the first (quoted in full in chapter 1) she asks him, "¿Cómo hacerle crer [sic] en [mi timidez] a usted, que sólo conoce la valentía de mi inconsciencia?" (How can I make you believe in my shyness, you who only know the valor of my thoughtlessness?) She goes on to answer: "Tal vez porque le reconocí más esencia divina que a todos los humanos tratados hasta ahora" (Perhaps because I recognized in you more divine essence than in all the human beings I have dealt with until now). In the second letter she is even more specific, telling him, "Si Darío es para el mundo el rey de los poetas, para mi [*sic*] es Dios en el Arte" (If Darío is for the world the king of poets, for me he is God in Art). That her god can also be her lover (a point that becomes significant later in this chapter) is made evident in the next sentence: "Y he visto a ese mi Dios, vivo, dulce y magnífico, que ha de amarse con el más vívido fervor celeste y la más blanca ternura humana" (And I have seen my living, sweet, and magnificent God, who should be loved with the most vivid, celestial fervor and the whitest human tenderness) (*Correspondencia íntima* 43, 46).

In "El arte," published five years before these letters were written, the poet/god may well allude to Darío, who nests within Agustini's art and leads the fight against the relentless enemies of verse, whether they be the linguistic and cultural limits against which both poets do battle or the verbal assaults of insensitive critics. This "bird that sings like a god" might also be Agustini herself, who aspires to sing like her personal "god," Darío, and who is distressed by what she has set out to achieve by pursuing the pure star of poetry. For Agustini, the anguish felt during the act of writing was more than metaphoric. It affected her well-being to the point that her mother confessed, "Her verses are her greatest pleasure, but also her torment. At times, her nervous tension is such that I would prefer that she not compose them, even though I understand that they are a necessity for her" (quoted in Silva, *Genio* 36).[23] Though the identity of the bird and the nature of its misery are left unresolved, the modernista faith in the power of art serves as compensation and solace, for the tree of art stands taller than the tree of life, offsetting the pain of exile into the post-Edenic world of loss and mortality.

Despite Agustini's faith in the divine mission of poets the agony of writing is so great that later in the collection, in "Siembra" [Sowing] (112–13), Agustini portrays the poetic process as a brutal, if sacred, sacrifice. She describes a farmer's attempts to achieve a magical harvest by planting his own blood, which flows from a gaping wound in his chest that resembles a mouth. In the exchange between the lyric voice and the male poet/gardener, he tells her that she will consider him a god once the land begins to bloom. She returns to find him dead in the middle of the field, which is now covered by strange, magnificent plants and illuminated by a heavenly light. In "Siembra" the poet/god is male, and the scene observed by the female novice is inspirational and devastating at the same time.

These poems, which for the most part appear at the beginning of Agustini's first published volume of verse, set the tone for the collection and for her career. They reveal her primary concern to be poetic discourse or, more specifically, how to imagine a female perspective and a female lyric voice in the context of modernismo. In them, she acknowledges, through the images and themes of her verse, her debt to Darío as well as her desire to break away from him and his overpowering influence. Even in these early poems, in which she hides behind the mask of the male poet, she develops a dialogue in which the erotic other is language conceived in human form. The other eventually becomes a strong, amorous male, the quintessential modernista, and the voice of patriarchy and sociolinguistic conventions. The other coalesces around the imposing figure of Darío.

One can see how tightly social and literary issues are woven together in a poem like "La musa" (The muse) (111), in which writing is a contradictory enterprise that finds pleasure, delight, and even transcendence in the pain it arouses. While the lyric voice is of an unspecified gender, the sexualized muse is emphatically not the gentle source of inspiration conventionally invoked. On the contrary, Agustini calls forth a demonic temptress ("Yo la quiero . . . con dos ojos de abismo" [I want her . . . with two abysmal eyes]) whose visionary promise ("con dos ojos que se vuelvan fanales" [with two eyes that become lanterns]) is mixed with references to abduction, assault, and injury. The lyric voice appears to welcome the bittersweet consequences of the task before her or him as if assuming that punishment signals success in piercing the calm surface of conformity and in disrupting normative behavior.[24] Dissatisfied with simple and pleasant models, Agustini sets out to translate into poetry a universe that goes beyond the harmonious ideals pursued by earlier modernistas, thereby anticipating the creative disruptions of the *vanguardia*. She prefers to portray the world as a complex medley of beauty, purity, enlightenment, and strife. As recognized by Patricia Varas, the muse of the title refuses to be confined to a domestic space (124).[25]

These issues and themes run throughout *El libro blanco (Frágil)*, in which more than two-thirds of the poems address Agustini's preoccupation with writing and with finding innovative means of expressing her desire to become fully involved in a culture that would keep her in the role of a passive, obedient child. She takes delight in violating norms, and she finds gratification in her defiance. The resulting reinvention of the language of literary paternity bristles with an aggressive vitality that explodes with erotic energy by the end of the collection. Throughout there are allusions to Darío's work, and I show that it is the reimagining of Darío, as man and as modernista, and his patriarchal language that propels Agustini to produce her greatest work. I want to focus now on those poems from *El libro blanco (Frágil)* that best illustrate how Agustini develops this dialogue with Darío and his modernista tenets. These poems exemplify how she reformulates his anxieties about writing, how she takes the dominant discourse of male power and female passivity and alters it to address her individual concerns about privilege, power, and poetry, and how she begins to establish for herself an enabling language for her independent and innovative perspective.

This iconoclastic point of view does not come without a price. "El austero" (The austere one) (102) addresses how the artist/lyric voice (who is described as "pálido" [pallid]) fuses with "his" art and how every failure or fear of failure is taken as a blow to his existence. In this poem the artist's response to the anguish of his endeavor is equally violent, converting the search for knowledge into a bloodletting of what stands for "Truth" and provoking a desire to file down the torsos of ancient statues. Thus disillusionment ("Murió el Ensueño" [The dream died]) is tied to the outdated models and deceptive appearances: the marble is cold with frenzy, and the flame of the candle is made of ice. Nothing is as it seems. For this reason he pursues transparency, rejecting the glow of gold in favor of the cross and star. "El austero," written from the perspective of a male poet, elaborates upon the tensions Agustini shared with Darío and offers in response both images of destruction and, at the end, the fusion of religion and art.

A more consistently optimistic take on this pursuit of revelatory insight is presented in the next poem, "Astrólogos" (103), which is based on the extended conceit that poets are like astrologers in their exploration and interpretation of heavenly events. Though literally "clouded" by envy and other quarrels, the process of artistic creation is presented as both awe-inspiring and supernatural. Through this juxtaposition Agustini once again aligns the artistic enterprise with extremes that ultimately translate into pleasure and pain. Pleasure emerges from the "conquest" alluded to in the first two lines of verse. The poem's nontraditional format—it is a sonnet of two quatrains, or *serventesios*, and three couplets, or *pareados*, grouped as a third quatrain and a single, final couplet—points to Agustini's experimentation with existing forms (not unlike that of her modernista colleagues), and its language underscores her wish to go beyond her predecessors. She begins by joining ranks with her fellow poets, "brothers" in the adventure before her:

> Venid, venid hermanos! Allá en la azul esfera
> Que eternamente explora nuestra ansia de conquista,
> Cual de una flor de fuego el gran botón que abriera,
> Surge una nueva estrella de lumbre nunca vista! (103)

[Come, come brothers! There in the blue heaven / that our yearning for conquest explores eternally, / as from a fiery flower that the great bud would open, / a new star of light never before seen emerges!]

Here Agustini emphatically signals Darío's presence. She reconfigures his "botón de pensamiento que busca ser la rosa" (bud of thought that seeks to be the rose) from "Yo persigo una forma . . ." (240), melding it with his various astral images of untouched and unencumbered inspiration, like the one in "Pegaso" (254). The bud becomes a fiery flower, a new star of previously unseen strength, and a symbol of having conquered the "blue sphere" of both the heavens and Darío's poetic reflection of their splendor. The star sheds new light and makes possible a new way of seeing. The lyric voice is the one to assert its existence, to call attention to it, and to take ownership of it. The star thus becomes both inspiration and poetic text, a text that, in the second stanza, Agustini declares to be beautiful but open to attack:

> Vedla! —Oh Dios, Dios cuán bella!— Y, ved allá, ya lista,
> La tempestad que avanza; jamás en mi carrera
> Yo vi que al nacimiento de un astro no asistiera
> La nube tumultuosa que alarma y que contrista. (103)

[See it! —Oh God, God how beautiful!— And, see there, already poised /
the storm that advances; on my journey / I never saw that the tumultuous
cloud that alarms and saddens / would not accompany the birth of a star.]

The storm that approaches and the cloud that obscures the light emanat-
ing from the newly formed star suggest the fragile balance in Agustini's
life between fame and notoriety, between adulation and vilification. This
vulnerability to criticism and misunderstanding, common to all innovative
and prescient poets as well as to rebellious women, is further developed in
the next poem, "Jirón de púrpura" (Purple pennant) (104), with an interesting erotic twist.

In "Jirón de púrpura" Agustini builds upon the language in Darío's famous retort "y si hubo áspera hiel en mi existencia, / melificó toda acri-
tud el Arte" (and if, in my existence, there was harsh bile / Art sweetened
all bitterness") (245) from "Yo soy aquel que ayer no más decía. . . ." She
creates a "noble abeja de ensueños" (noble honeybee of reveries), whose
sweet nectar she drinks in a poetic and erotic union:

> Deja llegar mis labios a tus panales de oro [*sic*]
> Ah yo sé bien el precio de esa inefable miel!
> Noble abeja de ensueños, del divino tesoro
> Yo tomaré una gota como un fino joyel.
>
> Yo doy miel por miel; guarda el aguijón sonoro
> A la carne burguesa que profana el vergel,
> A los que regatean tu vida en la miel de oro
> Calculando a la sombra sagrada del laurel.
>
> ¡Ah! esos labios gastados de cifras no aman mieles!
> Ritmo, línea, color, pagan con oropeles
> Y ese dinero encrespa al cóndor del blasón
> Que cela los bravíos linajes aguileños.
> —¡Ah! si quieres ser fuerte, noble abeja de ensueños,
> En mis odios aguza tu sonoro aguijón! (104)

[Let my lips reach your golden honeycombs. / Ah, I know the price of that
ineffable honey! / Noble honeybee of reveries, from the divine treasure / I
will take a drop like a fine jewel.

I give honey for honey; reserve the resonant stinger / for the bourgeois flesh that profanes the lush garden, / for those who barter your life in the golden honey / making calculations in the shade of the sacred laurel tree.

Ah! those lips wasted in numbers do not love honeys! / They pay in tinsel for rhythm, line, color / and that money irritates the condor of the coat of arms / that the brave aquiline bloodlines oversee. / —Ah! if you want to be strong, noble honeybee of reveries, / sharpen your resonant stinger in my hatreds!]

Her lips reach the honey of his beehive, and she offers him honey in return. Unfortunately, the sweetness of the artistic product is embittered by the relentless materialism of the bourgeoisie. Insensitive to the merit of "rhyme, line, and color," they denigrate the poet/bee's "ineffable honey," his "divine treasure," and his life's work in the "sacred shadow" of the honorary laurel. Since the two poets share the same love of art and the same anger at those who do not, the lyric voice offers the noble bee to sharpen his phallic, sonorous stinger within her or, more precisely, within the hate she shares with him for the philistines who surround them. This hatred, a constant lament of the modernistas, was succinctly captured in Darío's oft-quoted "¡Torres de Dios! ¡Poetas! . . ." (Towers of God! Poets! . . .) (256–57).[26]

"Jirón de púrpura" not only shows how Agustini imaginatively elaborates upon modernista imagery and how she pursues the thorny issues regarding the role of art in society, it also addresses the complex relationship between the concrete and the abstract. Resentment of the crass, unfeeling public plays into the poets' struggle with material reality, most particularly with how to make the materiality of the text consonant with the immaterial dreams and the transcendent levels of existence it seeks to capture. By extension the poem questions how to make those dreams and visions perceptible to the reader who recognizes only what is visible and palpable. By defining the longed-for partner of poetic bliss as a "noble abeja de ensueños" and the desired goal as "inefable miel," Agustini subtly draws attention to concerns which, as shown by Daniel Tiffany in his study *Toy Medium: Materialism and Modern Lyric,* have followed lyric poetry virtually from its beginnings but which become ever more problematic during the modern period.

"Al vuelo" (In flight) (108–9) continues the collection's focus on writing, this time emphasizing the failings of formal expectations and the deceitful superficiality they engender. The poem endorses, instead, spirit, vitality, spontaneity, and natural, unencumbered purity. The fourth and fifth stanzas declare,

> —Frente a la Venus clásica de Milo
> Sueño una estatua de mujer muy fea
> Oponiendo al desnudo de la dea
> Luz de virtudes y montañas de hilo!—
>
> Nunca os atraiga el brillo del diamante
> Más que la luz sangrienta de la llama:
> Ésta es vida, calor, pasión vibrante,
> Aquélla helado resplandor de escama! (108)

[—Facing the classic Venus de Milo / I dream of a statue of a very ugly woman / contrasting the nudity of the goddess / with the light of virtues and mountains of cloth!—

Never let the brilliance of the diamond attract you / more than the bloody light of the flame: / this one is life, heat, vibrant passion, / that one the cold splendor of scales!]

Agustini asserts her continued dissatisfaction with the rigid rules of artistic production. This time she goes one step further, rejecting traditional visions of feminine beauty and ideal form. As Marcella Trambaioli points out, "The 'I' affirms in an emphatic manner 'I dream of a statue of a very ugly woman,' contrasting her with the classic Aphrodite, who seems to her to be 'the cold splendor of scales'" (59).[27] By condemning the cold emptiness of brilliant execution and exalting the heat of flesh and blood passions, however defective that flesh and blood may be, Agustini ties modernismo's most fundamental aspirations to her new spirited sexual orientation.

At the same time, "Al vuelo" exposes fault lines that were beginning to surface within the movement. The formal perfection cultivated by the early modernistas in their pursuit of beauty and transcendence had begun to be copied by less talented practitioners. Agustini's injunction against false appearances addresses this problem and anticipates the position most

often identified with Enrique González Martínez and his famous "Tuércele el cuello al cisne . . ." (Twist the neck of the swan . . .) (116), published
four years later, in 1911. Whereas González Martínez's sonnet begins with
"Tuércele el cuello al cisne de engañoso plumaje / que da su nota blanca
al azul de la fuente," ("Twist the neck of the swan that, arrayed in deceptive plumage, gives its white note to the blue of the fountain"), Agustini's
ends with

> Desdeñad la apariencia, la falsía,
> La gala triste del defecto erguido:
> Menos tendréis que descubrir un día
> Desnuda el alma horrorizada, fría
> Ante el Supremo Tribunal temido! (109)

[Disdain appearance, falsehood, / the sad display of the elevated flaw: / you
will have less to reveal one day / with your naked soul horrified and cold /
before the feared Supreme Tribunal!]

Like González Martínez, she aspires to a purity of expression through
which she can achieve communion with the transcendental aspects of existence, but she also rejects the superficiality that is demanded of women.
She speaks out against the expectations that keep her focused on appearance rather than on achieving something of substance, and she aspires to
a life that reflects her personal truths. Hence the concluding reference to
judgment gives this declaration of poetic intention an interesting twist that
hints at Agustini's multiple, irreverent challenges to authority.

The poem that follows "Al vuelo" in the collection, "El hada color de
rosa" (The pink fairy) (110), further develops Agustini's position. It is an extraordinary testament to the fact that Agustini is not simply trying to be a
great modernista poet but has formulated a poetics in which she responds
to and even aspires to supplant Darío:

> El hada color de rosa que mira como un diamante,
> El hada color de rosa que charla como un bulbul,
> A mi palacio una aurora llegó en su carro brillante,
> Esparciendo por mis salas un perfume de Stambul.
>
> —Toma —y una esbelta lira de oro me dio—en ella cante
> La musa de tus ensueños sus parques, el cisne azul

Que tiende en los lagos de oro su cuello siempre al Levante,
Y Helena que pasa envuelta en la neblina de un tul.

Busca la rima y el ritmo de un humo, de una fragancia,
Y en perlas de luz desgrana las risas de Extravagancia
Que muestra los dientes blancos a Zoilo de adusto ceño.
Canta en la aurora rosada, canta en la tarde de plata
Y cuando el sol, como un rey, muera en su manto escarlata,
Mientras que la noche llega, ensaya un ritmo y un sueño! (110)

[The pink-colored fairy with a diamond-like look, / the pink-colored fairy who prattles like a nightingale, / arrived at my palace one dawn in her shining cart, / spreading through my rooms a perfume from Istanbul.

—Take this —and she gave me a slim golden lyre— with it let / the muse of your reveries sing her parks, the blue swan / that on the golden lakes always offers its neck to the East, / and Helen who passes by in a mist of tulle.

Seek the rhyme and rhythm of a trail of smoke, of a fragrance, / and in pearls of light scatter the laughter of Extravagance / who shows her white teeth to Zoilus of the dour scowl. / Sing during the pink dawn, sing in the silver afternoon / and when the sun, like a king, dies in his scarlet cloak, / while night arrives, rehearse a rhythm and a dream!]

The struggle with Darío emerges in the evocative dialogue between the poem's lyric voice and the pink fairy. Key images recall both Darío's "Sonatina" (187–88) and his "El reino interior" (The inner kingdom) (225–27), the last poem of the 1896 edition of *Prosas profanas*. All three poems have fairy godmothers, palaces, princesses, and references to exotic locations and products. In contrast to the "hada madrina" of Darío's "Sonatina," who speaks from a male perspective, silences the princess, and is implicitly blue—like the "azul celeste" and "cuentos azules" of "El reino interior," Agustini's pink fairy gives her princess a lyre and the opportunity to sing. Though this poetry still echoes with Darío's blueness and his iconic swan (l. 6), Agustini's poem offers her—supposedly female—lyric voice options and possibilities.

Agustini further signals her debt to Darío through her use of the exceedingly unusual "bulbul," which appears in "El reino interior" with a much-needed internal explanation of its meaning ("*Bulbules:* ruiseñores").[28] By means of this striking reference Agustini flags the interplay among these three poems and their shared focus on the nature of poetry. In both "Sonatina" and "El reino interior" the female prisoner is the poet's poetic other, the virginal starting point for male creativity. Linked with the artist's "soul," this "tender sister of the Sleeping Beauty of the forest" (227) dreams of escape from the materiality and rigidity of the golden cage in which she resides, symbolizing the reconciliation between passion and virtue, between free rein and control, between wild visions and established expectations.[29] What does the lyric voice of "El hada color de rosa" dream about? The answer is given indirectly. In Agustini's sonnet, perhaps one of the most graceful of *El libro blanco (Frágil),* the princess is not told to wait silently for her prince, nor is she locked within sleep. On the contrary, she is invited to take up the lyre and, with it, to give voice to the muse of her dreams, who will find her own way to sing about the blue swan and Helen. In other words, she is welcomed into the modernista fold.[30] She is encouraged to search for "the rhyme and rhythm of a trail of smoke, of a fragrance," the type of subtleties desired by the princess of "Sonatina" and sought after by Darío in "Yo persigo una forma . . ." (240). She is instructed to sing in the morning, to announce a new day, and to create through the night, as the "sun, like a king, dies in his scarlet cloak." Unwilling to overthrow Darío directly, Agustini hides her challenge to authority and veils her ambition behind the simile uniting the fading light of the afternoon sun with a dying king. This metaphor reappears in later works of hers in which there is, as noted, a clear dialogue between old and new, past and future, death and rejuvenation. In "El hada color de rosa" the struggle is masked by the normal flow of time, the natural stages of the day. Nevertheless, within the symbolic context of the poem the intent becomes clear. The pink fairy of the title invites the poet to practice her art as the light fades on the ruling authority. As an ensemble, the poem dethrones Darío, asserting a wish to reinscribe his dictates within a personal, feminine perspective that grants the privilege of poetic nobility to a new lyric voice.

Eventually these veiled statements of rebellion become directly aggressive and assertively sexual. The parks, swans, and lakes that the pink fairy would have her muse capture in song resurface in "Nocturno" (Nocturne) (254) and "El cisne" (The swan) (255–57) from *Los cálices vacíos* in defiant declarations of autonomy, becoming clearer and more patently rebellious as the attributes subtly signaled in the reference to Helen, in Greek mythology considered the most beautiful woman in the land, are more fully exploited. Behind this iconic association lurks the less emphasized detail that she was the product of a savage rape of the lovely Leda by Zeus, who had taken the form of a swan. While neither the "blue swan" of the sixth line nor the tulle-wrapped Helen of the eighth line calls attention to the patriarchal violence that hides within her story, this brutality (already evident in "El austero") appears here as the opening salvo in a battle for poetry that will leave many blood-stained combatants. In this regard, Agustini appears to respond to another poem from *Prosas profanas*, namely, "El cisne" (213), in which Darío announces his artistic goals. The "blue swan" of "El hada color de rosa" is the generative source of "Leda's blue egg" in Darío's poem. From this egg the spiritual and immortal Helen emerges as model and inspiration for the offspring between "la nueva Poesía" (the new poetry) and the new male inseminating force (Darío himself). Poet and Zeus fuse in the sexual embrace of language that hides its violence behind its assertion that beneath the white wings of the swan "the new Poetry / conceives in a glory of light and harmony / the eternal and pure Helen that embodies the ideal."[31] At this point Agustini does not, as she does later, unmask the lasting injury inflicted by this affirmation of male poetic power.

This engagement with the modernista conception of poetic authority develops further in "Mi oración" (My prayer) (121), in metaphors that reverberate with echoes of Darío's "La espiga" (The ear of wheat) (234–35) from the 1901 edition of *Prosas profanas*. Though there is a coincidence between the two descriptions of the temple-like countryside, each addresses a different facet of the scenes presented. Darío focuses on God's immanence in nature, leaving his role as initiate and guide implicit in his instruction to the reader to look and see. Agustini, however, emphasizes her hope of becoming the priestess of her temple by drawing from her muse the wisdom found in nature, a vision that seems to have arrived by way of Darío and Charles Baudelaire, particularly from Baudelaire's vastly influential "Correspondances." In "Mis ídolos" (My idols) (156–58) she achieves her objective. She sets up an altar for the new god of poetry, who is marked as a member of a "celestial race" and who reigns supreme over a thousand "singing voices." "Mis ídolos" ends with ten revealing lines:

Luego, con los brillantes escombros formé un claro
Altar para el dios nuevo que reinó, simple y fuerte,
En la belleza austera del templo de lo raro
Donde todo vivía como herido de muerte.
Y quité el polvo viejo, las corolas marchitas,
Y traje de los campos alegres margaritas
De vívidas corolas y de perfume santo.
Y ofrendé al nuevo dios mi corazón que abría
Como una flor de sangre, de amor y de armonía.

Y le adoré con ansias y le adoré con llanto! (157–58)

[Then, with the shining rubble I made a bright / altar for the new god who reigned, simple and strong, / over the austere beauty of the temple of the unusual / where everything lived as if fatally wounded. / And I removed the old dust, the withered flowers, / and I brought from the happy fields daisies / of vivid corollas and holy perfume. / I offered the new god my heart which was opening like a flower of blood, of love, and of harmony.

And I adored him with yearnings and I adored him with a flood of tears!]

Agustini worships in the temple of the "strange," the "unusual," that is, at the altar of the god of Darío's *Los raros*. She honors his disavowal of empty, formulaic phrases and formats by "removing the dust and withered flowers of the past," even if this means rewriting his now-established perspectives. She brings to the altar the color, vitality, harmony, and passion demanded of all true adherents. This poet/god reappears in "Ave de luz" (Bird of light) (152–53), another poem that elucidates the ways in which Agustini begins to turn from obedient priestess into seductive usurper.[32]

In "Ave de luz" Agustini develops the image of the bird of poetry that plays a central role in several of the poems already discussed, emphasizing its abilities as a magical force of poetic illumination and inspiration.[33] Through a virtuoso elaboration of the metaphor of light, she joins divinity with artistic ability and converts, once again, the poet into a type of god. In addition, she moves this enlightening force from the tree of art, where it took up residence in "El arte," into the poet's brain, thereby following the example set by Darío in his short story "El pájaro azul" (The blue bird), which was first published in 1886 and later collected in the 1888 edition of

Azul . . . In this story Garcín is a dedicated poet who pursues art in opposition to the desires expressed by his philistine father. The beloved poet equates his torturous aspirations with the "blue bird" locked within his brain. Garcín's "insanity" eventually ends with his shooting himself in the head, opening the door to the bird's cerebral cage.

While some critics have seen in the dismemberment of the human form that appears in Agustini's poem her struggle with the dominant patriarchal perspective,[34] I find her images to be particularly apt representations of her anguish over and obsession with artistic creativity, not unlike those of Darío's Garcín. These factors are particularly evident in the poem's last two stanzas:

> Postraos ante el hombre que lleva en su cerebro
> Esa ave misteriosa ¡manojo de fulgor!
> Que mata, que enloquece, que crea y que ilumina
> ¡Aquel en quien anida, es émulo de Dios!
>
> . . . .
>
> ¡Oh Genio! ¡extraña ave de vuelo inconcebible!
> De regias esbelteces, de olímpica actitud;
> Escucha: yo te brindo mis frescas ilusiones,
> Mis mágicos ensueños, mi rica juventud,
> ¡A cambio de un instante de vida en mi cerebro!
> ¡A cambio de un arpegio de tu canción de luz! (152–53)

[Kneel before the man who carries within his head / that mysterious bird, bundle of resplendence! / that kills, that maddens, that creates and illuminates / the one in whom it nests, is the rival of God!

. . . .

Oh genius! Strange bird of inconceivable flight! / Of royal slenderness, of Olympic attitude; / Listen: I offer you my fresh hopes, / my magic reveries, my rich youth, / in exchange for an instant of life in my brain! / in exchange for an arpeggio of your song of light!]

The poem confirms that the agony that comes from wanting to fuse with the true light of poetic perfection can lead to insanity, a very concrete fear expressed by Agustini's mother. In a passage quoted earlier in the chapter, she admits that she worries about her daughter's mental health (Silva, *Genio* 36). Yet, as the poem clarifies, the ecstasy of artistic success counterbalances all the risks and sacrifices. For this reason, "Ave de luz" ends with her willingness to forfeit her youth and dreams in order to carry in her head the strange and wonderful bird that currently sings in the brain of the godlike poet. The language she employs recalls the story of Lot's daughters and the seduction that promises access to knowledge and control of the future.

Though there can be little doubt that that poet is Darío, "Iniciación" (155) additionally supports this identification. In "Iniciación" Agustini places the bird/poet in the same "sacred forest" as the ones that appear in Darío's "Coloquio de los centauros" (204) and "Yo soy aquel que ayer no más decía . . ." (246). Through this imaginative interchange with Darío, Agustini finds her path to the new perspective that defined her work.

The seductive overtones at the end of "Ave de luz" become progressively more assertive and direct just a few pages later in the collection. In the seven poems of "Orla rosa" (Pink fringe), the concluding section of *El libro blanco (Frágil)*, and in the one immediately before them, "Misterio, ven" (Mystery, come) (159–60), Agustini goes beyond timid apprentice and begins the transformation of artistic model into amatory other and partner. While critics such as Arturo Visca and Girón Alvarado have recognized this section as the one that signals a transition to a more confident stance in Agustini's writing, they did not recognize to what extent it represents the culmination of what preceded it.[35] As my survey of the poems from the first part of *El libro blanco (Frágil)* makes abundantly clear, Agustini's primary, almost obsessive concern is with writing and with delineating her poetic vision and literary aspirations. Her ideals were established in an ongoing detailed conversation with Darío, whose prominence and recourse to the language of literary paternity could have, in another context and with a different poet, condemned her to an incapacitating sense of inadequacy, if not paralysis. Agustini nevertheless picks up her pen and begins to compose, claiming her right to be not only an engaged, sexual individual but also an active producer of culture who pushes the limits of what women can say. Her defiant rebellion against convention is written in many keys: the fanciful, the religious, and the erotic. She cleverly blends the language of fear, transgression, arousal, and seduction as she creates a voice that is both personal and poetic.

The new affirmation of self found in "Orla rosa" marks an internally consistent but nonetheless dramatic development in the formulation of her views on life, love, art, and writing. Unfortunately, many critics ignored the breadth of Agustini's contribution by reducing her visionary stance to issues of passion, emotion, and sexuality.[36] In this regard the archetype of the sexual seduction and conquest of the older male becomes a powerful conceptual tool, underscoring that her appropriative stance is undertaken in the name of cultural renewal. While the old ways lead to death, the reformulation of concepts, values, and language leads to (re)birth. In her poetry Agustini aspires to expand and renew modernista discourse as well as to alter the perspectives that that discourse communicated. Her goal is to open up language and possibilities. It is precisely this promise of empowerment that had such an impact upon other women writers and the reason she is judged to be a pioneer who influenced her compatriot and contemporary María Eugenia Vaz Ferreira as well as a large number of younger poets who continued the struggle to establish a voice for women, including Alfonsina Storni, Juana de Ibarbourou, and Gabriela Mistral.[37]

The tasks she has set for herself, however, are far from easy. She has to invent a language within which she can operate and that does not lock her within a projection of a false masculinity, as she had been for the greater part of *El libro blanco (Frágil)*. She has to conquer the fears that plagued so many women of her generation about being an unwanted interloper and spoiler who would fall victim to disapproval, scorn, and isolation. She has to slide out from under Darío's imposing presence and stand up against the terror of always being derivative and inferior.

Although "Íntima" (Intimate) (163–64), the first poem of "Orla rosa," speaks of reflection in its choice of words as well as in its form, it is not about passivity. On the contrary, it is a self-confident statement that reveals Agustini's approach to writing and her faith in her artistic abilities. The poem's twelve stanzas of four hendecasyllabic lines echo the early modernista concern with formal balance and perfection. The language Agustini uses and the anguish she seeks to express evoke Darío, for her suffering, like his, results from the frightening burden of poetic responsibility. Darío's "Melancolía" (286), published in *Cantos de vida y esperanza*, epitomizes these concerns:

> Hermano, tú que tienes la luz, dime la mía.
> Soy como un ciego. Voy sin rumbo y ando a tientas.

> Voy bajo tempestades y tormentas,
> ciego de ensueño y loco de armonía.
>
> Ése es mi mal. Soñar. La poesía
> es la camisa férrea de mil puntas cruentas
> que llevo sobre el alma. Las espinas sangrientas
> dejan caer las gotas de mi melancolía.
>
> Y así voy, ciego y loco, por este mundo amargo;
> a veces me parece que el camino es muy largo,
> y a veces que es muy corto . . .
>
> Y en este titubeo de aliento y agonía,
> cargo lleno de penas lo que apenas soporto.
> ¿No oyes caer las gotas de mi melancolía? (286)

[Brother, you who have the light, tell me mine. / I am like a blind man. I proceed without direction feeling my way. / I walk beneath storms and tempests, / blinded by reverie and mad with harmony.

That is my curse. To dream. Poetry / is the iron shirt of a thousand cruel barbs / that I wear upon my soul. The bloody thorns / are dripping with my melancholy.

This is how I travel, blind and crazed, through this bitter world; / at times the road seems very long, / and at times very short . . .

And in this vacillation between courage and agony, / I carry, full of grief, what I can barely endure. / Do you not hear the dripping of my melancholy?]

Agustini turns to Darío but not in an act of subservience. She speaks as a strong "I," asserts herself, and professes autonomy. She sees the role she has been given as a painfully difficult one, demanding of great sacrifice. She compares her artistic mission to an arduous path and her destiny with that of Christ and his followers. She also repeats other images that are associated with Darío, namely, the spiritual nudity ("mi alma desnuda") required to write and the "ivory tower" ("torre de marfil") of poetic isolation, alienation, and aspiration.[38] The poem begins with the following three stanzas:

> Yo te diré los sueños de mi vida
> En lo más hondo de la noche azul . . .

Mi alma desnuda temblará en tus manos,
Sobre tus hombros pesará mi cruz.

Las cumbres de la vida son tan solas,
Tan solas y tan frías! Yo encerré
Mis ansias en mí misma, y toda entera
Como una torre de marfil me alcé.

Hoy abriré a tu alma el gran misterio;
Ella es capaz de penetrar en mí.
En el silencio hay vértigos de abismo:
Yo vacilaba, me sostengo en ti. (163)

[I will tell you the dreams of my life / in the deepest region of the blue night . . . / My naked soul will tremble in your hands, / my cross will weigh upon your shoulders.

Life's peaks are so solitary, / so solitary and so cold! I enclosed / my yearnings inside myself; and I rose up, / all of me, whole like an ivory tower.

Today I will open the great mystery to your soul; / it is capable of penetrating into me. / In the silence one finds the giddy dizziness of the abyss: / I staggered, I am supported by you.]

In the sexual language of penetration and climax that will become the hallmark of her poetry, the third stanza reveals the poet's increased daring, even though she still leans on the other as she surveys, from the heights of poetic production, the artistic landscape that is fraught with fearsome visions and dangers of failure. The fourth stanza once again echoes Darío's "La fuente" (235) but in a newly defiant manner:

Muero de ensueños; beberé en tus fuentes
Puras y frescas la verdad: yo sé
Que está en el fondo magno de tu pecho
El manantial que vencerá mi sed. (163)

[I die of reveries; I will drink truth in your / pure and refreshing fountains: I know / that the spring that will conquer my thirst / lies in the great depth of your chest.]

Here, in contrast to the other poems in which Agustini alludes to "La fuente," her lyric voice proposes to drink from the pure, truth-providing spring that flows within the poetic other. She takes control of the situation, drinks from him, as she does his blood in "Supremo idilio" (Supreme idyll) (*Cantos de la mañana* 188), and draws from him the essence that will sustain her. In the next stanzas she further elucidates their relationship:

> Y sé que en nuestras vidas se produjo
> El milagro inefable del reflejo . . .
> En el silencio de la noche mi alma
> Llega a la tuya como a un gran espejo.
>
> Imagina el amor que habré soñado
> En la tumba glacial de mi silencio!
> Más grande que la vida, más que el sueño,
> Bajo el azur sin fin se sintió preso. (163)

[And I know that in our lives / the indescribable miracle of reflection was created . . . / In the nocturnal silence my soul / reaches yours like reaching a great mirror.

Imagine the love that I must have dreamed / in the glacial tomb of my silence! / Greater than life, more than the dream, / beneath the endless azure it felt imprisoned.]

This language of reflection represents increasing confidence (it is the result of a miracle) and an ever-greater sense of equality. If, like other women writers, she must first see herself in the language of patriarchy and of her male contemporaries, Agustini quickly understands that these are surface images she must hold up to scrutiny so that they can be recognized as the distortions they are. Here, however, she adds depth to the image. When she looks into his soul, she sees everything she has longed to be. She sees the artist she aspires to be. More important, it is through this reciprocity that she moves from silence to speech. Like a Sleeping Beauty who has not yet awakened, she had been locked within "the glacial tomb of . . . silence." The love that stirs her is not human; it drives her to pursue a superhuman existence, that is, the demanding, even tortured, life of the poet:

> Imagina mi amor, amor que quiere
> Vida imposible, vida sobrehumana,
> Tú que sabes si pesan, si consumen
> Alma y sueños de Olimpo en carne humana.

> Y cuando frente al alma que sentía
> Poco el azur para bañar sus alas,
> Como un gran horizonte aurisolado
> O una playa de luz, se abrió tu alma . . . (163–64)

[Imagine my love, a love that wants / an impossible life, a superhuman life, / you who know if the soul and dreams / of Olympus weigh upon and consume human flesh.

And when facing the soul that barely felt / the blue to bathe its wings, / Like a great golden horizon / or a beach of light, your soul opened up . . .]

These dreams of Olympus can be no other than her dreams of poetic success and of achieving the modernista perfection of the "olímpico cisne de nieve" (Olympic snow-white swan) of Darío's "Blasón" (Coat of arms) (188–89).[39] The previously insensitive wings of her soul fuse with those of the swan. The "you" of the poem, her amorous other, reveals the full expanse of his soul, like "the blue" of the heavens and the reflective waters of the seas. She blesses and embraces life, life that he has come to epitomize: "Bendije a Dios, al sol, la flor, el aire, / La vida toda porque tú eras vida!" (I blessed God, the sun, the flower, the air, / all of life because you were life) (164).

The next two stanzas speak to the conquering of her fears, anguish, and suffering as well as to her joyous engagement in the modernista movement. She seeks to move away from ordinary human interaction with its frighteningly intrusive noise and activity:

> Si con angustia yo compré esta dicha,
> Bendito el llanto que manchó mis ojos!
> ¡Todas las llagas del pasado ríen
> Al sol naciente por sus labios rojos!
>
> ¡Ah! tú sabrás mi amor, mas vamos lejos
> A través de la noche florecida;
> Acá lo humano asusta, acá se oye,
> Se ve, se siente sin cesar la vida. (164)

[If with anguish I purchased this joy, / blessed is the weeping that stained my eyes! / All the wounds of the past laugh / at the rising sun through their red lips!

Ah! you will know my love, but we are going far / across the flower-filled night; / here the human frightens, here one hears, one sees, one feels life without pause.]

By the end of the poem the lyric voice stands emboldened. She asserts her autonomy by rejecting all imitation, all echoes of others. She declares a virginal beginning to the love affair with her specially selected partner, a relationship that will eventually produce a superior, poetic race. She writes,

> Vamos más lejos en la noche, vamos
> Donde ni un eco repercuta en mí,
> Como una flor nocturna allá en la sombra
> Yo abriré dulcemente para ti. (164)

[Let's go farther in the night, let's go / where not even an echo reverberates in me, / like a nocturnal flower there in the dark / I will sweetly open for you.]

This imagery sexualizes the exchange she has had with her poetic other and begins to alter the language of male creativity into erotic metaphors that empower women as writers and lovers. Though she still awaits contact with the male, she takes the lead and turns the tables, silencing him as she seduces him.[40] Silence becomes the prelude to productivity, to speech, to the promise of fulfillment.

The erotic undertone of "Íntima" is also intense in "Misterio, ven" (Mystery, come) (159–60), the poem that precedes the concluding section of *El libro blanco (Frágil)*. Agustini's lyric voice addresses the "extraño amado de mi musa extraña" (the strange lover of my strange muse), who is the beloved of her personal, idiosyncratic muse, that is, he is desired by that part of herself that inspires her to write and that pushes her to be a poet. He is an appropriate object of her attentions for he is himself a gifted poet, as implied in lines nine and ten, "Ven, tú, el que imprimes un solemne ritmo / Al parpadeo de la tumba helada . . ." (Come, you, who prints a solemn rhythm / upon the flickering of the frozen tomb), and as clearly stated in line thirteen, "Ven, tú, el poeta abrumador, . . ." (Come, you, the overwhelming poet). His talents are unique; he achieves the objectives that Darío had set for himself and for other modernista writers. The lyric voice affirms his success in statements about him that echo Darío's language and poetic vision.[41] The verse of her "strange beloved" vibrates in consonance with the deep, silent rhythms of the universe and achieves harmonious accord with the soul. Ready to face the dark night of death and other tragic visions, he masters the cadence of existence. Agustini takes these objectives and adds a nuance of mystery and passion:

> Ven, tú, el que imprimes un solemne ritmo
> Al parpadeo de la tumba helada;
> El que dictas los lúgubres acentos
> Del decir hondo de las sombras trágicas.
> Ven, tú, el poeta abrumador, que pulsas
> La lira del silencio: la más rara!
> La de las largas vibraciones mudas,
> La que se acorda al diapasón del alma! (159)

[Come, you, who prints a solemn rhythm / upon the flickering of the frozen tomb; / you who pronounce the mournful accents / of the profound speech of the tragic shadows. / Come, you, the overwhelming poet, who strums / the silent lyre: the rarest one! / The one of the long mute vibrations, / the one that is tuned with the tuning fork of the soul!]

The lyric voice of the poem speaks in seductive whispers. She invites intimacy and passion as his strumming of the silent lyre produces orgasmic tremors of both body and soul. She sets out to conquer the poet and to draw from him his powers to capture and tame the unheard music of the spheres and the rhythm of existence:

> Ven, acércate a mí, que en mis pupilas
> Se hundan las tuyas en tenaz mirada,
> Vislumbre en ellas, el sublime enigma
> Del *más allá,* que espanta . . .
> Ven . . . acércate más . . . clava en mis labios
> Tus fríos labios de ámbar,
> Guste yo en ellos el sabor ignoto
> De la esencia enervante de tu alma!
>
> . . . .
> Ven, oye yo te evoco,
> Extraño amado de mi musa extraña! (159–60)

[Come, draw close to me, so that in my pupils / yours may sink in a tenacious gaze, / let there be discerned in them, the sublime enigma / of the *beyond*, that frightens . . . / Come . . . draw closer . . . drive into my lips / your cold amber lips, / Let me taste in them the unknown flavor / of the exhausting essence of your soul!

.   .   .   .

Come, listen, I call you forth, / strange lover of my strange muse!]

She invites him to find in her eyes the sublime enigma of life beyond the here and now. She is the one who holds the answers, which fuse desire and delight, life and death, pleasure, poetry, and knowledge. Nevertheless, she still wishes to drink the essence of his soul. She wishes to kiss his cold amber lips, lips that recall the lips of a swan, the modernista symbol par excellence.

The identification of these amber lips with those of a swan has a clear precedent in Darío's "Leda" (276–77), which was first published in 1892 and later collected in *Cantos de vida y esperanza* (1905). "Leda" begins with the following stanza:

> El cisne en la sombra parece de nieve;
> su pico es de ámbar, del alba al trasluz;
> el suave crepúsculo que pasa tan breve
> las cándidas alas sonrosa de luz. (276)

[The swan in the shadow appears to be of snow; / its beak is of amber, of the translucent dawn; / the gentle first light that passes so briefly / colors the white wings pink with light.]

Agustini draws upon and alters this description, turning the swan's beak into lips but keeping them cold and amber-colored. She thereby melds the modernista icon with the writer/lover of the poem. Through the image of the swan as sexual partner and poet, which, as we have seen, has already developed strong associations in Agustini's early texts, one begins to see how the poems of *El libro blanco (Frágil)* become the basis for her mature poetics.

Sylvia Molloy was the first scholar to point to the confluence of swan and sexuality in both Agustini and Darío. In a much-quoted article she shows how Agustini's swan differs from Darío's Leda-based version and its identification with male, voyeuristic sexuality. Referring to Agustini's "El cisne" (255–56), from her third collection, *Los cálices vacíos*, Molloy writes, "She gives voice to feminine eroticism that in Darío is lost, is squandered, for lack of a word. . . . The eroticism in Agustini needs to be said, to be inscribed, not as a complaint of a defeated woman that is lost in the wind but rather as a triumphant—and fearsome—pleasure" (66).[42] But as much as Agustini's poetry inscribes an enthusiastic feminine eroticism that lies beyond Darío's perspective, giving voice to what has traditionally been silenced, her greatest breakthrough is how she recasts the language of literary paternity from a woman's perspective, permitting her eroticism to capture her empowering vision for writing. Agustini fuses lover, poet, and symbol and begins to define her poetry as a celebration of self, sex, and voice. As suggested in my discussion of "Misterio, ven" and "Íntima," by the end of *El libro blanco (Frágil)* Agustini begins to demand full participation in life as a sexually aware, artistically adroit woman.

The fusion of love and poetry is so strong that it has confounded many informed readers. Indeed, Agustini's language of poetic yearning so thoroughly resonates with that of erotic ardor that passion appears to overshadow artistic aspirations in many poems. In "Explosión" (165), for example, Agustini describes with such exuberance the joy of life and the delight in existence once love is achieved that alternative interpretations tend to be crowded out.[43] Yet the poem ends with a celebration of song and language: "Mi vida toda canta, besa, ríe! / Mi vida toda es una boca en flor!" (My whole life sings, kisses, laughs! / My whole life is a mouth in bloom!), a declaration that suggests that poetic success is part of the fulfillment achieved.

"El intruso" (The intruder) (168) clarifies how Agustini weaves together her erotic and poetic perspectives. Although this sonnet opens with an apostrophe that deliberately merges the abstract concept of love with a possible individual, this other is primarily the force that animates the potential of the lyric voice, unlocking her limitations and inhibitions. The images of the first quatrain evoke both the passion of a sexual encounter and the sensual explosion of literary inspiration:

> Amor, la noche estaba trágica y sollozante
> Cuando tu llave de oro cantó en mi cerradura;
> Luego, la puerta abierta sobre la sombra helante
> Tu forma fue una mancha de luz y de blancura. (168)

[Love, the night was tragic and tearful / when your golden key sang in my lock; / then, the door opened over the freezing darkness / your form was a stain of light and whiteness.]

Agustini's statement is as dramatic as the question with which Gilbert and Gubar open their study. While they ask, "Is a pen a metaphorical penis?" (3), Agustini leaves little doubt that her singing key is simultaneously a metaphorical pen and penis with which she acknowledges the unavoidable penetration of traditional sexual arrangements and linguistic patterns. She does not, however, simply accept these conventions. She recasts them by having the male figure serve her, enabling what Maria-Elena Armstrong calls "the passionate exaltation of the feminine voice that narrates with eroticism the male–female relationship" (52).[44] But whereas Armstrong sees purification, I see illumination in which the male's form becomes a "stain of light and whiteness" that writes upon the freezing shadows of this dark night of her soul, the night of artistic frustration and despair. This "white stain," with its contradictory associations, invokes a blessed transgression, a crossing of normative boundaries that recalls the subtle allusion to immaculate conception in "Por campos de ensueño." The white stain, whether ink or semen, is offered as a source of hope and inspiration, and the beloved becomes a guiding beacon that awakens the speaker's visionary abilities. At the same time, the poem does not ignore the imposing nature of male authority. He lays his head, perhaps the one that carries within it the "ave de luz," next to hers on the white pillow of the poetic page, and she willingly sleeps at his feet in exchange for the insights she has achieved:

> Y hoy río si tú ríes, y canto si tú cantas;
> Y si tú duermes, duermo como un perro a tus plantas!
> Hoy llevo hasta en mi sombra tu olor de primavera;
> Y tiemblo si tu mano toca la cerradura
> Y bendigo la noche sollozante y oscura
> Que floreció en mi vida tu boca tempranera! (168)

[And today I laugh if you laugh, and I sing if you sing; / and if you sleep, I sleep like a dog at your feet! / Today I carry even in my shadow your smell of spring; / and I tremble if your hand touches the lock / and I bless the tearful and dark night / that your early mouth bloomed in my life.]

The poem ends on a joyous note, asserting that the female lyric voice has found a way to write, to sing, and to blossom as a poet.

The vacillation between reverence and rebellion continues in and dominates the final three poems of the collection. Of the three, the most hopefully independent is the first, "La copa del amor" (The goblet of love) (169–70), and the most cautiously restrained is the third, "Desde lejos" (From afar) (172). While the title of "La copa del amor" points to the amorous dimension of the relationship discussed, its references to "the illustrious goblet," its "rare liquor," "the indelible shadow of your palms," "the silent tomb of my days," the "voice" that "embroiders" "gloomy silences," "harmonious lips," and "daydreaming fingers" all redirect attention to language and writing:

> Bebamos juntos en la copa egregia!
> Raro licor se ofrenda a nuestras almas.
> Abran mis rosas su frescura regia
> A la sombra indeleble de tus palmas!
>
> Tú despertaste mi alma adormecida
> En la tumba silente de las horas;
> A ti la primer [*sic*] sangre de mi vida
> ¡En los vasos de luz de mis auroras!
>
> ¡Ah! tu voz vino a recamar de oro
> Mis lóbregos silencios; tú rompiste
> El gran hilo de perlas de mi lloro,
> Y al sol naciente mi horizonte abriste.
>
> Por ti, en mi oriente nocturnal, la aurora
> Tendió el temblor rosado de su tul;
> Así en las sombras de la vida ahora,
> Yo te adoro el alma como un cielo azul!
>
> ¡Ah, yo me siento abrir como una rosa!
> Ven a beber mis mieles soberanas:
> ¡Yo soy la copa del amor pomposa
> Que engarzará en tus manos sobrehumanas!
>
> La copa erige su esplendor de llama . . .
> ¡Con qué hechizo en tus manos brillaría!

Su misteriosa exquisitez reclama
Dedos de ensueño y labios de armonía.

Tómala y bebe, que la gloria dora
El idilio de luz de nuestras almas;
¡Marchítense las rosas de mi aurora
A la sombra indeleble de tus palmas! (169–70)

[Let us drink together from the illustrious goblet! / rare liquor that our souls are offered. / Let my roses open their regal freshness / to the indelible shadow of your palm branches!

You woke my drowsy soul / in the silent tomb of time; / For you the first blood of my life / in the glasses of light from my dawns!

Ah! your voice came to embroider with gold / my gloomy silences; you broke / the great strand of pearls of my tears, / and you opened my horizon to the rising sun.

Because of you, in my nocturnal East, the dawn / stretched out the pink trembling of her tulle; / therefore in the darkness of life at this moment, / I adore your soul like a blue sky!

Ah, I feel myself opening like a rose! / Come drink my unrivaled honeys: / I am the goblet of the sumptuous love / that will be mounted in your superhuman hands! /

The goblet erects its burning splendor . . . / With what enchantment it would shine in your hands! / Its mysterious excellence demands / daydreaming fingers and harmonious lips.

Take it and drink, that glory gilds / the radiant idyll of our souls; / Let the roses of my dawn wilt / in the shadow of your palm branches!]

Although the lover's successes cast a lasting shadow, the lyric voice expects that her roses will be able to bloom and to give off "their regal freshness." Agustini thus acknowledges the lasting presence of the past and of established male authority. At the same time she expresses her faith that she will be able to flourish. She rises from her deathlike sleep, offering the other, in an erotically explicit allusion, the first blood of her life in the goblets of light of her personal dawn.

The lyric Sleeping Beauty of the poem wakes to the special quality of his voice; her soul stirs as his words embroider with golden threads the silences she has endured. She finds in him inspiration and the promise of a glorious future. She ties her love to modernismo by telling him that she adores his soul like "a blue sky." If "he" represents Darío, she no longer subordinates herself to him. He is to drink her unrivaled, sovereign honeys, and his hands will become the setting that holds her precious offering, for she is now the empowering "goblet of love." She demands ("reclama") that he acknowledge her with his poet's hands and mouth ("dedos de ensueño y labios de armonía"). Her last command is that he take the goblet and drink so that glory will fall upon both of them, yet ultimately she is willing to see "the roses of [her] dawn" wilt in the shadow of his success. This is the same shadow that, in the first stanza, she had hoped would allow her flowers to bloom. The roses that open under his undeniable influence are permitted to die, not, I believe, in surrender or abdication of authority but rather in an act of joyful partnership, which is highlighted by the exclamation marks in the text. She is ready to discard the first blooms of youth, those most influenced by his presence. She appears ready to begin a new phase of her life, possibly emerging from his shadow into broad daylight.

As Agustini brings her collection to a close and begins to anticipate the future, she formulates a way through which she can detach herself from the imposing other. "Desde lejos" (172) becomes the first of her poems about a distant lover. In later collections, as Agustini's confidence grows, her lyric voice takes a more active role in exiling, eventually even killing her lover. In "Desde lejos," however, she still contemplates him with yearning. She still imagines her happiness and her poetry tied to their reunion:

> En el silencio siento pasar hora tras hora,
> Como un cortejo lento, acompasado y frío . . .
> ¡Ah! Cuando tú estás lejos mi vida toda llora
> Y al rumor de tus pasos hasta en sueños sonrío.
>
> Yo sé que volverás, que brillará otra aurora
> En mi horizonte grave como un ceño sombrío;
> Revivirá en mis bosques tu gran risa sonora
> Que los cruzaba alegre como el cristal de un río.
>
> Un día, al encontrarnos tristes en el camino,
> Yo puse entre tus manos pálidas mi destino!
> ¡Y nada de más grande jamás han de ofrecerte!

Mi alma es frente a tu alma como el mar frente al cielo:
Pasarán entre ellas tal la sombra de un vuelo,
La Tormenta y el Tiempo y la Vida y la Muerte! (172)

[In silence I feel hour after hour pass by / like a slow cortège, measured and cold . . . / Ah! When you are far away my whole life cries / and to the gentle sound of your steps even in dreams I smile.

I know that you will return, that another dawn will shine / on my horizon as serious as a gloomy scowl; / your great resonant laugh will return to life in my forests / that it crossed as happy as the crystalline waters of a river.

One day, upon our meeting, so sad, on the road, / I put my fate in your pale hands! / And nothing greater must they ever offer you!

My soul is before your soul like the sea before the heavens: / Adversity and Time, and Life and Death / will pass between them like the shadow of a flight.]

She waits for love and language, confident in the musical inspiration of her beloved's laughter, which she compares to the crystalline springs of earlier poems. She places her destiny in his hands for she has chosen him among all others to be the one to guide her. When she turns to him, it is with the assurance that she offers him as much as he provides her and that she is emerging as his equal. She states, "Mi alma es frente a tu alma como el mar frente al cielo. . . ." The majesty of this image confirms a breadth of optimism and mutual support that carry her forward despite the passing shadow of "La Tormenta y el Tiempo y la Vida y la Muerte," with which the sonnet ends. It can hardly be surprising that, regardless of her poetic talent and her growing self-assuredness, she would recognize the fragility of relationships, of the creative process, and of life itself. Yet she sees these fearsome concerns as temporary. The dark clouds will give way to the songs of a new morning in *Cantos de la mañana,* published three years later.

CHAPTER THREE

DRINKING FROM THE FOUNTAIN

OF THE OTHER

Cantos de la mañana

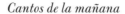

For Delmira Agustini writing is an all-consuming passion which she comes to equate with an erotic desire that promises ecstasy and produces anxiety. In *El libro blanco (Frágil)*, the still-tentative Agustini wavers between timidity and audacity, between fragility and assertiveness as she sets out to define her art and her role as poet. She discloses, in increasingly sexual terms, an attraction to a male other who functions as an ideal partner with whom she explores the possibility of reinventing what it means to be a *modernista*. The images that she turns to reveal the imprint of Darío's works, the power of patriarchy, and the influence of linguistic conventions. As Agustini begins to reconfigure these predominant patterns, erotic arousal and poetic aspirations crystallize around the figure of the great modernista poet. She envisions him as the supreme arbiter of aesthetic values and as a type of personal and artistic god. Darío becomes the one to seduce and ultimately to dominate.

In *Cantos de la mañana* (Songs of the morning), the more self-confident and independent Agustini of the concluding section of *El libro blanco (Frágil)* becomes progressively more autonomous. She no longer relies as heavily on Darío's poetry as a point of departure, but his presence is still felt, especially in the dialogic structures of many of the collection's poems and in the sexual imagery that continues to inform her response to his male perspectives on life, sex, and artistic creation. The daring way in which she formulates her challenge to social and aesthetic traditions gives her poetry a primacy, an originality, and an energy that distinguished her work and that drew attention to it from the beginning. Yet because of the numerous contextual factors discussed above, the breadth of this poetic endeavor was either inadvertently or deliberately misinterpreted by the earliest critics, most of whom were men and most of whom sought to sanitize her vision and her desires.[1] With changes in mores and advances in feminist criticism, readers have come to grasp the complexity of Agustini's sexually explicit verse, though many have tended to interpret her poetry in terms of biography or biology. Overlaid with violence, fragmentation, and pain, her poems reflect the extraordinary difficulties she faced as she tried to define herself as a poet and as a woman in turn-of-the-century Montevideo. While all modernista writers, indeed all romantic and postromantic authors, express the agony of striving to adjust the rigid structures of language to the free-flowing and musical qualities that they defined as the essence of literary discourse, her dark, tortured eroticism speaks to additional emotional and discursive battles.

Agustini, expressing her passion for life and writing, creates a vampiric seductress, who drinks the essence of the other, exerts her will, asserts her abilities, and extracts what has not been freely offered. This invasion of the body of the other is an aggressive violation of the literary tradition, the body of works, in which she began writing. It is an intrusion into the textual arena from which women poets had been barred.[2] Denied entry, she is forced to storm the gates of the dominant discourse or, to use a different metaphor more in keeping with her poetry, she is forced to mutilate this corpus of canonical texts. This body of writing constitutes an additional layer of associations to the multivalent other of her verse, whom she either dismembers or dramatically reconfigures.[3] She alternates between brazenly inflicting injury on and subtly appropriating male figures of creative empowerment such as Orpheus, Icarus, and Pygmalion.

While conflict with the prevailing patterns of perception and language dominates Agustini's poetry, wounding both actors, the "I" and "you" in the poetic dialogues of her poetry, there are moments of great exuberance, delight, and hope. During these moments Agustini draws upon more traditional images of illumination, growth, and renewal to express her greater faith in her abilities to take the lead at the dawn of the new poetic day that is proclaimed in the title of her second collection of verse, *Cantos de la mañana.* Nevertheless, even these more conventional (almost trite) affirmations acquire vibrancy when juxtaposed with the dark and pained declarations of anger and frustration. All these factors come together in a high-spirited demonstration of the poet's enhanced abilities as well as her continuing ambivalence toward her chosen vocation. In short, this slim volume of nineteen or twenty poems (depending on the edition used), published three years after *El libro blanco (Frágil)*, reveals her growing confidence and her ever-greater impatience with the inhospitality of the hegemonic culture.[4]

If one enters Agustini's volume through the front door of the prologue written by Manuel Pérez y Curis for the edition of 1910, one is immediately struck by the cultural context in which she wrote (see chapter 1). A single sentence captures the conflictive attitudes Agustini confronted at the beginning of the twentieth century in Montevideo. Pérez y Curis writes, "I do not find among the native poetesses of America a single one comparable to her for her originality of a good variety and for the virile arrogance of her songs" (178).[5] Women can be praised as authors only if their work appears sufficiently male. All honor and distinction come from being "virile." Today's reading public understands immediately that this language degrades women and turns the acclaim for the writer into a destructive force. A woman could only be deemed accomplished if she were not true to her sex. She had to behave and write like a man to receive critical approval. This situation also explains why Agustini, like many other women, felt compelled to hide behind a masculine persona, resulting in what critics have referred to as her transvestism.[6]

This strongly ambivalent position with regard to women was so common as to be part of the literary language of the day. In 1900, in "La mujer española" (The Spanish woman), Rubén Darío wrote, "In this century, the learned women and poets have been [as numerous as] an army, to such an extent that a certain author has published a volume with a catalogue of them—and he does not name them all!—. Among all the useless and thick foliage, the great trees rise up: Coronado, Pardo Bazón, Concepción

Arenal. These last two, in particular, virile minds, honor their fatherland. Regarding the countless majority of tacky Corinnas and Sapphos of puff pastry, they begin to form part of the abominable international sisterhood to which Great Britain has contributed greatly with its thousands of authoresses. To approach the palace of the much-discussed Eve of the future, these women have to exchange Pegasus for a bicycle" (*Obras completas*, 3: 361–62).[7] One can hardly ignore the reluctant praise Darío bestows on women, a point of view he repeats in his tepid endorsement of Agustini in his "Pórtico" to *Los cálices vacíos* (The empty chalices), her next collection of verse, published in 1913.

The unevenness of the inroads made against strongly patriarchal prejudices is evident as well in the equally inconsistent positions taken by Agustini. As mentioned above, in *Cantos de la mañana* the attitude she projects fluctuates between doubt, despair, and rebellious aggression on the one hand and a refreshing boldness and self-assuredness on the other. This vacillation is apparent at the start of the volume. The title of the collection self-assuredly extends the temporal frame of Agustini's "El hada color de rosa" from *El libro blanco (Frágil)* (110). She now sings throughout the night, well into the start of a new day. In contrast, the title of the first poem of the collection, "Fragmentos" (181–82), suggests a certain awareness that her poetic identity has its origin in "fragments," that is, in bits and pieces from elsewhere. Despite this decentering, the poem reveals a fundamentally optimistic assessment of who she is at this point. She declares her soul to be a guiding lantern to the wise ("fanal de sabios"), the heir to the now-deceased sun / god of "El hada color de rosa" (ll. 7–12), and the successor to the great poet/bird/gods of the previous collection (ll. 15–18). She also confidently asserts her adoption of the precepts that Darío had set down in "Ama tu ritmo . . ." (Love your rhythm) (236), where he advises,

> Ama tu ritmo y ritma tus acciones
> bajo su ley, así como tus versos;
> eres un universo de universos
> y tu alma una fuente de canciones.

[Love your rhythm and give rhythm to your actions / under its law, just as with your verses; / you are a universe of universes / and your soul a source of songs.]

Agustini responds, referring to herself:

> Alma que cabe en un verso
> Mejor que en un universo!
> —Instinto de águila real
> Que engarza en ave canora,
> Roja semilla de aurora
> En un surco musical! — (181)

[Soul that fits in a line of verse / better than in a universe! / —Instinct of a royal eagle / that places within the melodious bird, / the red seed of dawn / in a musical furrow!—]

No longer the pure and timid dove of "Por campos de ensueño" (96), her spirit is eaglelike, musical, and openly erotic. Nevertheless, by the end of the poem she turns her attention to the male "you" of the poem, perhaps the unnamed Spanish poet to whom the piece is dedicated.

In his edition of Agustini's *Poesías completas*, Alejandro Cáceres observes that the poem's dedication was added to the 1913 version (227). Despite this late addition (perhaps the result of an inadvertent omission during the first printing), the dedication seems to form an integral part of the poem, reinforcing the self-portrait of the lyric voice, her passionate embrace of the Spanish spirit, and her acknowledgment of the other's established literary authority. While this move to accept the legacy of Spanish verse was not at all unusual among modernista authors, especially after 1898, it is presented here as part of a passionate exchange in which her poetry supersedes his, as is evident in the poem's second section:

> * * *
> Mi sol es tu sol ausente;
> Yo soy la brasa candente
> De un gran clavel de pasión
> Florecido en tierra extraña;
> ¡Todo el fuego de tu España
> Calienta mi corazón!
>
> La plebe es ciega, inconsciente;
> Tu verso caerá en su frente
> Como un astro en un testuz,

Mas tiene impulsos brutales,
Y un choque de pedernales
A veces hace la luz! (181–82)

[My sun is your absent sun; / I am the red-hot ember / of a great carnation of passion / that bloomed in foreign soil; / All the fire of your Spain / heats my heart!

The common people are blind, thoughtless; / your verse will fall on their forehead / like a star on a brow, / but it has brutal impulses, / and a striking of flint / sometimes creates light.]

With this description Agustini implies that the other's influence is also fragmented, for it is affirmed and rejected at the same time. He is absent, but she reflects his light; she is the surviving force, the promise of rebirth of his disintegrating star. Unlike the insensitive masses, she feels the impact of his powerful verse, its ability to create sparks. Taken as a whole, this poem addresses Agustini's conflicted emotions about recovering the absent other. She is struggling with how to balance her desire to stand on her own and her discomfort with a total disavowal of the past, that is, with the type of deliberate forgetting she proclaimed in "Por campos de ensueño." She therefore creates an ambivalent middle ground between innovation and tradition, between independence and respect.[8]

To read this poem as reflecting Agustini's ambivalence toward all influence, including Darío's, is particularly illuminating. Like so many of her generation, she sought to follow the modernista precepts he had set out. These tenets included remaining faithful to oneself, aspiring to a greater truth through poetry, repudiating the unenlightened perspective of common people (the "plebe," who are blind), and rejecting bourgeois obedience to convention. In short, her affirmation of Darío's guidelines leads her, paradoxically, to break with the past; her position forms the basis of a type of love/hate relationship that, in turn, lends itself to the conceit of a sexual give and take—often between an established, older figure and a rebellious usurper of authority. This evocation of the story of Lot's daughters resonates emphatically in the next poem, "De 'Elegías dulces'" (About "Sweet elegies") (183).

The sexualization of tension between innovation and tradition is magnificently presented in the first section of "De 'Elegías dulces.'" By appropriating the myth of Orpheus, the emblematic poet of modernismo, and turning the other into the Eurydice figure, Agustini seems to end the reign of the male artist, condemning him to an eternity in the poetic nether-world of distant reverberations and vague recollections. Yet, notwithstanding the assertion that she is now on the "great path" toward the future, moving forward in the "bright and strong" sunlight of hope and vision, the poem maintains an achingly evocative tone of loss. She is paralyzed by her grief, held in place by her desire for what she can no longer have. Despite this anguish, declarations of confidence in the artistic independence of the lyric voice are scattered throughout the poem: in the reemergence of light at the end of the dark night of despair in the twelfth line, in the transition from silence, "muda como una lágrima" (mute like a tear), to speech, "hablemos de otras flores al corazón" (let us speak to the heart about other flowers), in the conversion of the golden leaves of autumn into the glow of new growth on old trunks, and in the reconstitution of the dismembered hours of the past into new flowers of the heart.

Even so, it is the haunting rewriting of the mythic representation of the eternal separation of lovers that gives this poem its majesty and colors it with nostalgia. This power begins with the brilliant combination of visual, auditory, and olfactory images, that is, in the synesthetic tour de force of the first stanza:

I

Hoy desde el gran camino, bajo el sol claro y fuerte,
Muda como una lágrima he mirado hacia atrás,
Y tu voz, de muy lejos, con un olor de muerte,
Vino a aullarme al oído un triste «¡Nunca más!»

Tan triste que he llorado hasta quedar inerte . . .
¡Yo sé que estás tan lejos que nunca volverás!
No hay lágrimas que laven los besos de la Muerte . . .
—Almas hermanas mías, nunca miréis atrás!

Los pasados se cierran como los ataúdes;
Al Otoño, las hojas en dorados aludes
Ruedan . . . y arde en los troncos la nueva floración . . .

—. . . Las noches son caminos negros de las auroras . . .—
Oyendo deshojarse tristemente las horas
Dulces, hablemos de otras flores al corazón. (183)

[Today from the great path, beneath the clear and powerful sun, / speechless like a tear I have looked back, / and your voice, from very far away, with a smell of death, / came howling to my ear a sad "never more."

So sad that I cried until I remained lifeless . . . / I know that you are so far away that you will never return! / There are no tears that can wash away the kisses of Death . . . / —Dear sister souls, never look back!

Pasts are closed like coffins; in Autumn, leaves tumble down in golden avalanches . . . / and the new flowering growth burns on the trunks of the trees . . .

—. . . Nights are dawns' black paths . . .— / Hearing the sweet hours sadly shed their leaves / let us speak to the heart about other flowers.]

The impact of the death of the other is simultaneously incapacitating and liberating. Through this description Agustini reveals her contradictory regard for the poetic practices of the past. In the quatrains the lyric voice is converted into silent pain and frozen sadness. The lost lover howls the inevitable "nunca más" that sentences the speaker to bereavement and paralysis but that also frees her to explore the options present in the tercets. The transition between these two sections is contained in the eighth line, which presents an ironic play on the command "don't look back." The poem thus combines Orpheus's longing for the beloved who is tragically doomed to remain in the underworld and the divine injunction to Lot's wife against returning to old, condemned patterns of behavior. Agustini's unique development of these mythic models underscores her simultaneous longing to follow and to reject Darío's imposing presence.

The famous "don't look back" is addressed to "almas hermanas mías." In this phrase Agustini cleverly draws upon the grammatical gender of "almas" to move the apostrophe to a female perspective, that is, to "her sisters" in poetry. While on first reading it seems to warn against Orpheus's tragic fate and the everlasting entombment of former lovers and previous voices, it actually exhorts her sisters not to repeat the mistake made by Lot's wife. She urges them not to turn to the past for models of inspiration, which will confine them to a position of inferiority or, worse, turn them into a worthless pillar of salt. As a transition to the tercets, it becomes an appeal to let the coffins of the past close, to move forward instead of backward, to become the new bearers of culture. The sonnet turns from silence and loss to renewal and hope in its final listening and speaking that enable the writing of the songs of this new morning.

While the optimism of this ending highlights the sweetness of the first section, the second is more mournful, more locked within the past, more haunted by the departed other:

II

Pobres lágrimas mías las que glisan
A la esponja sombría del Misterio,
Sin que abra en flor como una copa cárdena
Tu dolorosa boca de sediento!

Pobre mi corazón que se desangra
Como clepsidra trágica en silencio,
Sin el milagro de inefables bálsamos
En las vendas tremantes de tus dedos!

Pobre mi älma tuya acurrucada
En el pórtico en ruinas del Recuerdo,
Esperando de espaldas a la vida
Que acaso un día retroceda el Tiempo! . . . (184)

[My poor tears that slide / toward the dark sponge of Mystery, / without your doleful mouth, the mouth of one who thirsts, / opening in bloom like a purple treetop!

My poor heart that bleeds out / like a tragic hourglass in silence, / without the miracle of the inexpressible balms / on the trembling bandages of your fingers!

My poor soul of yours huddled / in Memory's ravaged portico, / hoping with its back turned to life / that perhaps one day Time will go backwards! . . .]

The section addresses the inhibiting effect of memory as the speaker clings to the past, huddled in the ruins of recollection. This image of a mendicant waiting for relief in the shadows of a faded structure is itself a remnant of an earlier version, which also clarifies the enigmatic double possessive of the ninth line. The final stanza of the original poem reveals the desires of the poetic voice to be graced with the leftovers of the other's dreams and irrationality, the other's poetry:

> Pobre mi vida toda acurrucada
> En el pórtico en ruinas del Recuerdo,
> Mendigando un despojo de tu locura
> Mendigando un harapo de tus sueños
> Mendigando en la flor de mi locura
> La caridad sombría de tu espectro! (184)

[My poor life all huddled / in the ravaged portico of Memory, / begging a scrap of your insanity / begging a tatter of your dreams / begging in the bloom of my insanity / the dark generosity of your ghost!]

Both "Fragmentos" and "De 'Elegías dulces'" imply a turning away from life in favor of images and words from the past, that is, the solace and support of dreamers, lovers, and poetic echoes.

The next three poems, "La barca milagrosa" (The miraculous boat) (185), "El vampiro" (186), and "Supremo idilio" (Supreme idyll) (187–89), reinforce the focus on poetic creation evident in the first two poems of the collection and are interconnected to them by themes and images. "La barca milagrosa" and "Supremo idilio" both envision poetry as a struggle between shadow and light, and both address many of the same concerns expressed in the final two tercets of Darío's "Yo persigo una forma . . ." (240–41), in which he states,

> Y no hallo sino la palabra que huye,
> La iniciación melódica que de la flauta fluye
> y la barca del sueño que en el espacio boga;
>
> y bajo la ventana de mi Bella-Durmiente,
> el sollozo continuo del chorro de la fuente
> y el cuello del gran cisne blanco que me interroga. (241)

[I find only the word that flees / the melodic introduction that flows from the flute / and the boat of reverie that sails on in space;

and below the window of my Sleeping Beauty, / the continuous sob of the fountain's flow / and the neck of the great white swan that questions me.]

Agustini's "miraculous boat" and its final line, "Yo ya muero de vivir y soñar" (I am already dying of living and dreaming), reverberate with Darío's "boat of dreams," which floats just beyond his control:

Preparadme una barca como un gran pensamiento . . .
La llamarán «La Sombra» unos, otros «La Estrella».
No ha de estar al capricho de una mano o de un viento:
Yo la quiero consciente, indominable y bella!

La moverá el gran ritmo de un corazón sangriento
De vida sobrehumana; he de sentirme en ella
Fuerte como en los brazos de Dios! En todo viento,
En todo mar templadme su prora de centella!

La cargaré de toda mi tristeza, y, sin rumbo,
Iré como la rota corola de un nelumbo,
Por sobre el horizonte líquido de la mar . . .

Barca, alma hermana . . . ¿hacia qué tierras nunca vistas,
De hondas revelaciones, de cosas imprevistas
Iremos? . . . Yo ya muero de vivir y soñar . . . (185)

[Prepare for me a boat like a great thought . . . / Some will call it "Darkness," others "The Star." / It should not respond to the whim of a hand or of a shifting wind: / I want it cognizant, unruly, and beautiful!

The great rhythm of a bleeding heart / of superhuman life will move it; in it I should feel / strong as if wrapped in the arms of God! Calm its flashing prow for me / regardless of the seas and the winds that blow!

I will load it with all my sadness, and, without direction, / I will proceed like the broken bloom of a lotus, / over the liquid horizon of the sea . . .

Boat, dear sister soul, . . . toward which never-seen lands, / of profound revelations, of unexpected things / will we go? . . . I am already dying of living and dreaming . . .]

Darío's complaint about his free-floating ship of dreams is answered by Agustini's hope that hers can be controlled. She does not want it to respond to the whim of some other guiding hand or to that of the random winds of fate (l. 3). On the contrary, she wants it to be "consciente, indominable y bella" (l. 4). These adjectives underscore her pursuit of an independence of thought, which appears to some as a frightening "darkness" and to others as an illuminating, guiding "star" (l. 2). These adjectives are the ones that Gwen Kirkpatick underscores in her insightful article on Agustini's challenging metaphorical journeys in search of transcendence through a highly physical and sexualized universe ("Prodigios de almas y de cuerpos" [175–76]).

"La barca milagrosa" as a whole elaborates upon Agustini's representation of poetry as a maritime journey to unknown lands that was central to "El poeta leva el ancla" of *El libro blanco (Frágil)* and fuses this metaphor with another of Darío's core images. She appropriates Darío's search for the rhythms of the great beating heart of the universe and makes it her own by having the transcendent heart bleed, as does her own in line 5 of the second part of "De 'Elegías dulces'" (184), thereby drawing attention to the anguish she feels in her life and in the world around her. Yet the lyric voice expects to find strength, security, and solace in the cadenced rocking that she senses and aspires to achieve in her art. Such movement and fluidity recall Darío's many fountains (the "chorro de la fuente" from "Yo persigo una forma . . ." and the "fuente de canciones" of "Ama tu ritmo . . ."), but here it will envelope her in a type of divine embrace and will become the depository of her sadness. From this perspective one can comprehend Tina Escaja's linking of ships and hearts with vaginas (108–10). The rocking motion of the ship, the embrace, and the promise of creation call to mind copulation and postcoital repose, as does the reference to "la rota corola de un nelumbo." The corolla is the hymenlike ring of petals that surround the reproductive organs of a flower. That it is broken speaks to Agustini's rejection of chaste behavior. On the contrary, together with the uncharted lands of the poem, it evokes the mysteries of erotic pleasure. Yet more than sensual delight, Agustini's ultimate goal, pursued equally through language and sexual freedom, is, not unlike Darío's, to enter a world, a transcendent realm, unseen by others.

This multilayered imagery aligns Agustini's work with that of other women writers of the period. As noted in chapter 1, so-called good women were traditionally condemned to obedience, purity, and selflessness, and attempts at independence, self-assertion, and writing were perceived as tearing the flesh of proper behavior. Despite the consequences—the sense of rupture, infraction, and ostracism—women continued to pursue writing and other unconventional endeavors. Some saw their lives as hideous wounds while others identified themselves with various monstrous representations of female autonomy. In the next poem, "El vampiro" (186), the desire for discursive control and independence expressed in line 4 of "La barca milagrosa" appears in the guise of the supreme nineteenth-century monster of rebellion, the vampire.

The prominence of the bloodsucking vampire in nineteenth-century literature exemplifies how an unusual interplay of science and prejudice worked to the detriment of women. As Bram Dijkstra has shown in his now-classic study *Evil Sisters: The Threat of Female Sexuality and the Cult of Manhood*, during the *fin de siècle*, the laws of evolution served to legitimate the patriarchal beliefs that men were the lords of human progress and that women were a lower order of humanity. Women, represented as volatile, emotional, unthinking reproductive tools of nature, were believed to demonstrate no interest in the elite, virile principle of evolutionary advance. They were seen, in short, as vampires of time and progress (26). To be good, women had to be properly acculturated to their subservient role in the monogamous structure of the nuclear family and had to be content to be governed by the superior judgment of their partners (42). Independent women were deemed to be sexual predators by instinct, intent upon depleting men's vitality and their economic potency as well as their seminal fluids (62, 114). To use Dijkstra's turn of phrase, these women were "unmasked as Dracula's daughters" and began to be portrayed as carnivorous panthers, spiders, and vampires alongside other cannibals of nature (64).

Agustini's recourse to the figure of the vampire has, as might be expected, attracted a good deal of critical commentary. Her decision to identify with this simultaneously repulsive and enticing creature offers a complex response to paternalistic language and beliefs of the nineteenth and early twentieth centuries. By defiantly allying herself with the male-created images of female rebelliousness and disobedience, she asserts her resistance to stereotypical concepts about women and cleverly co-opts the negativity of male criticism:[9]

> En el regazo de la tarde triste
> Yo invoqué tu dolor . . . Sentirlo era
> Sentirte el corazón! Palideciste
> Hasta la voz, tus párpados de cera,
>
> Bajaron . . . y callaste . . . Pareciste
> Oír pasar la Muerte . . . Yo que abriera
> Tu herida mordí en ella — ¿me sentiste? —
> Como en el oro de un panal mordiera!

Y exprimí más, traidora, dulcemente
Tu corazón herido mortalmente,
Por la cruel daga rara y exquisita
De un mal sin nombre, hasta sangrarlo en llanto!
Y las mil bocas de mi sed maldita
Tendí a esa fuente abierta en tu quebranto.

. . . .

¿Por qué fui tu vampiro de amargura?
¿Soy flor o estirpe de una especie oscura
Que come llagas y que bebe el llanto? (186)

[In the lap of the sad afternoon / I invoked your pain . . . To feel it was / to feel your heart! You grew pale / even your voice, your waxen eyelids,

were lowered . . . and you grew silent . . . You seemed / to hear Death pass by . . . I, who would open / your wound, bit into it —did you feel me?— / as if biting into the gold of a honeycomb!

I sweetly squeezed more, like a traitor, / your heart mortally injured, / by the cruel, rare, exquisite dagger / of a nameless curse, until bleeding it dry in tears! / And I spread out the thousand mouths of my damned thirst / at that open fountain of your grief.

. . . .

Why was I your vampire of bitterness? / Am I a flower or the stock of a dark species / that eats wounds and that drinks tears?]

The dramatically erotic female vampire addresses a male lover, whose suffering is the source of their attraction. While his torment might result from an unsatisfied sexual appetite or from any number of other causes, the modified sonnet signals its source to be creative anguish. The references to his fading speech, his wounding by a "rare and exquisite dagger," which is also an affliction that is not named, her conversion of his pain into broken speech ("llanto"), and her membership in a special, dark, and brooding race of individuals elucidate the nature of this eroticized encounter (with clear allusions to fellatio: "Y las mil bocas de mi sed maldita / Tendí a esa fuente abierta en tu quebranto") to be poetic.[10] The other's suffering fuses pen and penis, anticipating the critical leap made by Gilbert and Gubar in the 1970s.

Like all vampires, she sets out to draw the lifeblood from her victim in a voluptuous pursuit of domination and survival, and, consequently, her assumption of his injuries is less altruistic than self-serving. Her efforts to drink the essence of the male other at the fountainhead of his wounds emphatically evokes Darío's "La fuente," reminds the reader of her earlier statements in "La sed" and "Íntima" of *El libro blanco (Frágil)*, and affirms her desire to appropriate his artistic abilities. As a result, this poem, even more than an imaginative response to female sexual oppression, expresses a desire to wrest control of the images of productive creativity away from Darío and other male modernistas. The lyric voice of the poem rejects the soft, comforting, maternal overtones of the first line and quickly becomes a force of violent, if somewhat melancholic, usurpation. She cannibalizes his artistic anguish, biting into his wound and drawing from it the golden honey of inspiration, the same amber liquor of the poetic honeycombs that appear previously in Agustini's "Jirón de púrpura" (104). With sadistic assertion she asks if he felt her ("¿me sentiste?"). She longs to know that he is aware of her, that he senses her appropriation of his powers as he faces the end of his reign, as he hears the approach of death.

The speaker's ambivalence toward her vampirism, toward the recognition that to be a poet she must draw inspiration and insight from her predecessors, is picked up in the last two lines of the poem, where she asks: "¿Soy flor o estirpe de una especie obscura / Que come llagas y que bebe el llanto?" She questions if she is the new flowering or the latest descendent of a "dark species." David Spooner, in the six pages on Agustini in his *The Poem and the Insect*, sees in this "especie oscura" one of her many entomological references and a modernista, if not modern, questioning of the nature of the human species (117). I believe, however, that this doubting of her humanity is much more in keeping with Darío's own ambivalence toward the divinity of poets and the destructive pull of human passions, which is tied to his longing for success and salvation and his fears of failure and damnation. As in Darío's work, death and oblivion become a dual specter that takes up residence in the background of many of Agustini's poems. The possible impending demise of the other gives the lyric voice an excuse for cannibalizing him and for metamorphosing herself into the powerful partner in their relationship. She joins the "dark species" of writers who, like her, draw their sustenance and strength from those who came before them as well as from the way they address the difficulties of writing and the pain of the world around them. Perhaps it is this sense of being one of many that explains Agustini's selection of the masculine "el vampiro" for the title. The title may be Agustini's way of asserting that she is one among equals regardless of gender.

Implicit in the relationship described is an assumption that the survival of the other (and of his poetry) becomes dependent on her ability to absorb his anguish and to continue his endeavors. Lodged subtly within this symbolism is the question of immortality, the aspect of vampirism that seems to have survived most dramatically into its twentieth- and twenty-first-century science fiction versions. This heterodoxical vision of everlasting life first evolved in the context of eroding faith in traditional beliefs. Increasingly uncertain of answers provided by orthodox religions, many modernistas turned to art as a means of accessing the transcendent and of achieving immortality.[11] In a veiled way that evokes demonic as well as divine implications, "El vampiro" supplies a woman's response to the traditional male stance on the redemptive power of artistic production. Two of the most famous modernista declarations on the subject are Darío's "Yo soy aquel que ayer no más decía . . ." (244–47) and Manuel Gutiérrez Nájera's "Non omnis moriar" (161–62). With the subtlest of maneuvers, Darío joins poet and poetry with the male godhead and declares, "El Arte puro como Cristo exclama: / *Ego sum lux et veritas et vita!*" (Art, pure like Christ, exclaims: / I am the light, the truth, and the life!) (246). By changing "the way" (via) to "the life" (vita) Darío proclaims the power of art and the artist to reveal the path to eternal life. Gutiérrez Nájera has his female lover passively observe as the male asserts that their immortality hinges on *his* accomplishments. Addressing his companion, the lyric voice declares,

> ¡No moriré del todo, amiga mía!
> De mi ondulante espíritu disperso,
> algo en la urna diáfana del verso,
> piadosa guardará la poesía.
>
> . . . .
>
> Y porque alzo en tu recuerdo notas
> del coro universal, vívido y almo;
> y porque brillan lágrimas ignotas
> en el amargo cáliz de mi salmo;

Porque existe la Santa Poesía
y en ella irradias tú, mientras disperso
átomo de mi ser esconda el verso,
¡no moriré del todo, amiga mía!

[I will not die completely, dear friend, / compassionate poetry will hold in
safe keeping / something of my undulating scattered spirit, / in the transparent urn of verse.

.   .   .   .

And because I raise in your memory notes / of the universal chorus, vivid
and venerable; / and because unknown tears shine / in the bitter chalice
of my psalm;

because Holy Poetry exists / and in it you radiate, as long as poetry / may
hide a scattered atom of my being, / I will not die completely, my friend!]

Gutiérrez Nájera's female other silently waits and observes as the poet
manages to capture her divine essence in his art, by which he achieves
transcendence and immortality. In the case of "El vampiro," Agustini reconfigures the perspective of her predecessors. She consumes the essence
of the other, in a variation on transubstantiation, and thus his existence is
perpetuated through her body. She appropriates his pain, and his poetry
will live forever in a new feminized version, all part of an encounter that
takes on satanic overtones.

Though Agustini's language is innovative, especially with regard to her
empowerment of the supposedly female lyric voice of "El vampiro," she is
not the only modernista to blend eroticism, transcendence, and an alternative knowledge loosely tied to the black arts. On the contrary, this embrace of sexuality as a means to understanding the hidden, even dark,
forces of existence was quite a common characteristic of modernista verse.
In "Alaba los ojos negros de Julia" (Praise Julia's black eyes) (190–91), written in 1894, Darío converts a playful reference to Julia's eyes into a reflection on the opposing forces of illumination, the white light of reason and
spirituality and the black light of passion, physicality, and mystery. Not
simply a seductive piece of flattery, this poem endorses the life-affirming,
energizing passions that rise from the dark side, that contain profound
truths, and that lead the way toward creation. In "Misa negra" (Black
mass) (269–70), first published in *El País* in 1893 and later in the section

of *El florilegio* (Selected writings) entitled "Hostias negras" (Black communion wafers), the poet José Juan Tablada affirms his faith in sexual love as an alternative to traditional religious rituals. Closer in tone to Agustini's poem are the more disturbingly sinister sonnets that make up Leopoldo Lugones's "Los doce gozos" (The twelve pleasures) (117–24) from *Los crepúsculos del jardín* (The twilights of the garden), published in 1905. One of these twelve, "Delectación morosa" (Slow delight), suggests a mysterious, almost diabolical rite of initiation with its references to bloodless knees upon a pedestal base beneath a warped sky, revealing a universe that is less than perfectly harmonious. Like Agustini's, Lugones's fearsome vision offers an unnerving combination of revelation and revolution. Read in tandem with her fellow modernistas, Agustini's "vamping" exposes hidden dimensions to the eroticized play of language in the works of her contemporaries, a play that embraces forbidden roles and broken assumptions of acceptability.

The exchange between the injured male and the attentive revitalizing female that starts in "El vampiro" continues in the lengthy poetic dialogue of "Supremo idilio" (187–89) (see notes).[12] Through its setting and language Agustini points once again to the iconic Darío as the poetic male other, exposing his commanding presence and the way his goals come to define Agustini's vision of herself and her poetic endeavors. In particular, the final tercet of his "Yo persigo una forma . . ." echoes in the poem's opening stanza, revealing how much his language had become hers as well. The resulting back and forth of descriptions and desires as well as the conversation between an older male and a younger female lover simultaneously asserts and alters conventional modernista discourse. At the same time, the dialogic structure, its language of courtship and seduction, and its evocation of transcendental aspirations recall the Song of Songs.

The poem begins by rejecting the passivity of Darío's "Sleeping Beauty," who remains enclosed in her fortress, distant from the sad music of the spring, and disconnected from the conversation between the poet and the great white swan. The female voice of the dialogue no longer waits to be awakened, even though the world around her (the castle in which she resides) sleeps in a lulled complacency or a stupor of material excess. She is the shining white figure who engages the other in an active and assertive exchange of music and words, "they take turns singing" (Alternándose cantan, l. 5). The Darío figure becomes, in this new version, the dark body that stands under the romantic balcony, as Agustini replaces his projection of his artistic perfection with a faded, "murky" image. The complexity of the conversation that ensues emphasizes just how intertwined Agustini imagines the two identities to be. By the end, the poem fuses the two lovers into one chiaroscuro vision, two voices that sing as one.

Using the language of erotic arousal, the poem picks up the exploration of the dark side of survival begun in "El vampiro." In "Supremo idilio," however, the roles are reversed. He is now the tenebrous figure whose powers are satanic (l. 20). He drinks from her blood as she had drunk from his (ll. 28–29); she lives in him as he had come to live in her (l. 51). Tina Escaja understands this doubling to be central to the development of Agustini's poetry. She writes, "The parties involved in the debate of love wind up, therefore, in a mimetic, specular exchange, and inverting their respective roles to the point that the adversaries become doubles of each other. This defining is consistent with René Girard's theory about violence and the sacred, according to which the opposites in a conflict or debate, by acquiring a desired object, wind up looking like each other" (79).[13] But Escaja, while understanding the significance of this fusion of opposites, misses the point that the desired object is poetic discourse and that the masculine other is the figurative Darío, his artistic aspirations, and his poetic language.[14]

The duet Agustini creates focuses on what each means for the other. He speaks first, describing her in terms of fertility, regeneration, and the cultivation of a supreme race. The two speakers are joined to each other by his ability to strum her heart, that is, to produce in and through her a music that continues his art and defines her as a poet (ll. 6–10). She is the springtime flowering and resonance (ll. 6–10, 47) of his autumnal longing and despair (l. 23). Pale, enigmatic, injured, and possibly near death (l. 15), he is compared to an unknown portrait on a distant canvas. He has begun to fade, to slip between distinction ("un blasón") and suffering or, even worse, shame ("un estigma") (ll. 11–15). His response is, "Yo soy la Aristocracia lívida del Dolor / que forja los puñales, las cruces y *las liras* . . ." (ll. 17–18, emphasis added) (I am the livid Aristocracy of the Pain / that forges the daggers, the crosses, and the lyres . . .). His anguish, which forges his hope, his anger, and his art, embitters all who pursue his lead and contaminates those whom he has touched (stanzas 4–6). The female voice, by contrast, is presented as a resplendent dawn and as a promise of renewal, and her "new blood" (l. 29) offers him a reprieve from his frightening hell, his devastating winter.

She does not shrink from this role but rather exuberantly offers herself as an escape from his sterility and despair. Her heart, like the rudder of an "unconscious," rudderless ship (perhaps another "miraculous boat"), leads her to him and to his sinister charm. He is captivating, but, more important, she is a willing, active partner; she is the source of light and inspiration, and as she lays her head on his pillow her curls become an inseminating flood of golden illumination (stanzas 7, 8). These allusions, with their echoes of Lot's daughters, reveal how a zealous and forceful female can become the source of regeneration and even immortality.

By the fourteenth stanza the verbs appear in the plural, creating a binding union of "we." Though Agustini lets the male speak for both of the figures, she denies him exclusivity. Instead, she has him invite the female into a partnership of equals and has him suggest that together they "sow" the "blue-hued furrows of Dream" (los surcos azurados del Ensueño) (l. 66). The assertive masculinity of this image is combined with a neologism ("azurados"), which makes these furrows belong to a modernista, that is, a descendant of Darío and his groundbreaking *Azul.* . . . The expanded vision of the traditional "planting of seed" opens the door to female activity within a sexual/poetic realm that had previously been reserved for men. In this context the "love" that opens stanza fifteen evokes a doubly powerful impulse. It is that lustful urge toward transcendence that joins pleasure and pain, good and evil. The desires that motivate this poetry are felt somatically and excite both body and soul. They cannot be contained in the frozen forms of the past that are raised on high on an artificial base. They must soar with freedom and passion. The product of this multivalent love is an eternal fruit whose bloody juice is drunk by four lips (l. 75), the same four lips that produce the music that closes the poem.

"Supremo idilio" is followed by the poem "La intensa realidad de un sueño lúgubre . . ." (The intense reality of a gloomy dream) (190) that, because of its images, theme, and positioning, resembles a sorrowful postscript or afterthought.[15] The two six-line stanzas of this untitled poem present both a promising but troubling declaration of empowerment and a fearsome vision based on dismemberment and cannibalism.

> La intensa realidad de un sueño lúgubre
> Puso en mis manos tu cabeza muerta;
> Yo la apresaba como hambriento buitre . . .
> Y con más alma que en la Vida, trémula,
> La sonreía como nadie nunca! . . .
> ¡Era tan mía cuando estaba muerta!
>
> Hoy la he visto en la Vida, bella, impávida
> Como un triunfo estatuario, tu cabeza!
> Más frío me dio así que en el idilio
> Fúnebre aquel, al estrecharla muerta . . .
> ¡Y así la lloro hasta agotar mi vida . . .
> Así tan viva cuanto me es ajena! (190)

[The intense reality of a gloomy dream / put your dead head in my hands; / I grasped it like a starving vulture . . . / And with more soul than in Life, trembling / I smiled at it like no one ever did! . . . / It was so mine when it was dead!

Today I have seen it in Life, beautiful, courageous / like a sculptural triumph, your head! / It made me colder like that than in that mournful / idyll, upon clutching it dead . . . / And so I cry over it until I exhaust my life . . . / Thus, so alive, it is so alien to me.]

The impending death of the male other that "Supremo idilio" keeps at bay by drawing upon the strengths and vitality of the female lyric voice arrives through a mournful dream of assimilation and possession. This time the speaker takes hold of his "dead head," grasping it tightly, happily proclaiming that it is hers in death. She seizes it like a "starving vulture."

This disturbing vision coincides with the iconic Salome, who, dancing before Herod or holding the head of John the Baptist, is the embodiment of feminine seductiveness and of the power women have to make men forget their putatively superior, rational selves and in the process to lose, quite literally, their heads. The quintessential self-serving monster, Salome reappears in countless works at the turn of the twentieth century, capturing the anxieties men had about shifting social arrangements, their sense of moral disorientation, and their fears about the changing role of women.[16] Yet Agustini embraces the figure of Salome, as she did the vampire, as a way to assert herself and as a gesture of defiance against the widespread vilification of rebellious, independent women.[17] Alicia Ostriker considers the type of brutality (against others and herself) that surfaces in Agustini's poetry to be a constant of women's writings expressing rejection of the limitations imposed upon them. She explains "that violence against the self and against the other are equivalent expressions of rage at entrapment in the gender-polarized relationships, and that satiric and retaliatory poems which *dismantle* the myth of the male as lover, hero, father, and *God* are designed to confirm polarization and hierarchy as intolerable" (*Stealing* 11, emphasis added).

Two of the words in this quotation are relevant to Agustini's case: "dismantle" and "God." The need to dismember the body of male discourse is easily perceived in Agustini's floating heads and bleeding hearts, and this dismantling is just one of her responses to the ultimate male power play linking men with God. It is perhaps because of his imposing, godlike authority that the lyric voice of this untitled poem only feels comfortable claiming him as her own once he is dead (l. 6). When she awakes, however, she is forced to confront the even more frightening reality that he continues to reign.

Though initially the lyric voice seems pleased with the relationship she sets up with the "tú" of "La intensa realidad de un sueño lúgubre . . . ," her self-designation as a "starving vulture" reveals a tortured ambivalence. She is not the swan she hopes to become, the swan that hovers in her poetic imagination as an emblem of all that is possible for others; she is the bird of prey that waits for death and that eats the decaying flesh that is somehow left at the margins of respectable behavior and discourse. She is the dark bird of carrion as opposed to the "ave de luz" that she had, in the poem of that title from *El libro blanco (Frágil)*, aspired to hold in her head. These visions, however fearsome, are better, in her view, than total exclusion from the struggle to write, better than silence and the blank page. Writing, even when it becomes a type of desecration, a staining, and a deadly rupture, is the option she pursues. She therefore smiles as she looks down at the head in her hands. She smiles even as she picks the flesh from the poetry of her predecessors. But her struggles with the imposing presence of the other and with unrelenting rules and expectations ultimately lead to tears and exhaustion.

The gruesome severed head of this untitled poem is a persistently provocative metaphor in two additional poems from *Cantos de la mañana*, "Lo inefable" (The ineffable) (193–94) and "Tú dormías" (You were sleeping) (204). In these two poems the mix of aggressive eroticism and destructive revenge so emphatically present in all allusions to Salome is tempered by their encapsulation in a context of art, artistic aspiration, and dreamy desire. The horror of decapitation is mollified by poetic redirection that turns the reader's attention to other associations, including those of divine illumination. "Lo inefable" ends with an emotional expression of yearning that compares its desired objective to holding in her hands the head of God. This simile, the poem's title, and its references to unspoken and inexpressible thoughts declare that its focus is on poetry or, more specifically, on the agony of poetic creation. These elements also point to the lasting impact of the work of the late romantic poets Rosalía de Castro and Gustavo Adolfo Bécquer.[18] The anguish Agustini shared with her predecessors is made more acute by its transformation at the beginning of the sonnet into the strange death of the lyric voice; she is dying of a "thought, speechless [silent] like a wound" (193). The entire poem develops this conceit of spiritual maiming and sacrifice, culminating in the hope of a miraculous transformation:

> Yo muero extrañamente . . . No me mata la Vida,
> No me mata la Muerte, no me mata el Amor;
> Muero de un pensamiento mudo como una herida . . .
> ¿No habéis sentido nunca el extraño dolor
>
> De un pensamiento inmenso que se arraiga en la vida
> Devorando alma y carne, y no alcanza a dar flor?
> ¿Nunca llevasteis dentro una estrella dormida
> Que os abrasaba enteros y no daba un fulgor? . . .
>
> Cumbre de los Martirios! . . . Llevar eternamente,
> Desgarradora y árida, la trágica simiente
> Clavada en las entrañas como un diente feroz! . . .

Pero arrancarla un día en una flor que abriera
Milagrosa, inviolable! . . . Ah, más grande no fuera
Tener entre las manos la cabeza de Dios! (193–94)

[I die in a strange way . . . Life is not killing me, / Death is not killing me,
Love is not killing me; / I am dying of a thought, silent like a wound . . . /
Have you never felt the strange pain

Of an immense thought that takes root in your life / devouring body and
soul, and not achieving its bloom? / Have you never carried inside a sleeping star / that would burn you whole and would not give off light? . . .

Height of Martyrdom! . . . To carry eternally / the tragic seed, clawingly
destructive and dry, / nailed in your entrails like a ferocious tooth! . . .

But to extract it one day in a flower that would open, / miraculous and in-
violate! . . . Ah, it could not be greater / to hold in one's hands the head
of God!]

The thought she wishes to express but cannot penetrates her soul and eats
away at her flesh. It burns but fails to illuminate; it promises fertility and
growth but produces instead a barren hurt, for it is the thought that dead-
ends in a form that is not true to what is imagined.

Her anguish is described as "the tragic seed" "nailed in [her] entrails"
(ll. 10, 11), and this turn of phrase links her torment with the bitter sweetness of erotic love but also to a painful phallic presence that must be extir-
pated or, at the very least, reconfigured. This change is achieved through
the subtlest of allusions; the male seed embedded in her womb emerges
during a type of poetic childbirth as the head of a newborn, providing
another feminized response to the language of literary paternity. The resulting liberation is so empowering as to be like holding the head of God
in her hands. Consequently, the final godhead represents more than divine
inspiration. It simultaneously stands as a figurative castration, that is, the
undoing of male domination and an assertion of female authority. The
hope expressed is that, with the right words, the poet's vision would be
liberated from servile obedience to a male perspective and from all fear of
being forever inferior to the great modernista master; she would be able to
touch the face of God and to scale the heavens, a goal that echoes in "Las
alas" (The wings) and in its reworking of the myth of Icarus (see below).

Darío's "Yo persigo una forma . . ." addresses the same concerns as "Lo inefable," but differs greatly from it in intensity. Both poems employ images of natural growth, and both allude to language's escape from poetic control, but Darío's sonnet has nothing like Agustini's pain. Darío writes, "Yo persigo una forma que no encuentra mi estilo, / botón de pensamiento que busca ser la rosa; . . . / . . . / Y no hallo sino la palabra que huye . . ." [I pursue a form that my style cannot find, / bud of a thought that aspires to become the rose; . . . / . . . / I find nothing but the word that flees . . . (240–41)]. There is no devouring of body and soul, there is no burning destruction, and there is no tragic seed driven into his innermost parts like a ferocious tooth. Agustini's success is, somewhat ironically, tied to a nightmare of dismemberment and usurpation that she converts into a glorious dream of productivity.

"Tú dormías" (204) begins by comparing the disembodied head of the other to a precious gem that glows in the mounting of the hands of the lyric voice. This vision brilliantly intensifies the fusion of the erotic and poetic other as the object of a new and controlling female perspective:

> Engastada en mis manos fulguraba
> como extraña presea, tu cabeza;
> yo la ideaba estuches, y preciaba
> luz a luz, sombra a sombra su belleza. (204)

[Mounted in my hands, your head / gleamed like a strange jewel; / I designed cases for it, and I valued / its beauty light for light, shadow for shadow.]

This description of the head as a jewel of uncommon worth sets up the provocative metaphor in which her own poetry becomes a type of jewelry box intended to display his cognitive abilities and linguistic skills. His achievements shine in hers. Indeed, the poetics of one is reflected in the other, light to light and shadow to shadow. He becomes the admired gem in what Sylvia Molloy calls a "macabre reversal of *modernismo*'s basic situation, in which the male poet contemplates woman as precious bibelot" (Introduction 117). This role reversal is consistent with the way in which Agustini seeks to revise modernista assumptions about literary empowerment. The rest of the poem, however, addresses the fearsome endeavor of trying to take hold of the other:

En tus ojos tal vez se concentraba
la vida, como un filtro de tristeza
en dos vasos profundos . . . Yo soñaba
que era una flor de mármol tu cabeza . . .

Cuando en tu frente nacarada a luna,
como un monstruo en la paz de una laguna,
surgió un enorme ensueño taciturno . . .

¡Ah! tu cabeza me asustó . . . Fluía
de ella una ignota vida . . . Parecía
no sé qué mundo anónimo y nocturno . . . (204)

[In your eyes perhaps life was concentrated, / like a philter of sadness / in two deep glasses . . . I dreamed / that your head was a marble flower.

When on your forehead, made pearly by the moon, / an enormous taciturn fantasy sprang forth / like a monster on the tranquility of a lagoon . . .

Ah! your head scared me . . . From it / an unknown life flowed . . . It seemed / to be I know not what anonymous and nocturnal world . . .]

The poem moves from energy and illumination to stillness and darkness. Though she sees in his eyes the wisdom of life and a potion of sadness, she also imagines his head becoming a marble flower, frozen in time, unable to fulfill its destiny. In the tercets, the forehead of the severed head, iridescent with the light of the moon, appears as a silent, monstrous reverie. This vision addresses the inconsistencies that exist between the promise of becoming a poet and the realities attached to achieving it. More specifically, the poem evokes with nightmarish imprecision the struggle to produce lifelike vitality from the inanimate rigidity of language, the terror of digging beneath the placid surface of conventional truths, and the fear of artistic failure. On contemplating the sleeping other of the title, the lyric voice sees only a life that is unknown and perhaps unknowable. The more she stares at him, the more she sees the dark side of her attraction. Lover and poet become a threatening reality that she forces herself to confront.

These three poems with severed heads weave together issues of divinity, inspiration, and artistic authority. As a group they reveal an interesting link to "A una cruz" (To a cross) (191–92), the poem that precedes "Lo inefable" in the collection and that is subtitled "ex voto." In the broadest sense, an ex-voto is an offering to a church in fulfillment of a vow. In a more limited sense, it is an image offered to a deity or saint as a form of prayer or in thanks for desires fulfilled. The ex-voto appears to be the poem itself, which is presented in response to a prayer that has been answered, that is, to a miracle of sorts. This miracle is the same fusion of vitality, sexual passion, and poetic fulfillment that animates the core of Agustini's work.

In this poem the empowerment takes place in a religious context. The arms of the cross both embrace and shelter the speaker's injured soul. The refuge she takes magically joins the cross, a naturally phallic symbol, with the moon, which is traditionally linked to women in general and to the Virgin Mary in particular. This erotic tug is further elaborated as the moon is described as being engaged to "Mystery" and as wearing a bride's veil. The moonlight turns the sky into an "abismo de luz" (abyss of light). This revelatory abyss echoes the final line of Darío's "Venus" from *Azul* . . . , "Venus, desde el abismo, me miraba con triste mirar" (Venus, from the abyss, looked at me with a sad look) (175), and the entire poem resurrects Darío's tour de force of poetic layering: Venus is lover, goddess, and shining light of hope for spiritual salvation and poetic success. Similarly, Agustini sexualizes the universe and converts the nocturnal silence into a space in which she can hear the voice of God, making possible the miraculous conversion that is described in the final three stanzas of the poem and that clarifies the reason for the offering of the ex-voto:

> Y la Armonía fiel que en mí murmura
> Como una extraña arteria, rompió en canto,
> Y del mármol hostil de mi escultura
> Brotó un sereno manantial de llanto! . . .
>
> Así lloré el dolor de las heridas
> Y la embriaguez opiada de la rosas . . .
> Arraigábanse en mí todas las vidas,
> Reflejábanse en mí todas las cosas! . . .
>
> Y a ese primer llanto: mi alma, una
> Suprema estatua, triste sin dolor,
> Se alzó en la nieve tibia de la Luna
> Como una planta en su primera flor! (192)

[And the faithful Harmony that gurgles in me / like a strange artery, broke into song, / and from the hostile marble of my sculpture / a serene spring of weeping began to flow! . . .

In this way I cried the pain of the wounds / and the narcotic intoxication of the roses . . . / All lives took root in me, / All things were reflected in me! . . .

And at this first crying: my soul, a / supreme statue, sad without pain, / rose up in the lukewarm snow of the Moon / like a plant in its first bloom!]

Gratitude is expressed for the harmony that is converted into song, for the free-flowing weeping that breaks out of the rigid marble of artistic and so-cial conventions. In the ambiguous "embriaguez opiada de la rosas" (nar-cotic intoxication of the roses), Agustini seems to analogize the expansive energy of sexuality (possibly the intoxication of the loss of virginity and an awakening to erotic gratification) with the exuberance the speaker feels as she overcomes the bloody wounds she endures as she enters the forbidden realm of writing, in which she opens herself to the pain of others. As in "Lo inefable," injury results from her daring assertion of her independent nature, a dangerous undertaking that affords her access to a vision beyond herself and the ability to hold within herself all lives and all things. With this declaration the poet restates the modernista objective, summarized by Darío in "Dilucidaciones" (Elucidations), the prose introduction of 1907 to *El canto errante* (The wandering song). He states, "I have expressed what is expressible in my soul and I have wanted to penetrate the soul of others, and to submerge myself in the vast universal soul. . . . I have looked unself-ishly at what appears foreign to my being in order to convince myself that nothing is foreign to my self. I have sung, in my various ways, the multi-form spectacle of Nature and its immense mystery" (304).[19]

Moreover, in "A una cruz" the voice of the poem and of poetry, once an inflexible, inanimate statue, very much like the despised statue dis-cussed in chapter 2, is now a sensitive, organic entity. The earlier statue fails because it is form without feeling. This one comes close to equaling its model, the "statue made flesh," from Darío's "Yo soy aquel que ayer no más decía . . ." (245). It becomes a responsive being that is compared to a flowering plant, resolving the contradiction in the "marble flower" of "Tú dormías." As much as these final stanzas are about harmony, song, and universality, they maintain the sensual tone and sexual allusions that have dominated my reading of Agustini's poetry. The night, the warm light of the moon, the reproductive powers of the plant, and the sexual associations of the calyxes of flowers all suggest the blossoming to be both poetic and erotic.

Despite these moments of triumph, what is evident from the very beginning and throughout *Cantos de la mañana* is that Agustini's self-confidence invariably collides with the obstacles she perceives in paternalistic attitudes, social patterns, and linguistic constraints. This clash undermines the sense of achievement and belonging, creating, in turn, poems of doubt and despair. The final three poems I want to discuss here contain the full range of these ambivalent emotions and address Agustini's awareness of the impediments she must face. "Las alas" (199–200) recounts the joy of success as well as the disappointment of having to confront the continuing limitations imposed on women; "Primavera" (Springtime) (205–6) reflects Agustini's unbridled enthusiasm for her poetic accomplishments; and "Los relicarios dulces" (Sweet reliquaries) (207) examines the past with a mixture of nostalgia and hope for progress.

The dialogue between the two sides of the gender divide that structures "Las alas" (199–200) leads the reader beyond an implied conversation between the female lyric voice and the male other into a comprehensive intellectual exchange with Darío's "Sonatina," from 1893 (187–88).[20] Agustini evokes Darío's vision of poetic goals, enthusiastically grants the female writer the mantle of poetry, and emphatically claims for the female lyric voice a power equal to that of the male poet, seer, and savior. By the end of the poem, however, Agustini sees this power dissipate, and she appears compelled to acknowledge that social, emotional, and perhaps even literary constraints continue to limit a woman's options. Instead of enabling the poet, as it does in "Sonatina," love destroys the female poet's abilities. On her own, the female poet parallels Darío's male poet, but in the presence of the male beloved the results could not be more different.

Both Agustini's "Las alas" and Darío's "Sonatina" associate poetic abilities with having wings, an image Agustini cultivates from the beginning of her career. To her, wings are inherently poetic because they are associated with musical birds, divine ascent, and modernismo's emblematic swan. They offer an escape from mundane worries and material concerns. In "Sonatina" Darío identifies the conquering warrior as a poet by stating that "en caballo con alas, hacia acá se encamina" (he is headed in this direction on a horse with wings) (l. 44). The winged horse both affirms the masculine erotic energy of the much-awaited hero who comes to conquer the silenced princess (ll. 43–48) and represents the domination and spiritualization of his basic instincts and desires. More specifically, the winged steed is Pegasus, the horse of the Muses, the magical animal who, by striking the ground, created the spring beloved of poets. The resulting combination of spiritual control and artistic prowess contributes to the poet's ultimate victory over death itself (l. 47).

The spiritual energy and visionary powers of Agustini's lyric voice are as great as those of Darío's knight/poet; they are celestial in origin and are tied to her existence on an otherworldly plane. The first lines consist of clipped verses that, in their implied breakdown of linguistic cohesion, anticipate the loss that is announced at the end but that evidently precedes the beginning of the poem. These lines offer a series of defining metaphors and similes:

> Yo tenía . . .
>   dos alas! . . .
> Dos alas,
> Que del Azur vivían como dos siderales
> Raíces! . . .
> Dos alas,
> Con todos los milagros de la vida, la Muerte
> Y la ilusión. Dos alas,
> Fulmíneas
> Como el velamen de una estrella en fuga; (199)

[I had . . . / two wings! / Two wings, / that lived off the Blue heavens like two astral roots! . . . / Two wings, / with all the miracles of life, Death, / and hope. Two wings, / like lightning bolts, / like the sails of a fleeing star;]

Above all else, the talents of the crucially positioned "yo poético," the "I" that begins the poem, are linked with ascension, that is, with escape from the earthbound attributes of daily existence. Through this ascent she realizes for herself the desires of Darío's princess, who is tied to the material world and who can only dream of flight while waiting for her beloved (ll. 37–40). In Agustini's poem her gifts are associated with the starry light that penetrates the dark of the evening sky, and this image of illumination carries over into her ability to understand the workings of the world. By combining marine and astral images in the magnificent visual simile that compares her wings to the sails of a star that escapes its orbit, Agustini evokes the movement, the magic, and the supernatural qualities of a meteor and the seafaring associations of earlier poems about literary creation. This image also captures the fluidity and dynamism that she is so grateful for in "A una cruz" (191–92). In that poem the harmonious flow of existence is dammed up within a hostile marble sculpture that must be broken for the poet's music to be heard. This statue, which evokes the rigid sociocultural, linguistic, and artistic dictates of the day, holds the soul of the poet in the same way that the marble cage of the palace imprisons Darío's princess (ll. 31–36). If "A una cruz" is an expression of appreciation for liberation from previous constraints, "Las alas" offers an exuberant affirmation of the heights that can be achieved after breaking free.

Another feature that links "A una cruz" and "Las alas" is the way in which they define poetic insight. In both cases these abilities are tied to breaching the limitations of the individual's take on the world and the realization of a universal consciousness. In "A una cruz" she states, after being liberated, "Arraigábanse en mí todas las vidas, / Reflejábanse en mí todas las cosas! . . ." (192). In "Las alas" her poetry encompasses everything, good and evil, life and death, hope and despair, for her wings hold "todos los milagros de la vida, la Muerte / y la ilusión." Her vision is ultimately nothing less than cosmic, containing two firmaments and the full range of life's emotions. She ends the first section with three short lines:

> Dos alas,
> Como dos firmamentos
> Con tormentas, con calmas y con astros . . . (199)

[Two wings, / like two firmaments / with storms, with calm, and with stars.]

This final image subtly anticipates the central problem that emerges in the next section and that by the end becomes the focus of the poem. Agustini's world is not the fantasy imagined by Darío in "Sonatina," for it is filled with as much adversity as peace and with wonder. A possible source of her pain appears in the coupling of an unnamed "you" in the first line of the second section with the allusion to the fact that her wings are gone. This connection is established through the simple and evocative question, "¿Te acuerdas de la gloria de mis alas? . . ." (Do you remember the glory of my wings? . . .).

The rest of stanzas two and three continue to claim for her poetry the most desired qualities of modernista verse. Her poetry, under the aegis of her two wings, contains musicality, rhythm, color, and insight. The rhythm is golden, the color subtle, and the vision compatible with the future:[21]

> El áureo campaneo
> Del ritmo; el inefable
> Matiz atesorando
> El Iris todo, mas un Iris nuevo
> Ofuscante y divino,
> Que adorarán las plenas pupilas del Futuro
> (Las pupilas maduras a toda luz! . . .) el vuelo . . . (199)

[The golden chiming / of the beat; the ineffable / nuance amassing / the whole Rainbow, but a new Rainbow / dazzling and divine, / that the Future's complete eyes will adore / (the mature eyes in full light! . . .) the flight . . .]

From her heavenly position she declares her poetry to be on the side of future wisdom and understanding, offering new views on the nature of life and beauty. Her powers lead her out of a backward-looking worldview into a modern perspective. Futurity and modernity replace tradition and habit in an attempt to open both poetic and social possibilities. The flight is a departure from the weighty restrictions of long-held beliefs. For this reason, it (and, ultimately, her failure) recalls mythic examples of those who attempt to scale the heavens and who challenge divinely ordained limitations, most notably Icarus. Her ascent generates an uneasy response of newly awakened suns, comets, and storms. Nevertheless, she is able to achieve, at least for a moment, tremendous spiritual and creative powers:

> El vuelo ardiente, devorante y único,
> Que largo tiempo atormentó los cielos,
> Despertó soles, bólidos, tormentas,

Abrillantó los rayos y los astros;
Y la amplitud: tenían
Calor y sombra para todo el Mundo,
Y hasta incubar un *más allá* pudieron. (199)

[The burning, consuming, singular flight, / that long tormented the heavens, / woke suns, shooting stars, storms, / polished the lightning bolts and the stars; / and the spaciousness: they had heat and shadow for the whole World, / and they could even incubate a *beyond*.]

In this passage, Agustini expresses the most fundamental of modernista aspirations, namely, to provide a transcendental vision that breaks with the predominant positivistic ideology of the day. The materialism, pragmatism, and utilitarianism that informed daily activity are implicitly contrasted with a search for ultimate truths. Her focus is on what others cannot see. Her perspective reflects a dynamism and an eroticism that become all-consuming ("ardiente, devorante y único"). Equally significant is the way Agustini appropriates the sexual metaphors of creation previously used by male authors and makes them female and birdlike as well. She has the power to incubate a "beyond," that is, to hatch a vision that elevates her above the here and now. This semantic shift and the foregrounding of wings and flight hint at the emergence of a new swan of modernista verse, one that embraces women writers. Unfortunately, this flight ends like that of Icarus, who, by flying too close to the sun, lost his wings.

The myth of Icarus—his short-lived escape from the labyrinth, his overzealous flight, and his ultimate fall—appears to be an ideal metaphor for the struggle of women writers at the turn of the twentieth century. Before his fateful flight, both Icarus and his father, Daedalus, had been locked in the labyrinth created by Daedalus himself. Imprisoned within the confines of a father's mazelike rules and restrictions, the woman poet cannot easily find a way out. Even when given a means of escape, as Agustini herself was given by doting parents who encouraged her talents, women were often trapped by social and emotional constraints. The temptations that lead the lyric voice back to the restrictions from which she had broken free are suggested by Agustini's imagery. The apparent innocence of the lover's smile that wakes the sleeping poet is contrasted with the horrific outcome of their interaction. This juxtaposition raises further questions of responsibility. Like Icarus, she falls because her wings melt, but Agustini deliberately leaves unclear the source of the heat:

> Un día, raramente
> Desmayada a la tierra,
> Yo me adormí en las felpas profundas de este bosque . . .
> Soñé divinas cosas! . . .
> Una sonrisa tuya me despertó, paréceme . . .
> Y no siento mis alas! . . .
> Mis alas? . . .
>
> —Yo las *vi* deshacerse entre mis brazos . . .
> ¡Era como un deshielo! (200)

[One day, oddly / fainted on the ground, / I fell asleep on the deep plush textures of this forest . . . / I dreamed divine things! . . . / A smile of yours woke me, it seems to me . . . / and I do not feel my wings! . . . / My wings? . . .

—I *saw* them melt between my arms . . . / It was like a thaw!]

Do they melt because of the primal, erotic passion suggested by her fainting, by the "felpas profundas," and by "el bosque" mentioned in the poem? Does the power of the male's smile to wake imply a power to control and to deny? Does her love for him require that she relinquish her creative endeavors, despite her desire to hold on to them? Do her wings melt under the heat and pressure of domesticity, leaving her tied to the mundane? Or do they melt because she has attempted to fly too close to her personal sun, to Darío as model and source of inspiration? If Darío is both sun and lover, as suggested earlier, the implications are even more disturbing, especially if Girón Alvarado's assumption (131) that the final words are spoken by the male other is correct.

There is no horror, no apology, no lament, simply an accepting statement made by another. He looks on, quietly regarding as normal and appropriate the disintegration of her wings. His disparagingly matter-of-fact declaration reasserts the fundamental contention that a woman's role is to be passive and silent. Agustini thereby reveals her perception of the way the outside world views her aspirations to excel, to break free of traditional expectations, and to be a poet. All are of little importance, hardly worthy of note. The true tragedy is not that she falls but that her fall is deemed appropriate and even deserved. A sympathetic reader can only begin to imagine the hurt that is reflected in these final words. For Agustini the pain of poetic production that is common among all artists takes on a particularly tortured and tragic dimension in her work.

Despite all the seemingly insurmountable impediments, Agustini continues to strive and to hope for the dawning of a new day for *modernista* poetry and women alike. Invoking the illuminating flight and the "felpas profundas de este bosque . . ." of "Las alas," "Primavera" (205–6) offers an ebullient, uplifting antidote to the sad vision of poetic descent, a response that coalesces around the lyre, one of *modernismo*'s principal symbols of poetic aspiration. In "Primavera" the lyric voice self-assuredly takes possession of the Orphic instrument by converting it into a type of lover. She embraces both the lyre and the hardships that accompany it.

In the first stanza, her exuberant affirmation of the awakening of her poetic abilities is described in cosmic terms. The arms of the lyre are compared to resplendent wings directed toward the future, and the lyre's awakening to a new sun over a new world. This bold statement prepares the reader for the defiant tone of the second stanza, which rejects the passivity of earlier dreams and the dependence on others by presenting a series of rhetorical challenges to the many obstacles the lyric voice must overcome. She defies these obstacles to redouble their efforts, for she is certain of the curative and redemptive powers of her art, which figuratively fuses with the melodious rebirth of spring. By the end of the poem, the reawakening countryside provides organic images evocative of passion and eroticism:

> Los brazos de mi lira se han abierto
> Puros y ardientes como el fuego; ebrios
> Del ansia visionaria de un abrazo
> Tan grande, tan potente, tan amante
> Que haga besarse el fango con los astros . . .
> Y otras cosas más bajas y sombrías
> Con otras más brillantes y más altas! . . .
>
> ¡Oh! mi lira de brazos como pétalos
> ¡Flor la más rara de esta primavera! (206)

[The arms of my lyre have opened / pure and ardent like fire; intoxicated / with the visionary anguish of an embrace / so large, so powerful, so loving / that it makes the mud and the stars kiss each . . . / and other things lower and darker / with others more resplendent and higher! . . .

Oh! my lyre with arms like petals / the strangest flower of this springtime!]

Agustini turns the lyre into a sexual partner, dispensing with the male poet/model/lover of previous poems. She stands on her own and directly embraces poetry, through which she melds the human and the divine, the terrestrial and the heavenly, the erotic and the poetic. Nevertheless, she acknowledges those aspects of a woman's life that anchor her in the mud and dark and that give her work a uniquely defined perspective. The radiant hope tinged with doubt and fear of "Primavera," the penultimate poem of *Cantos de la mañana,* provides a preliminary conclusion to her collection.

The final poem, "Los relicarios dulces" (207), begins an exploration that continues into Agustini's next volume of verse. It examines the dilemma of the inescapable recollections of lost loves, past poems, and binding social expectations that reside beneath the surface of creative expression. The poem's title and its reference to a reliquary, that is, to a container or shrine where some physical remnant of a saint is kept, signals Agustini's meditation on Darío, all that he stands for, and his lasting impact upon her work. Her poem, like the ex-voto of "A una cruz," is the literary equivalent of the religious artifact. It contains the remains, the erasure, of another poet. The fusing of the other's "erased soul" with hers links the poem/reliquary to a palimpsest and acknowledges that, at least for her, traces of the past writings are the inevitable point of departure. Agustini nevertheless turns her belatedness, that is, her late arrival on the literary scene, into a strength. She writes, "Hace tiempo algún alma ya borrada fue mía . . . / Se nutrió de mi sombra . . ." (Long ago, some already erased soul was mine . . . / It fed on my shadow . . .). The earlier poet lives within her, nourished by her. With subtle echoes of a vampiric embrace, her struggle for ascendancy concludes with ambivalence:

Alma que yo ondulaba tal una cabellera
Derramada en mis manos . . . Flor del fuego y la cera . . .
Murió de una tristeza mía . . . Tan dúctil era,

Tan fiel, que a veces dudo si pudo ser jamás . . . (207)

[Soul that I made wavy like long hair / spilled in my hands . . . The fiery and waxen flower . . . / died of my sadness.

It was so malleable, / so loyal, that at times I doubt that it could have ever existed . . .]

The collection therefore elaborates upon the conflicted emotions of its second poem, "De 'Elegías dulces,'" a conflict that is signaled at the beginning and end by the adjective "dulces." As much as Agustini longs to hold on to the erotic other, the figurative Darío, she knows she has to find the appropriate balance of remembering and forgetting in order to become a spokesperson for the future. The struggle between inherited ideals and desire for change becomes more violent as Agustini becomes more confident in her ability to stand on her own. The title of her next collection, *Los cálices vacíos*, affirms her efforts to empty poetry of what came before in order to fill it with an innovative and expansive vision, one that is neither tidy nor pristine.

Figure 1. Delmira Agustini as a young woman. Courtesy of the Biblioteca Nacional

Figure 2. Delmira Agustini in Montevideo's Parque Giot. Courtesy of the Biblioteca Nacional

Figure 3. Celebration of the wedding of Delmira Agustini and Enrique Job Reyes.
Courtesy of the Biblioteca Nacional

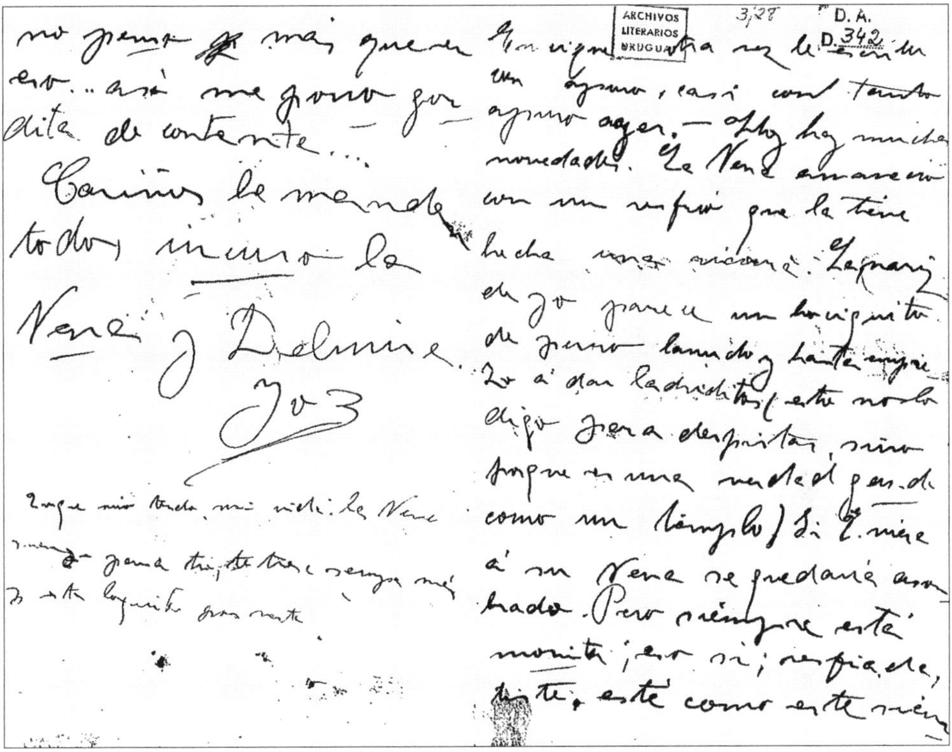

Figure 4. Postcard written by Agustini to Enrique Job Reyes
in which she refers to herself as la Nena.
Courtesy of the Biblioteca Nacional

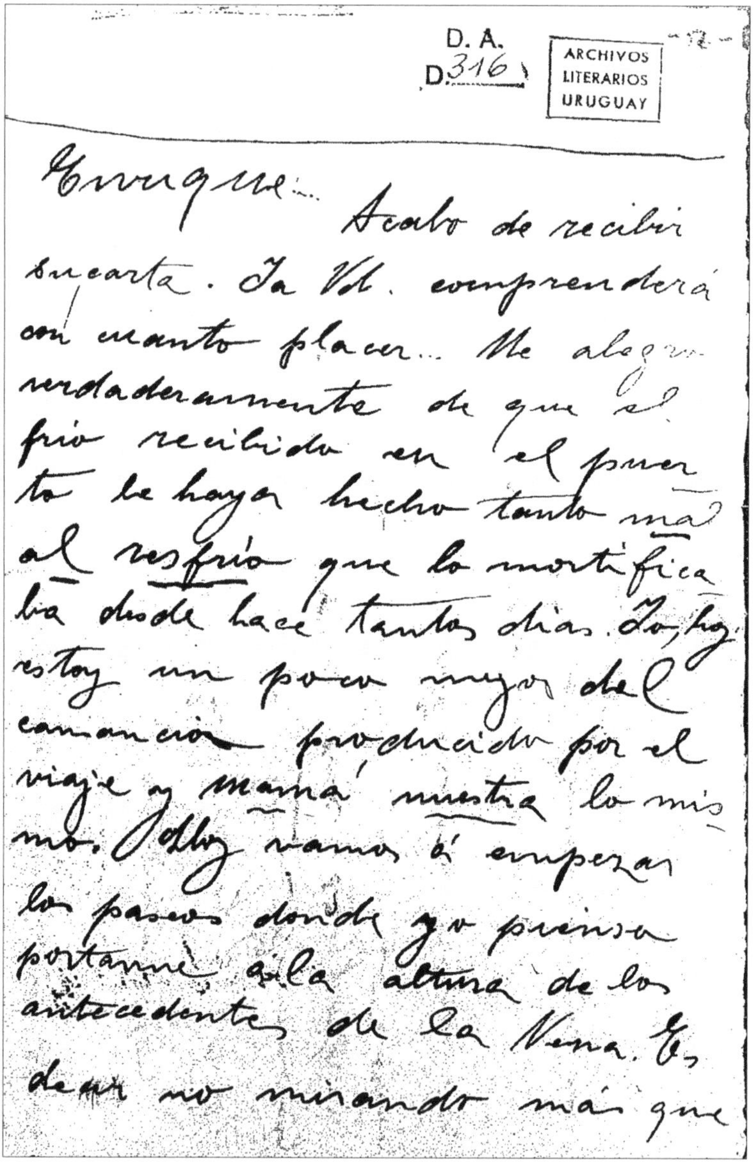

D. A.
D316

ARCHIVOS
LITERARIOS
URUGUAY

Enrique: Acabo de recibir su carta. Ya Vd. comprenderá con cuanto placer... Me alegro verdaderamente de que el frío recibido en el puerto le haya hecho tanto mal al resfrío que lo mortificaba desde hace tantos días. Yo, hoy estoy un poco mejor del cansancio producido por el viaje y mamá muestra lo mismo. Hoy vamos á empezar los paseos donde yo pienso portarme á la altura de los antecedentes de la Nena. Es decir no mirando más que

Figure 5. Two-page letter from Agustini to Enrique Job Reyes in which she expresses her affection for him. Courtesy of the Biblioteca Nacional

mi vuelta — si Dios quiere
importará al Uruguay el
resfrío más notable
que por allí se conozca. —
Pienso que Montevideo debe
de estar feo, feísimo con mi
ausencia. Estoy tan convenci-
da de que sin la Nena no sabe nada... Mañana espero conti-
nuar mis impresiones para
nuestro diario, y espero
también las suyas sobre Montevideo... Estoy por salir. — De mi
corazón no le digo nada porque
me cuesta un poquito hablar de
eso así... y por lo demás Vd. sabe
bien que es siempre, siempre
el mismo. Muchos recuerdos de todos
y mamá le reitera una vez más su
agradecimiento, sus recomendaciones etc, etc.
aplace el domingo — si Dios quiere e penquísimo

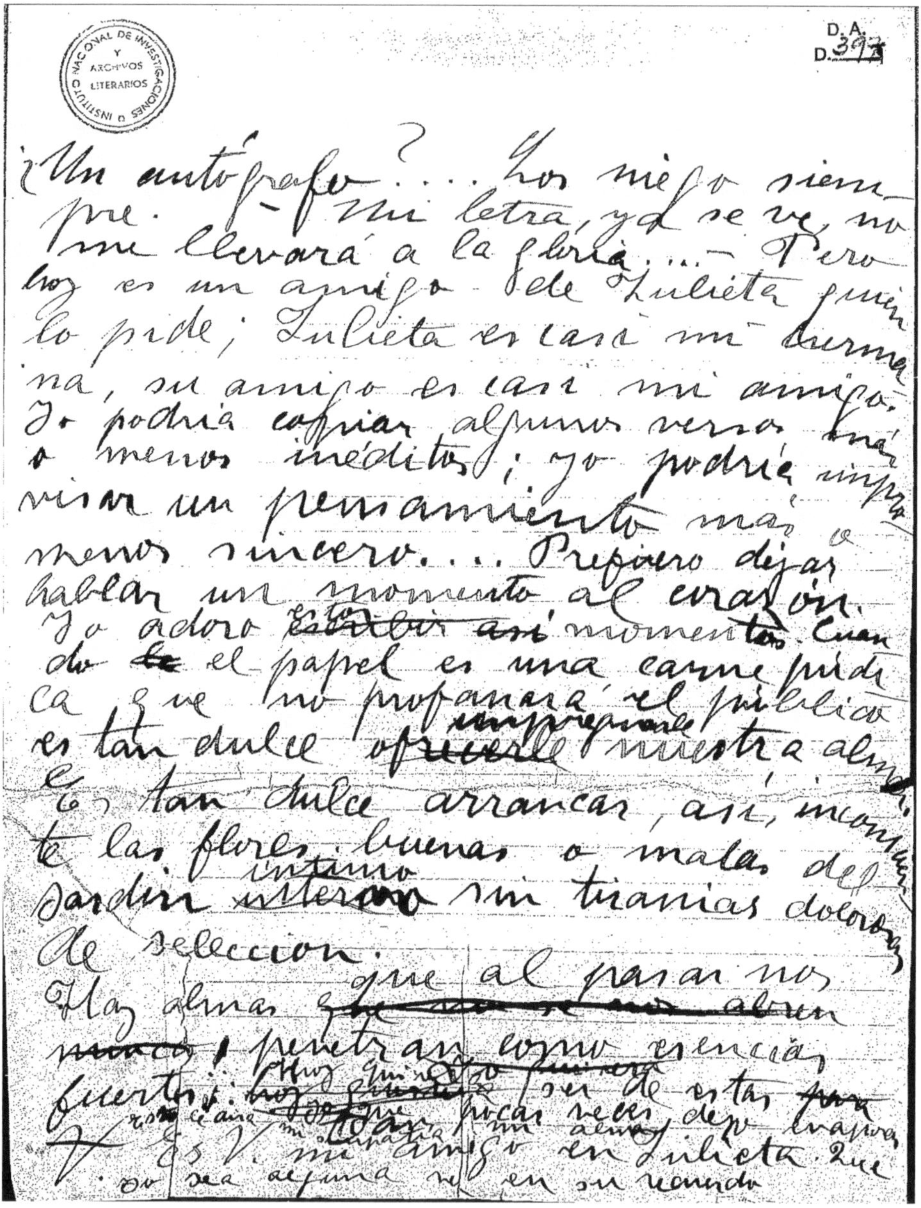

Figure 6. Letter Agustini wrote in response to a request for an autograph in which she comments on her hard-to-read handwriting.
Courtesy of the Biblioteca Nacional

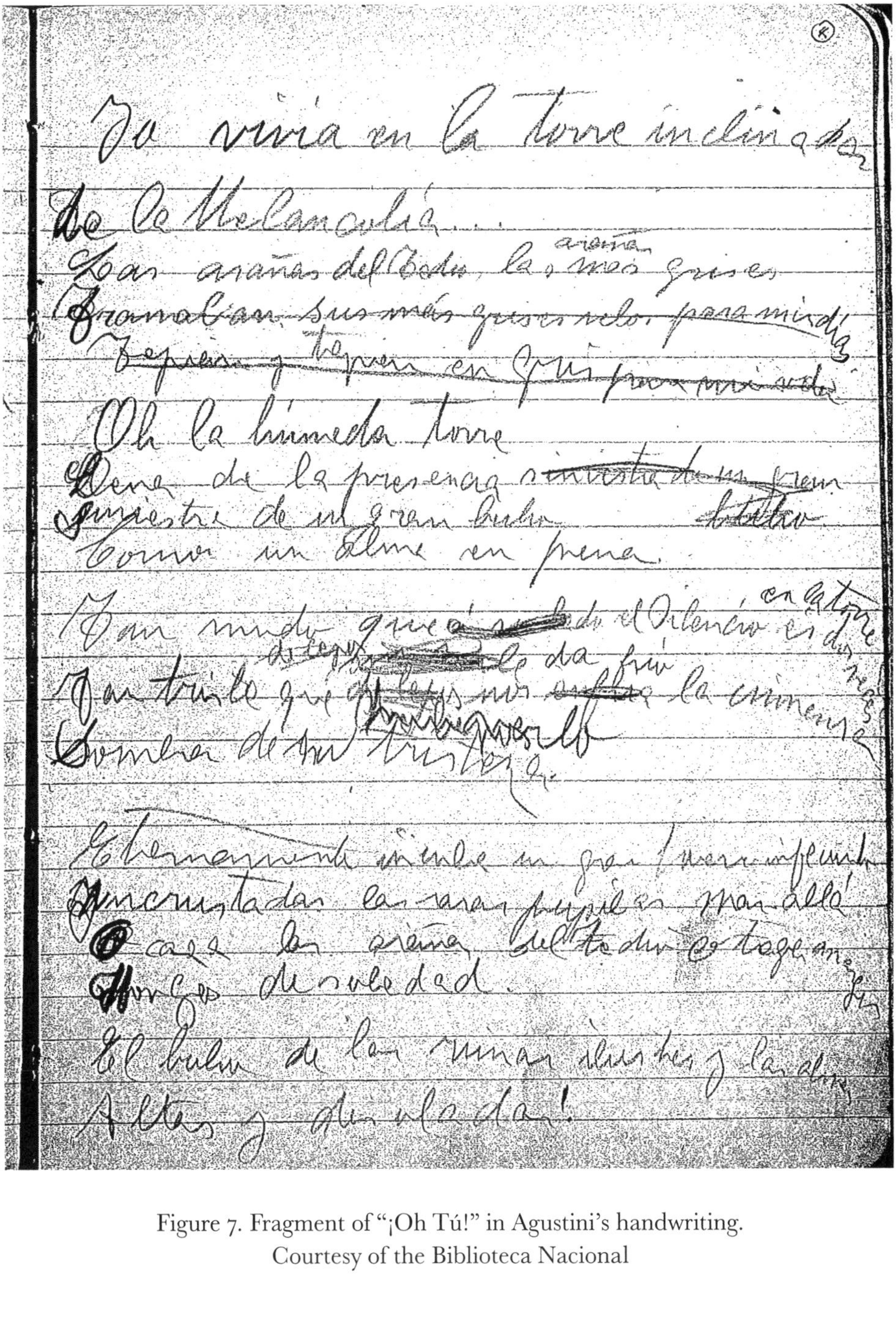

Yo vivía en la torre inclinada
de la Melancolía...
Las arañas del tedio, las más grises,
tramaban sus más grises velos para mí...

Oh la húmeda torre
llena de la presencia siniestra de un gran
siniestro de un gran búho
como un alma en pena.

Tan mudo que el silencio en la torre
tan triste que la inmensa
sombra de tu tristeza

Eternamente
incrustadas las raras pupilas más allá
de las arenas del tedio
de soledad.
El búho de las ruinas ilustres y las altas
Altas y desoladas!

Figure 7. Fragment of "¡Oh Tú!" in Agustini's handwriting.
Courtesy of the Biblioteca Nacional

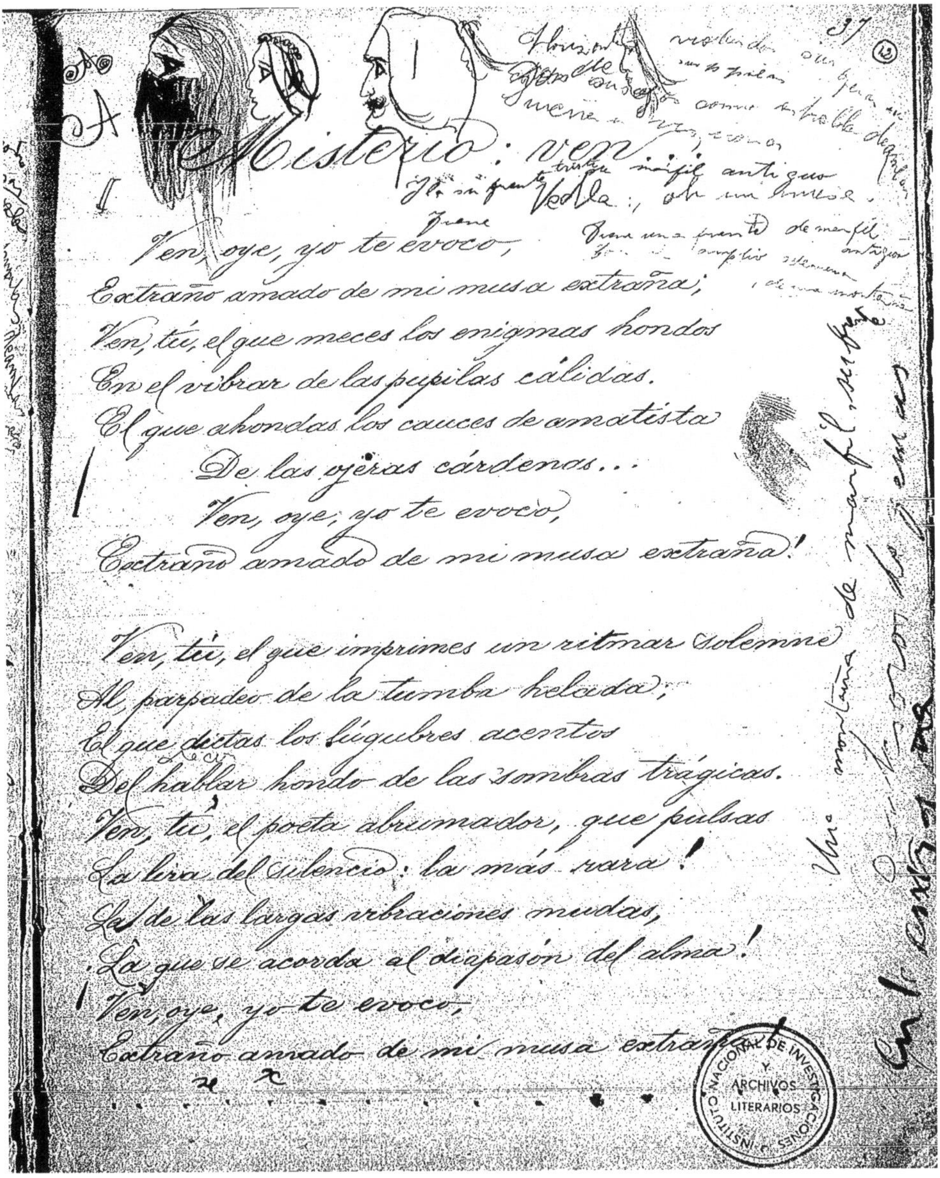

37

Misterio: ven

Ven, oye, yo te evoco,
Extraño amado de mi musa extraña;
Ven, tú, el que meces los enigmas hondos
En el vibrar de las pupilas cálidas.
El que ahondas los cauces de amatista
De las ojeras cárdenas...
Ven, oye, yo te evoco,
Extraño amado de mi musa extraña!

Ven, tú, el que imprimes un ritmar solemne
Al parpadeo de la tumba helada;
El que dictas los lúgubres acentos
Del hablar hondo de las sombras trágicas.
Ven, tú, el poeta abrumador, que pulsas
La lira del silencio: la más rara!
La de las largas vibraciones mudas,
La que se acorda al diapasón del alma!
Ven, oye, yo te evoco,
Extraño amado de mi musa extraña

Figure 8. First page of Agustini's father's rewritten copy of "Misterio, ven" with the poet's doodles. Courtesy of the Biblioteca Nacional

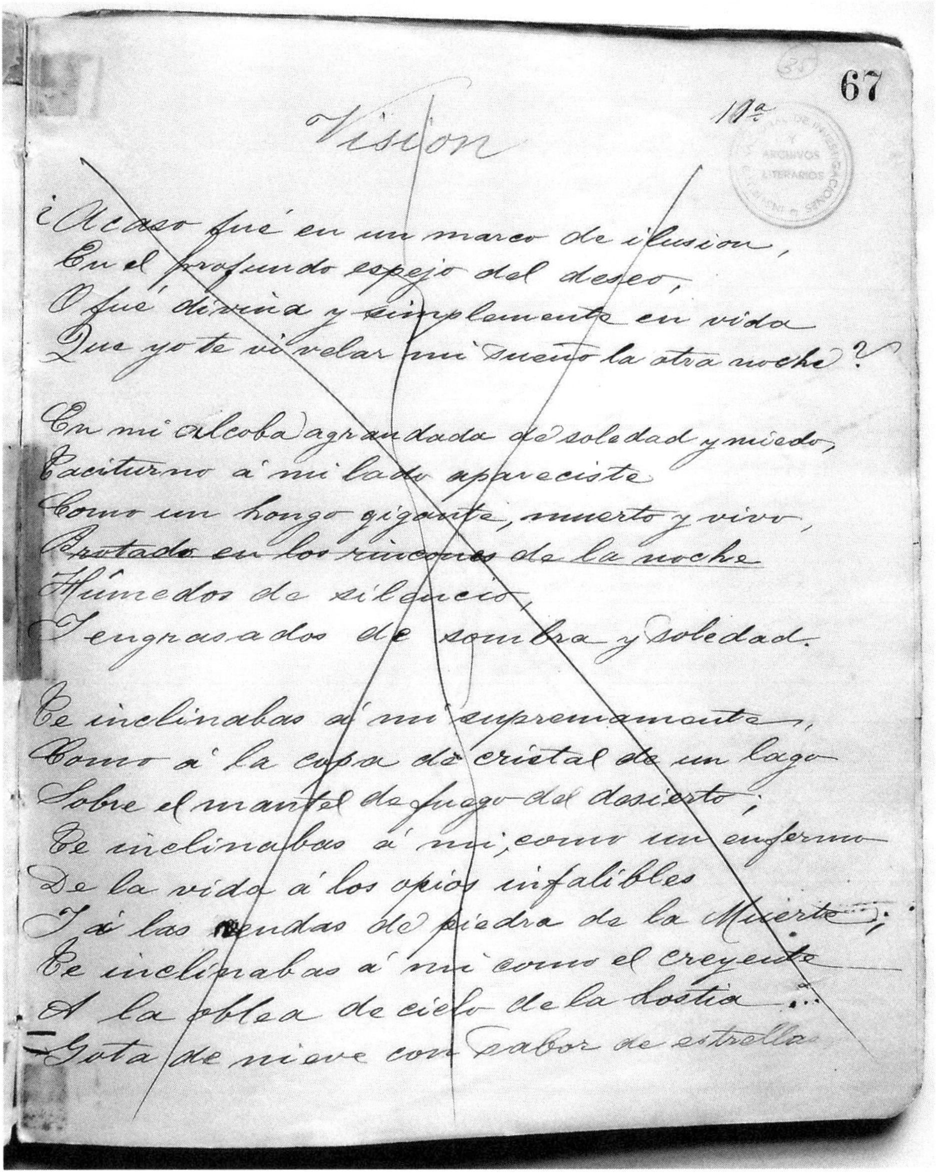

Visión

¿Acaso fué en un marco de ilusión,
En el profundo espejo del deseo,
O fué divina y simplemente en vida
Que yo te ví velar mi sueño la otra noche?

En mi alcoba agrandada de soledad y miedo,
Taciturno á mi lado apareciste
Como un hongo gigante, muerto y vivo,
Brotado en los rincones de la noche
Húmedos de silencio,
Y engrasados de sombra y soledad.

Te inclinabas á mí supremamente,
Como á la copa de cristal de un lago
Sobre el mantel de fuego del desierto;
Te inclinabas á mí; como un enfermo
De la vida á los opios infalibles
Y á las vendas de piedra de la Muerte;
Te inclinabas á mí como el creyente
A la oblea de cielo de la hostia...
—Gota de nieve con sabor de estrella

Figure 9. First page of Agustini's father's rewritten copy of "Visión" with printer's marks.
Courtesy of the Biblioteca Nacional

CHAPTER FOUR

TURNING LOSS INTO EMPOWERMENT

Los cálices vacíos

Delmira Agustini's tumultuous life, with its successes and tragic end, was shaped by both the opportunities and the dangers generated by the cultural shifts occurring in Uruguay at the beginning of the twentieth century. Her life also reflects the daring with which she sought to move beyond the entrenched social and conceptual conventions of her day. During the six years between the first and last books of verse published during her lifetime, she constantly reimagined her role as both a woman and a poet, seeking a symbolic strategy that would allow her to overcome personal and poetic limitations and conquer the private creative anxieties that she describes throughout her work. This quest reverberates through the core of her poetics and reveals her vision of art. By focusing on her passionate obsession with writing, this book opens a hitherto unexplored line of critical reading of her work that exposes her highly nuanced transformation of male-centered *modernista* tropes of artistic production. Just as her male predecessors imposed carnal and poetic longings upon the passive female body, Agustini forges a seductive verse through which she seeks to garner control over the other and the poetic process. This engaging, sexualized other whom she aspires to conquer is, as I have argued throughout, an amalgam that is the text and person of the idealized Rubén Darío. "He" is the object of her erotic desires, the embodiment of modernista perfection, the pinnacle of poetic success, and the body of hegemonic texts, myths, and symbols.

Perhaps the most striking change that takes place in Agustini's poetry during the three years between the publication of *Cantos de la mañana* (1910) and *Los cálices vacíos* (The empty chalices) (1913) is an ever-greater awareness of the dangers involved in transgressing the patriarchal rules of society. Struggling against what she comes to envision as the brutal imposition of restrictions against women, her language resonates with loss and injury at the same time that her images grow more assertively sexual and violent. Her willingness to suffer for what she most desires—art, independence, and love—becomes a battle between opposing forces of light and dark, death and resurrection, body and spirit. The imposing elements from the personal as well as cultural past emerge in different guises and to different effect throughout the collection. They might appear as a cruel current lover, a deceased husband, or a formidable statue of inherited social and artistic structures. Similarly, she is at times the victim and at others she triumphantly vanquishes the constraining forces that have prevented women from achieving sexual independence and creative empowerment. Her nocturnal forays into the world of poetic imaginings appear as a type of internal exile in which she mourns the death of a socially sanctioned "husband" even as she anticipates the liberating delight of erotic adventures and poetic promise. In short, she turns established linguistic and behavioral patterns to her advantage. She mourns a past that she has, in effect, chosen to terminate. Vampiric insults become a source of strength. Leda's and Galatea's passivity is rejected as gender boundaries are crossed. As she formulates ways to take control of her poetic language and fate, Agustini finds a new voice that, in her assertive rewriting of traditional male visions of love, lust, and artistic production, generates a new style. This new style allows violence and rebellion to enter the utopian sanctuaries of modernista interiors and landscapes and anticipates the fractured visions and psychological pain of the avant-garde.

Agustini opens *Los cálices vacíos* with a short, untitled poem in French which presents many of the themes and images that will reappear throughout the collection. The poem also affirms her participation in the widespread fascination with France and French culture encouraged and propagated by her compatriots and fellow modernistas:

> Debout sur mon orgueil je veux montrer au soir
> L'envers de mon manteau endeuillé de tes charmes,
> Son mouchoir infini, son mouchoir noir et noir
> Trait à trait, doucement, boira toutes mes larmes.
>
> Il donne des lys blancs à mes roses de flamme
> Et des bandeaux de calme à mon front délirant . . .
> Que le soir sera bon . . . Il aura pour moi l'âme
> Claire et le corps profond d'un magnifique amant. (225)[1]

The poem echoes the refined tone of the turn-of-the-century poetry and reflects the elaborately crafted nature of the popular art nouveau style. It also evokes a special type of spiritual openness and artistic awakening that, ironically, is unique to the night. As the harsh light of the physical world fades, the visionary sees beyond the surface, the superficial, and the routine. The night becomes a moment of spiritual insight. This quality made the hours after dark the conceptual centerpiece of numerous musical and poetic nocturnes of the period.[2]

This privileging of the night is visible in "Debout sur mon orgueil . . ." as well. Even though this eight-line piece includes a reference to an ambiguous "you," the night itself takes center stage as an alternative sexual partner who offers the speaker the pure soul and the profound body of a magnificent lover. The night offers her a welcoming refuge, a type of embrace, in which she can engage in the passionate—and private—enterprise of reverie and writing. "He" satisfies the fervent desires that are hidden by the daytime "cloak" of her public persona and her dutiful mourning of the absent you.

Through this reference to loss and implications of a type of widowhood Agustini establishes from the beginning of *Los cálices vacíos* an intricate grieving process that includes remembering and moving on and announces the delicate balance she attempts to establish between influence and independence (recalling the mournful lament of "De 'Elegías dulces,'" 183).[3] Her nocturnal contemplation of sexual victories and defeats, her ambivalence with regard to lost opportunities and lost loves, and her hunger to retain and to alter the memories of the past all echo within the darkened chamber of the poem. What is particularly revealing in this first poem is the way she fuses lust with the soulful enfolding of the night and its potential for creativity. She shows the night the reverse of her cloak, the possibly white interior, that is marked by what she is missing and mourning and what she seeks to capture on or through other white objects. She moves beyond the distant source of inspiration—the absent you, the now-iconic Darío—into the arms of a different type of partner, one that would allow her greater independence.

The infinitely black handkerchief that the night provides to "drink up all [her] tears" is the ambiguous darkness that wraps, isolates, and, to a certain extent, protects all artists. It offers consolation in the face of her distraught ambivalence. The fear of the consequences of breaking expectations lurks in the dark depths of the night, an image that anticipates the menacing abysses that reappear in other poems in the collection. Yet here, at the very beginning of *Los cálices vacíos*, Agustini's lyric voice emerges triumphant; in the second stanza she welcomes the white lilies and bandages, which calm her passions ("flaming roses") and her anxieties ("delirious brow"). Optimistically, almost arrogantly ("Debout sur mon orgueil"), she proclaims her ability to overcome her weaknesses and to achieve independence. She finds the night gentle, forgiving, consoling. The lilies and bandages will become the white pages on which she will resurrect the charms of her departed lover, his talents, and his successes. They complement the cloak in which she has dressed herself as the widow and heir. As she embraces the body and soul of the night, she moves beyond loss to hope for erotic and literary fulfillment.

As if to restart the collection, this time in Spanish, Agustini repeats much of the metaphoric language that undergirds "Debout sur mon orgueil . . ." in the next two poems of the collection, "Ofrendando el libro" (Offering up the book) (226) and "Nocturno" (Nocturne) (227). The images from the first poem are noticeably strong in "Nocturno," which begins with a provocative stanza of two lines: "Fuera, la noche en veste de tragedia solloza / Como una enorme viuda pegada a mis cristales" (Outside, the night in tragedy's dress sobs / Like a vast widow standing close to my window-panes). The cloak, the grieving, the loss, the tears are all attributed to the night, which now appears as a widow who peers in through the window. Agustini reinforces the allusion to widowhood from the first poem and presents separation, distance, and mournful recollection as the initial factors in the act of writing. The window from which the poet looks at the observing figure becomes a powerful statement about the creative process. The two women see each other and are drawn to each other but stand divided by a transparent line, in stark opposition to one another.

This dividing window becomes the poetic equivalent of Darío's "Palabras liminares." Whereas Darío transforms the adjective "liminar," which refers to an entry point, a door jamb and, by extension, a window frame, into a metaphor, Agustini signals her desire to express her own declaration of poetic intent by returning to the word's literal signification. When Darío begins *Prosas profanas*, his revolutionary second collection, with this strong, self-assured statement of poetic goals, he is not simply introducing his new volume of verse; he is crossing the threshold into a new creative period and, as he most certainly understood, into a defining moment for the new literary movement with which he is identified. Agustini's statement is more tentative, but in its own way announces a crossing over. Though she is haunted by the past, she signals a new beginning by keeping the past at bay—on the other side of the window, in the nocturnal and grief-stricken darkness—as she declares her own illuminated and vibrant revolutionary position, which includes her right to take possession of the discourse she had inherited. This assertion is represented in the second stanza in the description of the space inhabited by the lyric voice, a space that is simultaneously natural and luxurious:

> Mi cuarto: . . .
> Por un bello milagro de la luz y del fuego
> Mi cuarto es una gruta de oro y gemas raras:
> Tiene[4] un musgo tan suave, tan hondo de tapices,
> Y es tan vívida y cálida, tan dulce que me creo
> Dentro de un corazón . . . (227)

[My room: . . . / by a beautiful miracle of light and fire / my room is a grotto of gold and rare gems: / it has moss so soft, so deep with tapestries, / and it is so vivid and warm, so sweet that I believe I am / inside a heart . . .]

If the women of Darío's poems, poems that float through Agustini's nocturnal imaginings, represent the female consort of artistic creation, poetic inspiration, and language, in "Nocturno" Agustini makes her widow-like, bereft of a husband, tearful in her exploration of alternatives. The tradition-bound female figure looks in from the window because she does not belong in Agustini's reconfigured but clearly modernista chamber, for it has been prepared to receive the spirit of the departed partner. The room has been filled with light, warmth, and jewels, recalling, as Jorge Luis Castillo notes, the sumptuous bourgeois interior of Darío's "De invierno" from *Azul . . .* (176). It is also the space where she feels enveloped by the beating heart of the universe, the same heart that appeared in the rhythmic rocking of "La barca milagrosa" (185). Fusing the cosmic and the erotic, the poem converts the memory of the absent lover into a palpable presence, resurrected as the anticipated artistic and amorous partner, ready to inscribe himself on the whiteness of the not wholly innocent poet's bed:

> Mi lecho que está en blanco es blanco y vaporoso
> Como flor de inocencia,
> Como espuma de vicio!
> Esta noche hace insomnio;
> Hay noches negras, negras, que llevan en la frente
> Una rosa de sol . . .
> En estas noches negras y claras no se duerme. (227)

[My bed that is blank is white and vaporous / like a flower of innocence / like a foam of vice! / This night makes for sleeplessness; / there are black nights, black ones that carry on their forehead / a rose of the sun . . . / On these black and clear nights one does not sleep.]

The struggle between the dark, imposing forces of the past, on the one hand, and the light of the blank page and of illuminated poetic originality, on the other, is played out in Agustini's "Nocturno" during the nights of insomnia and artistic/sexual awakening. Even in this contextualization of her poetic efforts Agustini recalls Darío's work, especially his "Nocturno" of *Cantos de vida y esperanza* (291). In Agustini's case, nights of heightened clarity are the setting for her ardent pursuit of the perfect passion that melds opposites: what is inside and what is out, knowing and dreaming, innocence and vice, normative practices and innovation. This sexually productive encounter, this fusion of opposites, takes place on her blank, white bed, upon which she "writes" with roses and lilies: ". . . Amémonos por eso! . . . / Sobre mi lecho en blanco, / . . . / Caigamos en un ramo de rosas y de lirios!" (227) (Let us love each other for this reason! . . . / Upon my blank bed, / . . . / Let's fall upon a bouquet of roses and lilies!).

Agustini avoids the despair of Darío's poem and his nocturnal confrontation with the anxieties of poetic responsibility and its concomitant moral obligations. Whereas he is burdened by his thoughts of who he is, of how he has led his life, and of the uncertainty of the future, Agustini speaks with youthful enthusiasm and defiance. She conquers the night by taking a lover and giving herself over to the joy of creation. There is a sense of a physical and inspirational openness that arouses the reader and creates an erotic energy similar to the fitfulness of a sleepless night. In the fourth stanza she transforms her partner from black memory to a white presence appropriate for her bedroom by imagining him—in a metaphor that was first seen in *Cantos de la mañana* and that is repeated throughout this volume—as winter, old but wise, covered with the royal, weighty mantle of time:

> Y yo te amo, Invierno!
> Yo te imagino viejo,
> Yo te imagino sabio,
> Con un divino cuerpo de mármol palpitante
> Que arrastra como un manto regio el peso del Tiempo . . .
> Invierno, yo te amo y soy la primavera . . .
> Yo sonroso, tú nievas:
> Tú porque todo sabes,
> Yo porque todo sueño . . . (227)

[And I love you, Winter! / I imagine you old, / I imagine you wise, / with a divine body of throbbing marble / that drags like a regal cloak the weight of Time . . . / Winter, I love you, and I am the spring . . . / I color things pink, you make things white as snow: / because you know everything, / because I dream everything . . .]

If he is winter, she is the spring, the future, and the source of new growth. His is the majestic, rigid, erect body of pulsating marble. Hers is fecund, supple, and fragrant. By redefining the erotic other from whom she draws knowledge and pleasure, she turns herself into the ideal agent of a new type of artistic creativity. In a sexual and joyful pursuit of creativity that is as natural as the turning of the seasons, Agustini simultaneously embraces the past and declares a new beginning. Echoing the story of Lot's daughters, she happily produces with her older lover the next generation of modernista verse.

While both "Debout sur mon orgueil . . ." and "Nocturno" explore the potential of creative renewal embedded within separation and loss, "Ofrendando el libro" (226), the second poem in the collection, foregrounds the erotic figuration of poetic production through the combination of the title and the dedication to Eros. Agustini chooses Eros as the male counterpart to Darío's multifaceted Venus. This shift is significant, for as much as Venus and her flesh-and-blood equivalents arouse and animate, Darío remains the ultimate producer of culture. In Darío's poems "Coloquio de los centauros" (203) and "¡Carne, celeste carne de la mujer! . . ." (Flesh, celestial flesh of woman! . . .) (280–81), for example, Venus offers the male poet the universal patterns that he reads and translates into art, opening his vision to harmony, accord, and even solace in the face of death. The male author and the figure of Venus work in tandem in the context of an androgynous universe in which masculine and feminine are integrated. Yet his is clearly the voice that is heard. With creative dexterity Agustini slips the male Eros into Venus's metaphorical position, shifting the gender-aligned power structure and allowing the poet to speak with the same authority given to her masculine counterpart. She can comfortably assert her creative abilities as well as her erotic desires while repeating the modernista fusion of sexuality and art. Like Darío, she finds in love the model and metaphor for the magical energy of life and poetry.

The second stanza of "Ofrendando el libro" evokes the same life force that runs throughout existence (from the vegetative to the divine) in Darío's "Coloquio de los centauros" and suggests a type of healing not unlike the solutions alluded to in Darío's utopian poem:

> Porque tu cuerpo es la raíz, el lazo
> Esencial de los troncos discordantes
> Del placer y el dolor, plantas gigantes. (226)

[Because your body is the root, the essential / tie that binds the discordant tree trunks / of pleasure and pain, giant plants.]

Eros, the speaker's lover, her source of inspiration, and the promise of accord, reveals the deep-rooted but unobserved unity of the discordant pillars of pleasure and pain. The poem concludes with her becoming, under his influence, a seer ("te diviso") and a witness to the complexity of her existence:

> Porque sobre el Espacio te diviso,
> Puente de luz, perfume y melodía,
> Comunicando infierno y paraíso.
>
> —Con alma fúlgida y carne sombría . . . (226)

[Because I discern you hovering above Space / the bridge of light, perfume and melody, / connecting paradise and hell.

—With a resplendent soul and dark flesh . . .]

Eros offers a way to unite life's divergent aspects. From a more personal perspective, "he" offers a path over the rugged terrain of her experiences with love and writing, experiences that generate the book she offers him. If Eros is the "bridge of light, perfume and melody" that leads from heaven to hell and back again, if he can tame the savage lioness, if he can tether her with his embrace (as in the first stanza), then "she" must follow his lead. She must find salvation in the reconciliation of opposites. The high-energy dance of polarities—life and death, pleasure and pain, heaven and hell—that is so prominent here infuses the poem and the entire collection with its imaginative dynamism and anticipates many of Agustini's most striking images. Love and poetry come together in their abilities to transform, to elevate, to redeem, and to instill an otherworldliness, all of which is summarized by the poem's last four lines (quoted above).[5]

The final images also recall Darío's most famous pronouncements about poetry (quoted above): "Como cada palabra tiene un alma, hay en cada verso, además de la harmonía verbal, una melodía ideal. La música es sólo de la idea, muchas veces" (Since each word has a soul, in each verse there is, in addition to verbal harmony, an ideal melody. Often the music is only from the idea) (180). Agustini points to the dark body, the element that is implied but omitted in Darío's statement, because for her the somatic nature of words casts a highly menacing specter over her efforts. She understands that the normalization of male authority and desire means that all female assertion is by nature transgressive. As a result, she calls attention to the infernal aspects of the flesh. Despite the obstacles that must be overcome, including the inflexible physicality of language that plagues Darío's "Yo persigo una forma . . . ," Agustini finds hope.[6] Author and inspiration, language and thought are drawn together, seemingly conquering the dichotomous worldview grounded in masculine domination and feminine subjugation.

If the first three poems of *Los cálices vacíos* reveal Agustini's subtle commentary on life, love, and art, she draws attention to the dangers of her endeavors in the fourth, "Tu boca" (Your mouth) (228). If in the first three poems she minimizes the strength of the other by relegating him to the past or converting him into a force that empowers her, in "Tu boca" the perils of her encounter with him are made real and immediate. This short but powerful piece addresses Agustini's efforts on the edge of the abyss of artistic aspiration, which she defines as nothing less than a "divine labor":

> Yo hacía una divina labor, sobre la roca
> Creciente del Orgullo. De la vida lejana,
> Algún pétalo vívido me voló en la mañana,
> Algún beso en la noche. Tenaz como una loca,
> Seguía mi divina labor sobre la roca.
>
> Cuando tu voz que funde como sacra campana
> En la nota celeste la vibración humana,
> Tendió su lazo de oro al borde de tu boca;
>
> —Maravilloso nido del vértigo, tu boca!
> Dos pétalos de rosa abrochando un abismo . . .—
>
> Labor, labor de gloria, dolorosa y liviana;
> ¡Tela donde mi espíritu se fue tramando él mismo!
> Tú quedas en la testa soberbia de la roca,
>
> Y yo caigo, sin fin, en el sangriento abismo! (228)

[I was carrying out a divine task, on the rising precipice / of Pride. From the distant life, / some vivid petal flew toward me in the morning, / some kiss in the night. Tenacious like a madwoman, / I continued with my divine task on the precipice.

When your voice that fuses, like a sacred bell, / human vibration into celestial music, / extended its golden bond to the edge of your mouth;

—Marvelous, dizzying nest, your mouth! Two rose petals fastening up an abyss . . .—

Labor, glorious, painful, and libidinous labor; / canvas upon which my spirit was weaving itself! / You remain at the arrogant head of the precipice,

And I fall, endlessly, into the bloody abyss!]

There are echoes here of a Promethean undertaking (as there are later in "Otra estirpe" [243]), a "divine task" that, because it challenges the gods, leads to the hero's suffering on a craggy cliff. The moving mixture of audacious pride and punishing injury that fills the story of the compassionate Titan was, for Agustini, as for her romantic, postromantic, and modernista predecessors, a perfect analogue for the poet's fate (see Abrams, *The Mirror and the Lamp*, 280–81). This identification also appears in Darío's memorable "En las constelaciones" (In the constellations), a poem that was written in 1908 but was never incorporated in his later volumes of verse.[7] In this sonnet Darío declares a conflicted stance toward his poetic drive and destiny similar to Agustini's. In the second quartet, he states,

> Sé que soy, desde el tiempo del Paraíso, reo;
> sé que he robado el fuego y robé la armonía;
> que es abismo mi alma y huracán mi deseo;
> que sorbo el infinito y quiero todavía . . .

[I know that, since the time of Paradise, I am a criminal; / I know that I have stolen fire and I stole harmony; / that my soul is an abyss and my desire a hurricane; / that I soak up the infinite and I still want . . .]

Agustini appropriates and personalizes key Promethean traits by brazenly affirming her poetic and erotic desires, both of which she links with a type of divinity and danger. Though in "Tu boca" the lyric voice appears willing to accept risks and suffering, she is unprepared for the territoriality evident in the other's behavior as well as his blatant lack of compassion (similar to the cold aloofness of the male lover at the end of "Las alas" [199–200]). The unexpected turn of events is communicated by the suddenness of their introduction in the poem. What starts off as a gentle and amorous seduction becomes a pernicious enterprise that leads to the downfall of the lyric voice. The "tú" remains where the "yo" labored to be, that is, at the top of the cliff looking down with arrogance at the battered exiled poet. She falls from the heights of her ambitious climb into the abyss of real or imagined failure, recalling the abysses of Darío's sense of artistic and spiritual inadequacy.

While in "Ofrendando el libro" the other can be recognized as a poet because of the presence of the writer's hand, a hand that is capable of disclosing truths about life and death, in "Tu boca" his vocation is divulged by his mouth, which comes to her as a sensuous petal of recollected verse and a kiss in the night as well as through his voice, which echoes with the sacred sounds of celestial harmonies and the music of human desires, the musicality of great modernista verse. In short, his mouth offers a synthesis of spirituality and physicality through poetry and passion. This conquest of contradictory orientations is echoed in the image of his two lips, which embrace and envelop the dark abyss of ineffectuality and damnation. ("—Maravilloso nido del vértigo, tu boca! / Dos pétalos de rosa abrochando un abismo . . .—"). The mouth that promises the giddy, dizzying exaltation of song, verse, and passion is also the gaping orifice that can swallow the aspiring artist. This abyss reemerges at the end as the lyric voice alone suffers the consequence of her ambitions. Despite her efforts to stay on track, to continue to "weave" the "canvas" of her spirit, to remain true to her glorious, painful, and libidinous course ("Labor, labor de gloria, dolorosa y liviana"), she falls victim to the other's assertion of power, and she winds up as bloodied as the eagle-ravaged Titan, looking up at the one who had seemed to offer a type of salvation.

"Tu boca" speaks to Agustini's awareness of the hazards of overstepping the confines of womanly submission and poetic deference. This recognition seems to intensify in the course of her poetic production. Even more than the tragic conclusion to "Las alas" (see chapter 3), "Tu boca" confirms the disastrous consequences of pursuing aspirations designated for men.[8] Yet Agustini does not dwell on defeat. While this, the fourth poem of the collection, focuses on doubts and despair, the fifth, "¡Oh tú!" (Oh you!) (229–30), quickly revisits the promise of hope and escape from the confines of silence and despair.

These alternating reactions to the imposing power of patriarchy seem to reflect the inconsistency of change during Agustini's times. The discourse of male domination was being met with calls for equality, and some progress was actually being achieved in the Uruguay of the day (see chapter 1). On a personal level, as much as Agustini's success as a modernista must have seemed extremely difficult and unlikely, she managed to find a troubled freedom in the very act of writing, and through her poetry she was able to enter the predominantly male intellectual circles of her day, escaping, like the lyric voice of "¡Oh tú!" that flees the gloomy tower, her prosaic surroundings. Modernismo in general and Darío's verse in particular provided models of innovation and creativity that, to use the metaphors of this poem, illuminated her world and expanded the realm of what she could envision as possible. The uneasy, complex, and intricate fusion of artistic and erotic goals gives Agustini's enterprise a startling richness and sophistication.

"¡Oh tú!," with its emphasis on sunlit inspiration, explores the poet's efforts to emerge from the dark, confining structures that inhibit insight and creativity. Anticipating the macabre insects of surrealist images like those found in the paintings of Salvador Dalí, Agustini presents a vision of her emotional life:

> Yo vivía en la torre inclinada
> De la Melancolía . . .
> Las arañas del tedio, las arañas más grises,
> En silencio y en gris tejían y tejían.
>
> ¡Oh, la húmeda torre! . . .
> Llena de la presencia
> Siniestra de un gran búho,
> Como un alma en pena;
>
> Tan mudo que el Silencio en la torre es dos veces;
> Tan triste, que sin verlo nos da frío la inmensa
> Sombra de su tristeza.
>
> Eternamente incuba un gran huevo infecundo,
> Incrustadas las raras pupilas *más allá;*
> O caza las arañas del tedio, o traga amargos
> Hongos de soledad.
>
> El búho de las ruinas ilustres y las almas
> Altas y desoladas!
> Náufraga de la Luz yo me ahogaba en la sombra . . .

En la húmeda torre, inclinada a mí misma,
A veces yo temblaba
Del horror de mi sima. (229)

[I was living in the leaning tower / of Melancholy . . . / The spiders of boredom, the grayest spiders, / were spinning and spinning in the silence and grayness.

Oh, the humid tower! . . . / full of the sinister / presence of the great owl, / like a soul in torment;

so mute that the Silence in the tower is double; / so sad, that, without seeing it, the immense / shadow of its sadness makes us cold.

It eternally incubates a great infertile egg; / its strange eyes embedded *beyond;* / it either hunts the spiders of boredom or it swallows bitter / mushrooms of loneliness.

The owl of the illustrious ruins and the / high and disconsolate souls! / I, a castaway of the Light, was drowning in the darkness . . . / At times I trembled from the horror of my chasm.]

In this, the first section of "¡Oh tú!," Agustini's lyric voice lives isolated, separated from what is real and meaningful. Like the famous princess of Darío's "Sonatina," she is in need of saving. Unlike her, however, Agustini's female speaks, expressing her point of view about both her melancholic dissatisfaction and the dismal leaning tower in which she resides surrounded by spiders, silence, and gloom. Whereas Darío's princess is burdened by an excess of glittering wealth and ponderous materiality that obstructs her contact with the transcendent elements of existence, Agustini's lyric voice is tortured by the most mundane tedium, an existence without poetic vitality, enlightenment, or production. She shares this horrid tower with a great, sinister owl that lays eggs that will never produce offspring. The owl can see only the "ruins" of the past and joyless souls. She calls them ruins because she finds them to be in need of repair. In other words, like the modernistas before her, the speaker in Agustini poem decries the gloom that limits perception as well as the outmoded and uninspired rules that throttle creativity. She wants to break the double silence of banality and rigidity and seeks to leave behind her existence as a "castaway" from the world of light ("Náufraga de la Luz"), floating adrift on a sea of darkness. In this pursuit of light, Agustini rejects the *posmodernista* owl as formulated by Enrique González Martínez; she opts once again to align herself with Darío and his iconic swan.[9] The owl and its association with the solitude and shadows of the night offer Agustini only a frightening, unproductive vision that must be corrected by the true and elegant aquatic bird, that is, the poetic alter ego of her model, mentor, and lover, who comes to her aid in the second section of the poem:

> ¡Oh, Tú que me arrancaste a la torre más fuerte!
> Que alzaste suavemente la sombra como un velo,
> Que me lograste rosas en la nieve del alma,
> Que me lograste llamas en el mármol del cuerpo;
> Que hiciste todo un lago de cisnes, de mi lloro . . .
> Tú que en mí todo puedes,
> En mí debes ser Dios!
> De tus manos yo quiero hasta el Bien que hace mal . . .
> Soy el cáliz brillante que colmarás, Señor;
> Soy, caída y erguida como un lirio a tus plantas,
> Más que tuya, mi Dios!
> Perdón, perdón si peco alguna vez, soñando
> Que me abrazas con alas ¡todo mío! en el Sol . . . (229–30)

[Oh, you who pulled me from the strongest tower! / who gently raised the darkness like a veil, / who succeeded in creating roses in the snow of my soul, / who succeeded in producing flames in the marble of my body; / who made a whole lake of swans from my tears . . . / You who in me can do it all, / in me you should be God! / From your hands I want even the Good that does evil . . . / I am the brilliant chalice that you will fill to overflowing, Lord; / I am, fallen and risen up like a lily at your feet, / more than yours, my God! / Forgive, forgive if I sin some time dreaming that you embrace me with wings, all mine!, in the Sun . . .]

By the end of the second part of the poem, her savior becomes swanlike and delivers her from imprisonment. He, the "tú" of the poem, becomes all hers as she dreams of his enveloping her between his wings, thereby bringing her into the modernista fold. She is filled to overflowing by his divine inspiration in an image that clearly refers to the title of the volume. She starts out as one of the *cálices vacíos* but finds fulfillment by breaking free from the structures that would hold her back and by receiving all he has to offer. With this imaginative mix of metaphors, Agustini, like Darío in "El cisne" (213) (as I mentioned in chapter 2), subtly rewrites the erotically charged myth of Leda to create a new Helen of immortal beauty. Whereas Darío fuses male poet and Zeus in order to impregnate "the new Poetry," Agustini's lyric voice becomes the new Leda; she asserts her acceptance of the "God" (her god), the promise of fertility, and the dream of an egg from which she will hatch another new Helen, finding a direct answer to the large infertile egg of the first section of the poem.

This deification of the other is consistent with Agustini's hyperbolic references to Darío. As I noted above, six months before the publication of *Los cálices vacíos*, in August of 1912, she wrote to Darío, "If Darío is for the world the king of poets, for me he is God in Art" (*Correspondencia íntima* 46).[10] By drawing upon multivalent images in "¡Oh tú!," Agustini elaborates upon this identification and turns him into a figure resembling Zeus: god, poet, and sexual partner, who embraces her with the wings of a swan, filling her chalice with a generative fluid that satiates all desire. Both fallen and raised by his presence ("Soy, caída y erguida como un lirio a tus plantas, / Más que tuya, mi Dios!"), she ends the poem with a creative play on words, one in which her dream of making him hers in the bright sunlight merges with the myth of Icarus. Perhaps drawing upon the phonetic overlap between *abrasar* and *abrazar* in Uruguayan Spanish, she has the two lovers embracing and fusing in a combustible burst of erotic and poetic energy that rivals Icarus's sun-bound escape from terrestrial limitations.

Agustini's rapture with the other continues in and becomes the focus of "En tus ojos" (In your eyes) (231–32), an eight-stanza poem that consists of two sets of three quatrains, each followed by a five-line stanza. The unexpected regularity of its structure and rhyme scheme declares an aspiration to artistry that is reinforced by the poem's culminating stanza:

> . . . lámparas votivas
> Que se nutren de espíritus humanos
> Y que el milagro enciende; gemas vivas
> Y hoy por gracia divina, ¡siemprevivas!
> Y en el azur del Arte, astros hermanos! (232)

[. . . votive lamps / that are nourished by human spirits / and that the miracle ignites; living gems / and today by divine grace, eternal! / and in the blue of Art, twin stars!]

The final five lines retrace the poem's move from the human to the transcendent as the two eyes of the title become two stars that shine in the blue heaven of Art, underscoring that the "tú" of all the initial poems of *Los cálices vacíos* is not simply a projection of a beloved, real or imagined. Agustini once again converts the sexual language of artistic production into a fiery exchange between two lovers in which the desirous gaze of—as well as the erotic contact with—the other becomes a source of inspiration and empowerment. Like the eponymous star of Darío's "Venus," the "tú" is elevated to heavenly status and becomes a spiritual guide.

While the poem opens with a series of attempts to characterize the pull and power of the lover's eyes, the fourth stanza breaks the list of metaphors with a question that reveals the inadequacy of all definitions as well as the ambivalence, if not the fear, that the lyric voice feels as she stares into his eyes:

> ¿Sabes todas las cosas palpitantes,
> Inanimadas, claras, tenebrosas,
> Dulces, horrendas, juntas o distantes,
> Que pueden ser tus ojos? . . . (231)

[Do you know all the throbbing things / inanimate, bright, gloomy, / sweet, horrifying, close together or far apart, / that your eyes can be? . . .]

The question asking what his eyes might be generates another list of wide-ranging metaphors, but the most revealing are the first ones:

> . . . Tantas cosas
> Que se nombraran infinitamente! . . .
>
> Maravilladas veladoras mías
> Que en fuego bordan visionariamente
> La trama de mis noches y mis días! . . .
> Lagos que son también una corriente . . . (231)

[. . . So many things / that to name them would have no limit! . . .

My astonished bedside lamps / that embroider in fire with visionary skill / the plot of my nights and my days! . . . / Lakes that are also a stream . . .]

By playing with the dual meaning of *trama*, both "plot" and "weft," Agustini brings together in a single image her art with her fate. He embroiders the plot/weft of her days and nights with the ardor of his gaze, and he lights the way for her as she struggles to write the text of her life. She finds in his eyes beacons that allow her to see what others cannot and that allow her to be the insightful poet she longs to be. The metaphoric fusion of lakes and streams further enhances what she believes she can attain under his influence. Deep and placid, shallow and swiftly moving, these two types of water float at the end of the stanza, blending the lyric voice, the other, and the resulting texts of their lives. She finds in his eyes a surface in which she is reflected, a depth hidden from view by the superficial reflection, and a current that defies all attempts to be captured or contained. These features drift unanchored to a specific target, emphasizing not only the intricate interweaving of the two lovers and their texts but also the reflectivity and reciprocity that are essential to the equation. Her ultimate desire is to draw strength and wisdom from the other and thereby open the way for her to write poems that reveal simultaneously the fluid, visible world around her and the profound truths that, for the most part, go unobserved.

Through this sophisticated fusion of eyes and lakes, perception and reflection, life and literature, Agustini once again turns to reflectivity as a source of empowerment. She sees and is seen and takes control of the images that emerge in the text.[11] This melding of seeing and being seen is also found in "La ruptura" (The break) (235), a short, two-stanza poem that approaches the issue of the imposing forces of the past from two different angles:

> Érase una cadena fuerte como un destino,
> Sacra como una vida, sensible como un alma;
> La corté con un lirio y sigo mi camino
> Con la frialdad magnífica de la Muerte . . . Con calma[12]
>
> Curiosidad mi espíritu se asoma a su laguna
> Interior, y el cristal de las aguas dormidas,
> Refleja un dios o un monstruo, enmascarado en una
> Esfinge tenebrosa suspensa de otras vidas. (235)

[It was a chain strong as a destiny, / sacred as a life, sensitive as a soul; / I cut it with a lily and I continue on my way / with the magnificent coldness of Death . . . With calm curiosity my spirit appears at its interior / lake, and the mirror of the sleeping waters, / reflects a god or a monster, disguised in a / gloomy Sphinx hanging from other lives.]

At the start, Agustini inverts the familiar simile comparing one's destiny with a type of bondage, in this case with an imposing chain. With allusions to sacred sensibilities, she refines the evocative power of the comparison. The undefined chain comes to symbolize the moral and personal obligations that control and restrain and shape individuals.

The next two declarations reinforce the metaphorical nature of the constraints as well as the lyric voice's cold determination to break with them, regardless of the consequences. She cuts the chain with a lily and, once free, she continues on her way "with the magnificent coldness of Death." This "coldness" conjures up the resolve with which she faces the future as well as an emotional calm, if not numbness, that comes from having endured hardships. She faces death as stoically as she does the obstacles in her life, including the limitations imposed upon her and the conflicted image she sees in the lake of her soul in the second stanza.

When she looks within herself, she sees a split image she cannot reconcile, for it is shaped by the contradictory ways in which the world has come to define her; it is "suspended from the lives of others."[13] As she struggles to define herself, she sees the incongruities of her life. The reflection holds a poetic god or a usurping monster dressed in the traditional patriarchal metaphor of the sphinx.[14] In the guise of the ancient feminine figure of the arcane and the unknowable, she acknowledges those forces that change her into an idea, a representation of the hopes and fears of the society in which she lives.

In "Tres pétalos a tu perfil" (Three petals to your profile) (234), the poem that precedes "La ruptura," Agustini addresses from a different perspective the poet's struggle with socially prescribed behavior and gender-defined roles:

> En oro, bronce o acero
> Líricos grabar yo quiero
> Tu Wagneriano perfil;
> Perfil supremo y arcano
> Que yo torné casi humano:
> Asómate a mi buril.

Perfil que me diste un día
Largo de melancolía
Y rojo de corazón;
Perfil de antiguos marfiles,
Diamante de los perfiles,
Mi lira es tu medallón!

Perfil que el tedio corona,
Perfil que el orgullo encona
Y estrella un gran ojo gris,
Para embriagar al Futuro,
Destila, tu filtro oscuro
En el cáliz de este lis. (234)

[In lyric gold, bronze, or steel / I want to engrave / your Wagnerian pro-file; / supreme and mysterious profile / that I made almost human; show yourself at my chisel.

Profile that you gave me one day / long with melancholy / and red with heart; / profile of antique ivories, / diamond of the profiles, / my lyre is your medallion!

Profile that boredom crowns, / profile that pride enflames / and a great gray eye smashes, / in order to intoxicate the Future, / it distills your dark potion / in the calyx of this lily.]

In this poem Agustini transforms the myth of Pygmalion, inverting the traditional associations linking women with passive objects and men with active creation. While a number of critics have explored this aspect of Agustini's poetry (see Tina Escaja, John Burt, and Maria-Elena Armstrong), they have overlooked one lesser-known detail about the sculptor from Cyprus, namely, that he hated women of flesh and blood and resolved never to marry. The misogynistic protagonist of the tale dedicated himself instead to art. He spent several months working on the statue of the ideal woman, one that was flawlessly beautiful and perfectly silent. He ultimately came to fall madly in love with his own creation and prayed to Venus for it to be turned into a living being. She took pity on him and brought the statue to life.

   With the subtlest of allusions to the more obscure aspect of the myth, Agustini draws attention to the fact that she is writing more about the artistic process than about an individual. The poem explores the transmutation of the specific and temporal into the essential and eternal through verse. In other words, "Tres pétalos a tu perfil" is a poem about poetry and its distillation of the present into the purity of art. Like her modernista colleagues, Agustini sees the individual through the filter of the centuries of art that preceded her (cf. Darío's "Divagación," 183–87). By describing her medium as "lyric" gold, bronze, and steel, she joins ranks with artisans and artists in their attempts to embed the unique and elusive within the universal and timeless. She seeks to create, as Pygmalion did, the "ideal, sculpted lover" (as stated in the fifth line of "El surtidor de oro" [The golden fountain] [247], from later in *Los cálices vacíos*), that is, to produce a piece of work so credible that it eventually comes to life in the minds of her readers.[15] Her success has, somewhat ironically, meant that biography has often overshadowed her serious contemplation of the nature and goals of poetic discourse. The aspiration to create a lifelike, vibrant, organic art is underscored by the three petals of the title, which, like the three stanzas of the poem, come together in the poem's final lines to form the calyx of a lily (l. 18) and which hold the essence of the other. Poem and poet fuse in a white embrace of the ideal, "Wagnerian" lover, echoing the statement of "¡Oh tú!" in which she is a sexual and creative "chalice/calyx" filled to overflowing.

The wide-ranging references to the nature of poetry that run throughout the first nine poems of *Los cálices vacíos* and that develop the imagery of earlier collections converge in "Visión" (236–37), the last poem of the collection's first section. In it, the mirror, bedroom, humid silences, lakes, godlike other, bedsheets, statues, printing, wings, and distant lover of previous poems coalesce to produce (in that order) a moving, mysterious statement about artistic inspiration and aspiration. "Visión" is about receiving, transforming, and giving back in a context that is fraught with ambivalence and tension. It therefore represents a type of midvolume (and what should have been a midcareer) reassessment and restatement of Agustini's poetics formulated in union with a great, energizing, but now-distant sexual partner.[16]

The poem opens with a four-line stanza that immediately directs attention to Agustini's belief in the reciprocal and interactive nature of poetic production:

¿Acaso fué en un marco de ilusión,
En el profundo espejo del deseo,
O fue divina y simplemente en vida
Que yo te vi velar mi sueño la otra noche? (236)

[Was it perhaps in a framework of hope, / in the deep mirror of desire, / or was it divinely and simply in life / that I saw you watch over my sleep the other night?]

She follows the creative process as it starts in the "mirror of desire," that is, in that moment when the poet, upon mobilizing the linguistic resources at her command, finds herself looking into the reflective surface of the poetry and poetic discourse she has inherited. These traditions are epitomized in "Visión" by the lover who has slipped into her private chamber—if not into her consciousness. He enters her bedroom in the same way he did in "Nocturno," but here his presence is different. He has an effect similar to the confines of the dank tower in "¡Oh tú!" He sheds no light, and he offers no companionship. He simply stands as a witness to her dreams. She feels, instead, fear and loneliness as she confronts him and what he means for her artistic aspirations. This sense of her being on her own is appropriate, for he is no longer the engaged lover of before. Though Agustini repeats "Te inclinabas a mí . . ." (You were leaning over me), assigning to the lyric voice the passivity of the reclining position, it quickly becomes clear that she is the one in control.[17] In the third stanza she defines him as ill, weak, parched, and in search of salvation, and she begins to imagine herself as the source of strength and as a transcendental solution to his quest. She compares herself to a communion wafer through which he seeks redemption:

Te inclinabas a mí como el creyente
A la oblea de cielo de la hostia . . .
—Gota de nieve con sabor de estrellas
Que alimenta los lirios de la Carne,
Chispa de Dios que estrella los espíritus.— (236)

[You were leaning over me like the believer / over the heavenly wafer of the Eucharist . . . / —A drop of snow with the flavor of stars / that nourishes the lilies of the Flesh, / a spark of God that shatters the spirits.—]

She no longer identifies with the male other's images of women but with his authorial authority and, as a result, with the role of godlike savior/creator that she had assigned to him previously. By means of the same simile, the *modernista* metaphors of artistic insemination and male reproductive supremacy become ingestion and spiritual awakening in which she is the generative source of power and transcendence.[18]

By the end of the stanza she is ready to assert her autonomy as a poet. She now controls his fate, writing his destiny on the dark page of her bed with her body and revealing the spiritual beyond. This avowal of self grows stronger and more defiantly sexual in the sections that follow. She writes,

> Te inclinabas a mí como si fuera
> Mi cuerpo la inicial de tu destino
> En la página oscura de mi lecho;
> Te inclinabas a mí como al milagro
> De una ventana abierta al más allá.
>
> ¡Y te inclinabas más que todo eso!
>
> Y era mi mirada una culebra
> Apuntada entre zarzas de pestañas,
> Al cisne reverente de tu cuerpo.
> Y era mi deseo una culebra
> Glisando entre los riscos de la sombra
> A la estatua de lirios de tu cuerpo!
>
> Tú te inclinabas más y más . . . y tanto,
> Y tanto te inclinaste,
> Que mis flores eróticas son dobles,
> Y mi estrella es más grande desde entonces.
> Toda tu vida se imprimió en mi vida . . . (237)

[You were leaning over me as if / my body was the initial of your destiny / on the dark page of my bed; / you were leaning over me as over the miracle / of a window open to the beyond.

And you leaned more than all that!

And my gaze was a snake / aimed, among the bramble of eyelashes, / at the reverent swan of your body. / And my desire was a snake gliding among the crags of the darkness / toward the lily statue of your body!

You leaned more and more . . . and so much, / so much you leaned, / that my erotic flowers are double, / and my star is greater since then. / All your life was printed on my life . . .]

The role reversal becomes complete. His body fuses with the swan's as she appropriates the phallic symbol of the snake. She penetrates him with her gaze, turning her own eyes into the force that were his in "En tus ojos." Her desire slips through every dark, erotic crevice, returning her to the image she had created of him in "Tres pétalos a tu perfil." She does not, however, simply change places with the male poet. She insists that she be recognized as a woman writer by brazenly alluding to tumescent female genitalia ("mis flores eróticas son dobles"), yet her increased powers, as much as they are presented in terms of a sexual encounter, are poetic. She shines because his life has been printed upon hers, that is, she has assimilated his art and is ready to be the active producer of new culture.

The final images of "Visión," while assertive and self-affirming, are tinged with disappointment and loss. The lyric voice envisions her ability to engender a new race, that is, to be the mother of the next generation of poets. Yet her hopes seem to be betrayed by his fading presence:

> Yo esperaba suspensa el aletazo
> Del abrazo magnífico; un abrazo
> De cuatro brazos que la gloria viste
> De fiebre y de milagro, será un vuelo!
> Y pueden ser los hechizados brazos
> Cuatro raíces de una raza nueva:
>
> Y esperaba suspensa el aletazo
> Del abrazo magnífico . . .
> Y cuando,
> Te abrí los ojos como un alma, ví
> Que te hacías atrás y te envolvías
> En yo no sé qué pliegue inmenso de la sombra! (237)

[Suspended I waited for the flapping of wings / of the magnificent embrace; an embrace / of four arms that glory dresses / with fever and miracle, it will be a flight! / And the enchanted arms can be / four roots of a new race:

Suspended I waited for the flapping of wings / of the magnificent embrace . . . / And when, / I opened your eyes up like a soul, I saw / that you
moved backward and you wrapped yourself / in I do not know what immense fold of darkness!]

The embrace she expects is that of the flapping wings of the modernista
swan with which she would achieve flight and the fulfillment of her elevated aspirations. It never comes, for he has receded into the dark, leaving
her torn between her sense of self and the slippery nature of the poetic
accomplishment. The male poet whom she has chosen as a partner is no
longer as strong and vibrant as he once was. She no longer feels confident
in their union or that it will bring her success. The tone is subdued and the
fate she faces uncertain. As he backs away, she is left with no choice but to
deal with his absence and to create her own artistic domain.

Agustini accomplishes this task in the remaining poems of the collection, in some cases by picking up and rounding out what she alludes to in
"Vision." For example, the failed flight of "Visión" is achieved at the end
of the volume in the second "Nocturno" (254). The promise of a new race
comes closer to fruition in "Otra estirpe" (Another race) (243), and the assumption of the authority that had previously been her lover's takes place
in "Con tu retrato" (With your portrait) (241). "Con tu retrato," the opening poem of the "Lis púrpura" (Purple lily) section of *Los cálices vacíos*, also
provides a glimpse into the twofold arousal that fuels Agustini's melding
of artistic and sexual gratification. The thrill of achieving a level of artistic
excellence that rivals or exceeds that of her model and mentor becomes
indistinguishable from the sexual excitement, the consummation, and the
petit mort of intercourse:

> Yo no sé si mis ojos o mis manos
> Encendieron la vida en tu retrato;
> Nubes humanas, rayos sobrehumanos,
> Todo tu *Yo* de emperador innato
>
> Amanece a mis ojos, en mis manos!
> Por eso, toda en llamas, yo desato
> Cabellos y alma para tu retrato,
> Y me abro en flor! . . . Entonces, soberanos

De la sombra y la luz, tus ojos graves
Dicen grandezas que yo sé y tú sabes . . .
Y te dejo morir . . . Queda en mis manos

Una gran mancha lívida y sombría . . .
Y renaces en mi melancolía
Formado de astros fríos y lejanos! (241)

[I do not know if my eyes or my hands / ignited the life in your portrait; / human clouds, superhuman thunderbolts, / all your "I" of natural-born emperor

Dawns in my eyes, in my hands! / For that reason, all in flames, I undo / my hair and soul, for your portrait, / and I open myself in full bloom! . . . Then, sovereigns /

Of the darkness and the light, your serious eyes / say splendors that I know and you know . . . / and I let you die . . . A great, livid, and dark stain

Remains on my hands . . . / and you are reborn in my melancholy / formed from cold and distant stars!]

The poem suggests that what arouses the lyric voice most is her ability to dominate the situation and to energize the life force that runs between them, awakening the fervor of "superhuman lightning bolts." She derives pleasure from creating the image of who he is and knowing all that he knows. She (and he in turn) is ablaze, that is, physically aroused by her audacity and assertion. Though he is the natural-born emperor, she commands, and, in commanding, she unleashes her soul "for [his] portrait." Artist as well as lover, she gives of herself and in the process opens herself to him and to gratification.

The "letting him die" that follows fulfillment is, on a poetic level, the letting go that Agustini has sought ever since the beginning of the collection. What remains is the ink stain of the past that she rewrites and through which he is born again. On a sexual level, she lets her partner slip away emotionally and perhaps even physically after the blood- or semen-stained encounter and the delights of intercourse. Little of the grandeur of the moment remains. She fills the melancholy that she experiences with a vision of him that has now turned cold. The joy of the instant is followed by a sadness that lingers in the text. The poem, therefore, reveals an interesting position regarding the power of poetry to capture and maintain the dynamism of life. Agustini suggests that in both life and art even the most dynamic experiences turn into memories, but memories that can be resurrected by maintaining the distant glow of extinguished stars.

If "Con tu retrato" takes passion and turns it into text, "Otra estirpe" (243), the third and final poem of the section, anthropomorphizes art and turns it into offspring. As one of Agustini's most quoted poems, "Otra estirpe" has drawn attention to the originality of her perspective, to her sexualized language, and to her daring eroticism:

> Eros, yo quiero guiarte, Padre ciego . . .
> Pido a tus manos todopoderosas,
> Su cuerpo excelso derramado en fuego
> Sobre mi cuerpo desmayado en rosas!
>
> La eléctrica corola que hoy desplego
> Brinda el nectario de un jardín de Esposas;
> Para sus buitres en mi carne entrego
> Todo un enjambre de palomas rosas!
>
> Da a las dos sierpes de su abrazo, crueles,
> Mi gran tallo febril . . . Absintio, mieles,
> Viérteme de sus venas, de su boca . . .
> ¡Así tendida soy un surco ardiente,
> Donde puede nutrirse la simiente,
> De otra Estirpe sublimemente loca! (243)

[Eros, blind Father, I want to guide you . . . / I ask of your all-powerful hands, / for his sublime body drenched in flames / over my body, fainted on roses!/

The electric corolla that today I unfurl / offers the nectary of a Wives' garden; / for his vultures in my flesh I surrender / a whole swarm of pink doves!

Give to the two cruel serpents of his embrace / my great feverish stem . . . Pour for me / absinthe, honeys from his veins, from his mouth . . . / Stretched out in this way I am a burning furrow, / where the seed of another Race, / sublimely insane, can be nourished!]

While the new breed that the lyric voice hopes to conceive appeared before (see "Noche de Reyes" (Epiphany night) [97], "La estatua" [101], "La barca milagrosa" [185], "El vampiro" [186], and "Supremo idilio" [187]), it is presented here with more defiantly erotic details, and the heightened eroticism of the text makes this response to literary paternity more assertively about female empowerment. The poem reorients the metaphoric universe conventionally dominated by the act of impregnation, placing gestation and birth at the center. The resulting shift is evident from the start, when the lyric voice tells Eros that she wishes to be in control. She demands a sexual engagement that will produce the new breed that is "sublimely insane," unfettered by tradition and practice. She audaciously declares her arousal and fertility ("La eléctrica corola que hoy desplego / Brinda el nectario de un jardín de Esposas") and links her rebelliousness with the destructive nature of uncontrolled passion as well as with the nobility of Prometheus's endeavors ("Para sus buitres en mi carne entrego / Todo un enjambre de palomas rosas!"). She offers herself to the serpents of his embrace, eagerly awaiting the moment of insemination and her ability to nurture and nourish her unique progeny. The offspring project a vision of the future and provide a new beginning that will evolve beyond the current species.[19]

This unsettling iconoclastic poem closes the middle section of *Los cálices vacíos*. The title of its final section, "De fuego, de sangre y de sombra" (Of fire, of blood, and of shadow), brings into sharp focus the disruptive and fearful passions that undergird the entire collection. While in "Otra estirpe" Agustini blatantly challenges the conventions of poetic discourse and authority, in "El surtidor de oro" (The golden fountain) (247), the first poem of the section, she subtly explores the fusion of sexuality and inspiration. The readily identifiable figures of the muse, the sculpted lover, and a new god that is—in a double assertion of dominance—the product of the poet's mind and imagination leave no doubt that "El surtidor de oro" is about artistic production.[20] The first of the poem's two stanzas begins with the lyric voice's request that her muse "let the golden fountain vibrate the pink cup of [her] mouth with kisses" (247):

> Vibre, mi musa, el surtidor de oro
> La taza rosa de tu boca en besos;
> De las espumas armoniosas surja
> Vivo, supremo, misterioso, eterno,
> El amante ideal, el esculpido

En prodigios de almas y de cuerpos;
Debe ser vivo a fuerza de soñado,
Que sangre y alma se me va en los sueños;
Ha de nacer a deslumbrar la Vida,
Y ha de ser un dios nuevo!
Las culebras azules de sus venas
Se nutren de milagro en mi cerebro . . . (247)

[Dear muse, let the golden fountain vibrate / the pink cup of your mouth with kisses; / let the ideal lover, the one sculpted / in miracles of body and soul, / spring forth alive, supreme, mysterious, and eternal / from the harmonious foam; / he should be alive by the effort of being dreamed, / that blood and soul flow from me in my dreams; / he must be born to dazzle Life, / and he must be a new god! / The blue snakes of his veins / are nourished by the miracle of my brain . . .]

The golden fountain ("el surtidor de oro") that gives the poem its title and that overshadows the entire piece is a variation on the Neoplatonic symbol that appears throughout romantic and modernista verse. It represents the divine one that is identical with the good and beautiful and the source of knowledge and art that enlightens the mind of the artist.[21] Agustini turns to the fountain to express her hope that she will receive the energizing inspiration that will allow her to be a modern-day Pygmalion, capable of creating an ideal, living, and eternal simulacrum of the perfect lover and that she will forge a statue that will resonate with her own, personal vision and with godlike powers to enlighten. She aspires to an enlightenment that will flow from the source through her mind into her creation and then beyond. Her inclusion of the prepositional phrase "de oro" echoes the romantic blending of metaphors and underscores the polyvalent nature of the central image. The references to "espuma" (froth or foam) and "culebras azules de sus venas" (the blue snakes of his veins) suggest that the fountain and its pulsating waters have a sexual dimension, becoming an inseminating flow of insight and creativity. By opening herself to the knowledge and language that pour into her, the poet/speaker is able to conceive and give birth to a powerful new and divinely inspired vision. The poem thereby subtly builds on the gestational associations of "Otra estirpe."

The second of the two twelve-line stanzas begins with the request that the muse let the golden fountain "seal" her mouth with kisses. The verb "sellar" in Spanish (and its English equivalent, "to seal") is ambiguous. It can mean to "close securely" or "to attach an authenticating mark." Agustini appears to be playing with this ambiguity. Uncertain whether she wants this poem to represent a beginning or an end, that is, an initial success or a final accomplishment, Agustini seems to waver between the two meanings:

> Selle, mi musa, el surtidor de oro
> La taza rosa de tu boca en besos;
> El amante ideal, el esculpido
> En prodigios de almas y de cuerpos,
> Arraigando las uñas extrahumanas
> En mi carne, solloza en mis ensueños;
> —Yo no quiero más Vida que tu vida,
> Son en ti los supremos elementos;
> Déjame bajo el cielo de tu alma,
> En la cálida tierra de tu cuerpo!—
> —Selle, mi musa, el surtidor de oro
> La taza rosa de tu boca en besos! (247)

[Dear muse, let the golden fountain / seal the pink cup of your mouth with kisses; / The ideal lover, the one sculpted / in miracles of body and soul, / embedding his extrahuman fingernails / in my flesh, sobs in my dreams; / —I do not want more Life than your life, / the supreme elements exist in you; / Let me stay beneath the heaven of your soul, / in the warm land of your body!— / —Dear muse, let the golden fountain seal / the pink cup of your mouth with kisses!]

While the dramatic achievement described here could be deemed an appropriate endpoint, Agustini leaves open the possibility that her concern is with the ongoing power of poetic inspiration.[22] The ideal lover/sculpture, the product of the lyric voice's ability to receive the inspiring emanation, rises from her and then invades her being. His "extrahuman fingernails" dig into her flesh at the same time that he sobs that she is everything he longs for. She is simultaneously tortured, exalted, and amorously engaged by the work of art she has produced. He wishes to "remain beneath the heaven of [her] soul, in the warm land of [her] body." Proud that she is both transcendent and immediate and that he finds refuge in her soul and in her welcoming physicality, she asks that the muse's lips be sealed, continuing the play on the word "sellar." It remains deliberately unclear whether she seeks a respite from the agony of artistic production or ongoing contact with the divine.

"Fiera de amor" (Wild animal of love) (248), the next poem in the volume, appears at first glance to be a straightforward continuation of "El surtidor de oro," for it offers an ongoing exploration of the creative process, repeating the language and imagery of the previous piece. At the same time, however, it presents an imaginative reworking of the divide between nature and culture, between social and artistic structures, and even between male and female, a reworking that is simultaneously disorienting and energizing. This disorientation is central to Agustini's vision, one that, as I stated at the beginning of the chapter, reveals the cracks and fissures in the modernista pursuit of perfection and that opens the way for the disjointed visions and broken mirrors of the avant-garde:

> Fiera de amor, yo sufro hambre de corazones.
> De palomos, de buitres, de corzos o leones,
> No hay manjar que más tiente, no hay más grato sabor;
> Había ya estragado mis garras y mi instinto,
> Cuando erguida en la casi ultratierra de un plinto,
> Me deslumbró una estatua de antiguo emperador.
>
> Y crecí de entusiasmo; por el tronco de piedra
> Ascendió mi deseo como fulmínea hiedra
> Hasta el pecho, nutrido en nieve al parecer;
> Y clamé al imposible corazón . . . la escultura
> Su gloria custodiaba serenísima y pura,
> Con la frente en Mañana y la planta en Ayer.
>
> Perenne mi deseo, en el tronco de piedra
> Ha quedado prendido como sangrienta hiedra;
> Y desde entonces muerdo soñando un corazón
> De estatua, presa suma para mi garra bella;
> No es ni carne ni mármol: una pasta de estrella
> Sin sangre, sin calor y sin palpitación . . .
>
> Con la esencia de una sobrehumana pasión! (248)

[A wild animal of love, I endure a hunger for hearts. / Whether of doves, of vultures, of deer, or of lions, / there is no food more tempting, there is no flavor more pleasing; / I had already ruined my claws and my instinct, / when erect on the almost otherworldliness of a plinth, / a stature of an ancient emperor dazzled me.

And I grew with enthusiasm; along the stone torso / my desire climbed up to his chest / like a shining ivy, nourished apparently by snow; / and I cried out to the impossible heart . . . the sculpture / preserved its glory so serene and pure, / with its forehead in Tomorrow and its soles in Yesterday.

Constant, my desire has remained fixed like / a bloody vine on the stone torso; / and ever since, while dreaming, I bite a statue's heart, / the supreme catch of my beautiful claw; / it is neither flesh nor marble: a starry paste / without blood, without heat, and without a beat . . .

With the essence of a superhuman passion!]

In contrast with the one in "El surtidor de oro," the statue in "Fiera de amor" does not belong to the lyric voice but is the one she aspires to conquer and control. The vocabulary she adopts to overtake established aesthetic values and to penetrate and defeat the rigidity of convention has, quite ironically but also appropriately, phallic overtones. The "and I grew with enthusiasm" that begins the third stanza and the "stone torso" (tronco de piedra) of the fourth recall a subtext of masculine domination that she aspires to appropriate and overthrow. The poem's title and its emphasis on savagery refer to more than erotic hunger. It anticipates the efforts by the lyric voice to erode inherited social and poetic structures. These structures are represented by the statue of an ancient emperor that comes into sight and becomes the focus of her pursuit, replacing other objects that could satisfy her hunger. It is entirely reasonable to identify the ancient sovereign with Darío, for he was the ruling poet of the day, and, despite his poetic innovation and originality, Darío comes to embody the enduring and unbending ideological and linguistic patterns Agustini aspires to alter.

As far-reaching as the poem is, its specific focus remains spiritual and artistic aspirations. The female lyric voice looks to penetrate the heart of the sculpture in an embrace that strives to sap the essence of its/his greatest accomplishments.[23] She hopes to draw from him the lifeblood that runs through his veins (very possibly the same lifeblood that courses through

the veins of her own sculpted creation in "El surtidor de oro"). She becomes a bloodthirsty vine that scales the "stone torso" and seeks out its
"impossible heart," which, together with its "glory," is locked within the
mass. By choosing the verb "custodiar," Agustini turns the statue into a
vessel that resembles a monstrance, holding divinity within its rigid framework, an allusion that is reinforced by the end of the poem. The last line of
the third stanza reveals that the art which the lyric voice pursues, like the
cultural context that it reflects, is quite literally grounded in the past but
open to the future. Though hidden by its wintry, rigid exterior, the statue
still speaks to the soul of "tomorrow's" artists.

The violence of the vine's penetration is juxtaposed with the spirituality
of its purpose, accentuating the poet's willingness to transgress normative
behavior in the pursuit of artistic insight. The intensity of her physical
ferocity equals the exaltedness of her goal. The final three lines of verse
define the core of poetic inspiration as neither flesh nor stone. It is the
essence of stars. As much as poetry draws on the language of erotic desire,
it can be reduced neither to sexual passion nor to a petrified vision. It is
the distillation of all that moves the human spirit; it is superhuman and
eternal. It is the living stone and the magical substance of stars that define
modernista verse.[24]

This fusion of astral and poetic power stands at the center of Agustini's
suggestive and enigmatic "Nocturno" (254). It is the key to the poem's
structuring image, the mysterious "lago de tu alma," which both reflects
and lights up the firmament:

> Engarzado en la noche el lago de tu alma,
> Diríase una tela de cristal y de calma
> Tramada por las grandes arañas del desvelo.
>
> Nata de agua lustral en vaso de alabastros;
> Espejo de pureza que abrillantas los astros
> Y reflejas la sima de la Vida en un cielo! . . .
>
> Y soy el cisne errante de los sangrientos rastros,
> Voy manchando los lagos y remontando el vuelo. (254)

[The lake of your soul is mounted (like a jewel) in the night; / one would
say a canvas of glass and calm / woven by the great spiders of watchfulness.

The best of the purifying water in an alabaster vessel; / mirror of purity, with which you polish the stars / and reflect the abyss of Life in a heaven! . . .

And I am the wandering swan of the bloody trails, / I proceed staining lakes and soaring in flight.]

This tightly constructed poem takes a number of Agustini's more recurrent references, including modernismo's swan, weaves them together, and exploits their iconoclastic potential. The lake of the other's soul is a reflective surface, like the mirrors, streams, fountains, and crystalline grottos of earlier poems. It is the discursive plane in which the lyric voice seeks to find herself. It is set off by the darkness of the night and is mounted like a valuable jewel. The poem specifies, "One would say a canvas of glass and calm" (Diríase una tela de cristal y de calma). This allusion turns the lake into a work of art; it is a cloth, a canvas of crystal "woven by the great spiders of watchfulness" that fill the poets' nights of insomnia.

In the next stanza the other's poetry becomes the "nata de agua lustral en vaso de alabastros." In this remarkable metaphor Agustini subtly develops the associations with the adjective "lustral" at the same time that she links this poem with the title of her collection. The lake/poem represents the very best, the richest essence of the cleansing waters of lustration, a ritual of spiritual purification that goes back to Roman times. By invoking the verb "lustrar" and by placing these waters within a white alabaster vessel, Agustini endows them with a trifold power to purify. The cleansing waters of the lake are placed in the whitest of vessels, reflecting the purest of visions. Yet if this luminous receptacle can hold only a sanitized version of reality, it will not be able to accommodate what she has to say. She will feel compelled to empty the "vasos," the "cálices" (the glasses or chalices), that have been handed to her, something she does in the title of the volume, with which she offers the promise of the alternative possibilities contained therein. Sylvia Molloy makes a similar point in her seminal article on this and the poem that follows. She finds that they "break with Darío using his text, not by throwing it out, but by emptying signs in order to fill them in accord with other drives. Not in vain these two poems belong to *Los cálices vacíos*, a title that already announces, recalling Darío's 'full' chalices — *Las ánforas de Epicuro*, for example — , the diverging intention of the texts that it heads" (64).[25]

In the final two lines of the second stanza Agustini shifts the focus from the "lake of your soul" to the "you" that has created it. She merges, as she did in "Fiera de amor," product and producer, accentuating once again to what degree the other of her poetry is as much the work of art (and the social structures it embodies) as the artist. The lyric voice reveals that he is a mirror of purity that brightens the stars. He enhances the splendor of the night sky, recalling the intensity of the light that results in the "luminous blindness" of "Ceguera" (Blindness) (249). More significant from the point of view of a woman poet, however, is the fact that he reflects the abyss of life in a textual heaven that glosses over the pain felt by others. This point is reinforced by the choice of the word "sima" for abyss, which invokes its homonym "cima" and the idea that "abyss" and "summit" depend on point of view.

If, as suggested here, the lakelike modernista poem makes the stars shine and turns the abyss of life into a heaven, Agustini is not content to remain passively adrift upon its surface. The poem's concluding two lines reveal that she is already bloodied by her fight to create a space for herself in a world that would silence women. Throughout her career she insisted upon exposing the less-than-perfect reality obscured by the brilliant modernista vision of her male contemporaries. In "Nocturno" she is even more as-sertive. She defiantly reconfigures the icon of modernista perfection. She ends this short poem as a bleeding swan that takes flight, and the verbal structures, the "voy manchando . . . remontando," turn this action into a Sisyphean endeavor of never-ending efforts.

Significantly, the blood that is a marker for both her pain and her rebel-liousness is also a marker for her gender—monthly cycle, loss of virginity, childbirth. In this way, she conflates her injuries as an aspiring poet with being a woman.[26] She bleeds as she tears herself from Darío, her poetic model, mentor, and lover, and as she struggles to be included in the liter-ary universe that would exclude women.[27] For this reason, writing becomes for her, as for so many other women writers before her (see chapter 1), a harmful act. Her writing stains the smooth surface of patriarchal discourse which calmly reflects its own version of the cosmos. Her ascent toward cre-ativity leaves a trail of anguish that simultaneously reveals the advances attained and the limitations that still exist.

A more optimistic but not untroubled vision is presented in the next poem, "El cisne" (The swan) (255–57), which contains possibly her most famous sixty lines of verse. In "El cisne" Agustini focuses on her abilities and sees herself as a powerful respondent to the forces around her. She weakens the image of masculine supremacy through the portrayal of an exhausted lover, who, because of his identification with the swan, evokes above all else Darío and modernista verse.[28] In my translations, though tempted to refer to the swan as a "he," I have kept the less anthropomorphic "it," in order to underscore the poetic implications of this erotic tour de force. Agustini writes, "Hunde el pico en mi regazo / y se queda como muerto . . ." (It sinks its beak into my lap / and it is left as if dead . . .). While Molloy sees the swan's exhaustion as a result of the male poet's inability to cope with the urgency, energy, and ardor of his female lover, she overlooks the other dimensions to this metaphor. Although the allusion is definitely among Agustini's most explicitly sexual, the swan's exhaustion is as much literary as it is erotic. Through its arresting images "El cisne" proclaims Agustini's power to represent her own worldview as well as to overturn the patriarchal perspective of her contemporaries. Her appropriation of the swan is therefore an even more rebellious statement about poetry than González Martínez's famous "Tuércele el cuello al cisne" (Twist the neck of the swan) (116).[29]

This rebelliousness begins to emerge within the first of the poem's seven stanzas:

Pupila azul de mi parque	1
Es el sensitivo espejo	2
De un lago claro, muy claro! . . .	3
Tan claro que a veces creo	4
Que en su cristalina página	5
Se imprime mi pensamiento.	6 (255)

[The blue pupil of the eye of my park / is the sensitive mirror / of a clear, very clear lake! . . . / So clear that at times I believe / that on its crystalline page / my thought is printed.]

These six lines set up a number of key symbols that evolve throughout the poem. The reflective lake is the eye of her orderly, cultivated, and well-designed poetic universe, an artistic cosmos captured with brilliant concision by the "park" of the first line. This surreal pupil both holds within itself the modernista landscape and sees beyond it. Eye and lake fuse and become the page upon which the lyric voice writes; it is the surface that reflects her literary context and upon which she projects her personal visions and sensibilities. As was the case in "El surtidor de oro," Agustini subtly but forcefully comments on the role of the poet, marking the modern and *modernista* shift from imitation to expression, the move from the mirror to the lamp.[30]

The soul of the lake, the spirit that influences what and how she writes, is a swan "with two human eyes, / serious and kind like a prince." The swan's humanity and human identity are barely hidden. The images resonate with echoes of Darío's verse (most especially "Yo persigo una forma . . .") and recall the poet himself. The swan appears as the force that animates her erotic imagination and her poetic production. It initiates the process that culminates in poetry:

Flor del aire, flor del agua,	7
Alma del lago es un cisne	8
Con dos pupilas humanas,	9
Grave y gentil como un príncipe;	10
Alas lirio, remos rosa . . .	11
Pico en fuego, cuello triste	12
Y orgulloso, y la blancura	13
Y la suavidad de un cisne . . .	14
El ave cándida y grave	15
Tiene un maléfico encanto;	16
—Clavel vestido de lirio,	17
Trasciende a llama y milagro! . . .	18
Sus alas blancas me turban	19
Como dos cálidos brazos;	20
Ningunos labios ardieron	21
Como su pico en mis manos,	22
Ninguna testa ha caído	23
Tan lánguida en mi regazo;	24
Ninguna carne tan viva,	25
He padecido o gozado:	26
Viborean en sus venas	27
Filtros dos veces humanos!	28 (255)

[Flower of the air, flower of the water, / the soul of the lake is a swan / with two human eyes, / serious and kind like a prince; / lily wings, rose oars . . . / a burning beak, a sad and proud / neck, and the whiteness / and the softness of a swan . . .

The guileless and serious bird / has an evil charm; / —Carnation dressed as a lily, / it smells of flames and miracle! . . . / Its white wings disconcert me / like two warm arms; / no lips blazed / as did its beak in my hands, / no head has fallen / as listless into my lap; / no flesh as lively, / have I suffered or enjoyed: / doubly human potions / snake in my veins!]

The images here fuse sexual desire with artistic longing, erotic arousal with poetic inspiration. The act of literary creation is achieved, as it is in Darío, in union with an enabling, eroticized other.

The tensions that emerge in these two stanzas coincide with the contradictions of Agustini's life. Sexual prohibitions and privileges, artistic opportunities and constraints, promises of heaven and hell, desire and disappointment, all reverberate in these lines of verse. Physical love and her love of poetry offer her the greatest pleasure and the most disturbing torment. She feels that the one who inspires her is both harmful and empowering; he "smells of flames and miracles," of salvation and damnation. Regardless of this ambivalence, the lyric voice makes clear that he moves her like no other lover, that she prefers him to all others. She offers "Todo el vaso de mi cuerpo" (l. 36) (the whole receptacle of my body), but she is not a silent recipient. She goes on to question and to create, affirming the ownership of her poetry and her ultimate assertion of authorial autonomy. The final stanza declares,

Al margen del lago claro	45
Yo le interrogo en silencio . . .	46
Y el silencio es una rosa	47
Sobre su pico de fuego . . .	48
Pero en su carne me habla	49
Y yo en mi carne le entiendo.	50
—A veces ¡toda! soy alma;	51
Y a veces ¡toda! soy cuerpo.—	52
Hunde el pico en mi regazo	53
Y se queda como muerto . . .	54
Y en la cristalina página,	55

En el sensitivo espejo	56
Del lago que algunas veces	57
Refleja mi pensamiento,	58
El cisne asusta de rojo,	59
Y yo de blanca doy miedo!	60 (257)

[At the edge of the clear lake / I question it in silence . . . / and the silence is a rose / over its fiery beak . . . / But it speaks to me in its flesh / and I understand it in my flesh. / —At times, completely!, I am soul; / and at times, completely!, I am body.— / It sinks its beak into my lap / and it is left like dead . . . / and on the crystalline page, / on the sensitive mirror / of the lake that sometimes / reflects my thought, / the swan frightens with its redness, / and I, with my whiteness, am frightening!]

The unequivocal description of the amorous encounter reveals her womanly nature, but she is not passive; her response is assertive and authoritative. After penetration, the swan/Darío appears dead; "he" is limp and unresponsive. "His" energies have been spent within the context of her poetry, in the realm of the crystalline page/sensitive mirror of the lake that reflects her thoughts. He is no longer the white, guileless bird but a red swan that is both injured and injuring. Both he and she are locked in a passionately erotic encounter that ultimately revolves around artistic control. His condition is alarming, as is her own whiteness. He is defeated and she emerges as the new white emblem of poetry, frightening those around her. She assumes authorial authority and inherits the full weight of his responsibilities. She must create, regardless of how difficult and terrifying that prospect may be—to her and to others. Paradoxically, by engaging the master, she becomes the carrier of his heritage as well as the vehicle of her own poetic innovation.

The critical attention this poem has garnered is well deserved. It exemplifies the generational struggle of poets with the added poignancy of the threat to the balance of power between men and women. It runs the gamut of emotions from joy to fear to arousal to satisfaction back to fear again as the lyric voice strives to turn the mirror/page into a vision of herself and of the new verse she aspires to delineate. All the while she refuses to ignore the dangers and pitfalls of her endeavor.

Agustini's dread of failure is further developed in "Plegaria" (Prayer) (258–59), the next to the last poem of *Los cálices vacíos*. Agustini returns to

the lament of "La estatua" (101) from *El libro blanco (Frágil)* and its disturbing assessment of what it means to fail as an artist. Her greatest anxiety
stems from the prospect that the work of art will remain lifeless, never to
be animated by the creative spark associated with love and sexual passion.
This troubling concern is expressed in "Plegaria" in an opening question
to Eros: "—Eros: did you never by chance feel / pity for statues?" While
the title implies a traditional Christian context, this question redirects the
prayer for divine compassion and mercy to Eros, the god of sexual attraction and love, whose passion for life is contrasted with the unfeeling nature
of the statue. As I mentioned in chapter 2, the figure of the statue recalls,
among others, the evocative lines from Darío's "Yo soy aquel que ayer no
más decía . . . ," in which he proclaims the success that Agustini worries
she may not achieve. He writes, "En mi jardín se vio una estatua bella; /
se juzgó mármol y era carne viva" (245). His statue lives; marble becomes
flesh.[31] If Darío implicitly challenges all later poets to turn stone into flesh,
Agustini responds in "Plegaria" with trepidation. As becomes evident in
the first section of the poem, her fear that instead of creating life she will
destroy it takes on the quality of a death watch:

> —Eros: ¿acaso no sentiste nunca
> Piedad de las estatuas?
> Se dirían crisálidas de piedra
> De yo no sé qué formidable raza
> En una eterna espera inenarrable.
> Los cráteres dormidos de sus bocas
> Dan la ceniza negra del Silencio,
> Mana de las columnas de sus hombros
> La mortaja copiosa de la Calma,
> Y fluye de sus órbitas la noche:
> Víctimas del Futuro o del Misterio,
> En capullos terribles y magníficos
> Esperan a la Vida o a la Muerte.
> Eros: ¿acaso no sentiste nunca
> Piedad de las estatuas?— (258)

[—Eros: did you never by chance feel / pity for statues? / One might call
them stony chrysalises / of I know not what formidable race / in eternal,

indescribable waiting. / The sleeping craters of their mouths / produce the black ash of Silence, / the abundant shroud of Calm / flows from the columns of their shoulders, / and night flows from the sockets of their eyes: / victims of the Future or of Mystery, / in terrible and magnificent cocoons / they wait for Life or for Death. / Eros: did you never by chance feel / pity for statues?—]

The faces of the statues come to resemble skulls whose lifelike features are converted into craters and in whose mouths silence becomes black ash. From their shoulders flows a shroud of unearthly calm, and they are described as victims of the future, awaiting—wrapped within their cocoons—their sentence of life or death.[32]

Agustini's artistic anxiety is also expressed in another, more decidedly feminine vision. She worries that the superhuman race, the "sublimely insane" offspring of poet and poetic inspiration, will be stillborn, more precisely, will be locked forever within their stony chrysalis, never to emerge as full-fledged entities. The haunting beauty of this metaphor captures the possibility that these works will be unable to escape their formal structures and to achieve freedom and flight. To make this point, Agustini turns to the "chrysalis," a word closely associated with Darío and his unswerving desire to make his poetry escape its earthbound restrictions and limitations. The chrysalis and the spirit that emerges from it are constants in Darío's poetry from the time that he first published "Venus" in 1889 and later in the second edition of *Azul . . .* in 1890. In Darío's famous sonnet Agustini would have found not only the dramatic butterfly imagery but also the fusion of erotic longing with artistic aspirations and angst, particularly in its concluding tercets:

> "¡Oh, reina rubia!, —díjele—, mi alma quiere dejar su crisálida
> y volar hacia ti, y tus labios de fuego besar;
> y flotar en el nimbo que derrama en tu frente luz pálida,
>
> y en siderales éxtasis no dejarte un momento de amar".
> El aire de la noche refrescaba la atmósfera cálida.
> Venus, desde el abismo, me miraba con triste mirar. (175)

["Oh, blonde queen!, —I said to her—, my soul wishes to leave its chrysalis / and to fly toward you, and to kiss your fiery lips; / and to float in the halo that spills pale light on your brow, and in starry ecstasy to not stop loving you for a moment." / The night air cooled the warm atmosphere. / Venus, from the abyss, looked at me with a sad look.]

Simultaneously ideal lover and poetic perfection, Darío's Venus becomes the desired object that is always beyond reach. Heaven becomes an abyss as the poet confronts the goddess's twofold unattainability.

For her part, Agustini never loses sight of the difficulty of achieving her mission. Starting with the second section, the concern for the statue's lack of vitality and humanity encompasses individuals who have rejected Eros's other life-affirming benefits. The lyric voice focuses on those that have distanced themselves from the heat of passion and have enveloped themselves in multiple layers of frigidity and sanctity:

> Piedad para las vidas
> Que no doran a fuego tus bonanzas
> Ni riegan o desgajan tus tormentas;
> Piedad para los cuerpos revestidos
> Del armiño solemne de la Calma,
> Y las frentes en luz que sobrellevan
> Grandes lirios marmóreos de pureza,
> Pesados y glaciales como témpanos;
> Piedad para las manos enguantadas
> De hielo, que no arrancan
> Los frutos deleitosos de la Carne
> Ni las flores fantásticas del alma;
> Piedad para los ojos que aletean
> Espirituales párpados:
> Escamas de misterio,
> Negros telones de visiones rosas . . .
> ¡Nunca ven nada por mirar tan lejos! (258)

[Pity for the lives / that do not gild with fire your successes / nor scatter or tear apart your storms; / pity for the bodies cloaked / in the solemn ermine of Composure, / and the lit brows that bear / great marble lilies of purity, / heavy and glacial like icebergs; / pity for the hands gloved / with ice, that do not pick / the pleasing fruits of the Flesh / nor the fantastic flowers of the soul; / pity for the eyes that flutter / spiritual eyelids: / scales of mys-

tery, / black curtains of pink visions . . . / They never see anything for looking so far!]

The images of numbing cold and marmoreal purity reinforce those of lifelessness from the first section. To reject the delectable pleasures of the flesh
and the passionate strivings of the soul and to lock oneself within the glacial confines of unresponsiveness become here another form of death. The
poem goes further by expressing pity for people with "spiritual eyelids," for
they become the black curtains that drape over rosy visions and that prevent them from seeing anything because they are constantly looking beyond what is before them. With clever metaphors and brilliant linguistic
subterfuge, "Plegaria" couches in the language of compassion its condem-
nation of those who do not allow themselves to succumb to Eros's powers.
They are judged incapable of understanding the world around them, unable to achieve moral insight, satisfaction, and success. In defiance of normative standards, the poem disparages individuals who, in their hardened
purity, stand for the moral high ground, pursue the celestial promise of the
Eucharist, reject the ravishing quest of the vampire, and cling to chastity
as if it were tied to the heavens:

> Piedad para los labios como engarces
> Celestes donde fulge
> Invisible la perla de la Hostia;
> —Labios que nunca fueron,
> Que no apresaron nunca
> Un vampiro de fuego
> Con más sed y más hambre que un abismo.—
> Piedad para los sexos sacrosantos
> Que acoraza de una
> Hoja de viña astral la Castidad; . . . (259)

[Pity for the lips like celestial / settings where / the invisible pearl of the Eucharist shines; / —lips that never were, / that never captured / a fiery vampire / thirstier and hungrier than an abyss.— / Pity for the sacrosanct sexes /
that Chastity covers with armor made of a / leaf from an astral vineyard; . . .]

In short, "Plegaria" offers an openly rebellious stance, reflecting Agustini's attempts to break out of the inflexible, moral code dictated by male

self-interest that keeps women passionless, artificially pure, and unable to create art or generate life.[33]

Agustini closes her collection with "A lo lejos" (In the distance) (260), a poem that brings *Los cálices vacíos* full circle, back to the widows of the first poems, and that moves the discussion from multilayered rebelliousness to the dual impact of separation. Creation appears as a product of reflection and recall, which is colored by nostalgia and pain. This dichotomous perspective is embedded in the opening description of the absent other:

> Tu vida viuda enjoyará aquel día . . .
> En la gracia silvestre de la aldea
> Era una llaga tu perfil arcano;
> Insólito, alarmante sugería
> El esmalte de espléndida presea
> Sobre un pecho serrano. (260)

[Your widowed life will bejewel that day . . . / On the untamed grace of the village / your arcane profile was a wound; / unusual, alarming it suggested / the enamel of a splendid jewel / on a mountain chest.]

Uncertain as to how to deal with loss, the lyric voice feels that the other's memory is a wound. It hangs in the atmosphere, invading the tranquil countryside like the lacerations inflicted by his bladelike profile. It produces a bloody stain that is compared to a piece of fine jewelry. Recollections of the other harm and embellish, prevent the poet from being whom she wishes to be and yet continue to bestow grace. The enigmatic and distant future to which the lyric voice alludes is that moment, suggested in the penultimate stanza, when the chalices of modernista discourse can no longer hold her spirit:

> —¡Oh beso! . . . flor de cuatro pétalos . . . dos de Ciencia
> Y dos iluminados de inocencia . . .
> El cáliz una sima embriagante y sombría. —
> Por un milagro de melancolía,
> Mármol o bronce me rompí en tu mano
> Derramando mi espíritu, tal un pomo de esencia. (260)

[—Oh kiss! . . . flower of four petals . . . two of Knowledge / and two lit by innocence . . . / The chalice an intoxicating and dark abyss. — / By a miracle of melancholy, / marble or bronze I broke apart in your hand / spilling my spirit, like a jar of essence.]

Wiser because of her encounter with the inspiring other ("por un milagro de melancolía"), she recalls the embrace in which she shatters like a marble or bronze vessel. Despite the destruction that the image implies, it also suggests escape, like the liberation of a butterfly from its cocoon or a genie from a bottle. Once she has broken the mold which has held her, her essence is able to flow free. She will be able to create a work that will be bejeweled by the memory of the other. She is appreciative of all he has taught her, so she affirms his impact upon her life and poetry by repeating the first line of verse at the beginning of the final stanza:

> Tu vida viuda enjoyará aquel día . . .
> Mi nostalgia ha pintado tu perfil Wagneriano
> Sobre el velo tremendo de la ausencia. (260)

[Your widowed life will bejewel that day . . . / My nostalgia has painted your Wagnerian profile / on the enormous veil of absence.]

She converts his memory into a synesthetic Wagnerian profile painted on the canvas of absence. Yet sorrow and hurt are the emotions that dominate "A lo lejos." As the other recedes, the lyric voice seeks to fill what she sadly recognizes to be a possibly unbridgeable gap between the idealized past (the youthful exuberance of sexual love and the perfection of Darío's poetry) and the imperfect future (married life and ongoing fears of inadequacy).

The prose coda to the collection reinforces this Janus-like perspective of looking forward and backward at the same time. Agustini clarifies in a brief statement that the publication of *Los cálices vacíos* in 1913 contained a second edition of *Cantos de la mañana* and of parts of *El libro blanco (Frágil)*. The coda also announces the upcoming publication of "Los astros de abismo" (The stars of the abyss) (261). This new volume was to offer a new chapter in Agustini's work that would parallel the new chapter in her personal life, namely, her upcoming marriage to Enrique Job Reyes.

CHAPTER FIVE

ASPIRATIONS AND ABIDING DISAPPOINTMENTS

Los astros del abismo

Over the course of her career, as she becomes a more confident and self-reliant poet, Agustini finds creative ways to express her efforts to break away from the dominant writers of the day and their imposing perspective. In *Los cálices vacíos* she seeks autonomy from her lover/model/mentor by imagining him dead, mourning his demise, locking him in tomblike structures, and then moving on. His death makes room for a new generation of aspiring artists, who take the opportunity to fill the void left by his departure. In *Los astros del abismo*[1] (The stars of the abyss) she expands this vision, but she also begins to anticipate, prematurely and presciently, her own demise. The emphasis on the end of life and its multiple struggles cannot be disentangled from Agustini's personal tribulations following her marriage to Enrique Job Reyes or from her troubled relationship with her literary vocation. Nevertheless, the looming presence of death points to Agustini's continuing meditation on the nature of life, poetic influence, literary achievement, and the price that must be paid for transgressive behavior. The personal and literary tensions between hope and despair are evident in the title Agustini originally selected for the volume. The allusion to "los astros del abismo" underscores her belief that the pursuit of her desires, whether poetic or erotic, is a type of reaching for the stars that ultimately ends with dejection and the type of catastrophic fall that appear throughout earlier collections. This dichotomous perspective is hardly unique to Agustini. The stars and abyss of the title call to mind, for example, Darío's "Venus," a poem that reverberates, as I indicated in chapter 4, in many of the pieces in *Los cálices vacíos* in their fusion of love and art, ascent and descent, optimism and despair.

Though I prefer, along with Alejandro Cáceres, the title *Los astros del abismo*, most editions of Agustini's work put the subsection of five short poems entitled "El rosario de Eros" (Eros's rosary) at the beginning of the volume and call the whole collection by that name.[2] By starting with these pieces, editors have either intentionally or inadvertently emphasized the contemplative nature of the collection. The five poems correspond to the five large beads of what is known as a five-decade rosary, and the title of each begins with the word "cuentas," or beads, by which Agustini seems to refer to the ten smaller beads strung between each of the larger ones. In the last of the five poems, she refers to "tu sonrisa de cincuenta dientes" (281) (your smile of fifty teeth). For the observant Catholic, the prayers of each decade are accompanied by a meditation on one of the Mysteries of the Rosary, which include events in the lives of Jesus Christ and his mother, the Virgin Mary. Agustini turns from the religious to the worldly, seeking meaning and possible transcendence in the elements that have structured her life and work. She makes this a secular, erotic rosary in the style of Darío's *Prosas profanas*, his profane hymns.

When Darío refers to the content of his collection and its title, he directs attention toward a sexual passion that is inextricably linked to art, poetry, music, and religion. He writes, "I have said, in the pink Mass of my youth, my antiphons, my sequences, and my profane proses. . . . Ring, bells of gold, bells of silver; ring every day, calling me to the party in which eyes of fire shine, and the roses of mouths bleed unique delights" (*Poesía* 180).[3] The "proses," like the antiphons and sequences, are verses or hymns said or sung during the Mass. Darío invokes Catholic liturgy to break expectations regarding the genre in question, to defy accepted norms and values, and to challenge the social limits, restrictions, and constraints imposed on behavior, language, and vision. Agustini emulates Darío's creative maneuver and turns each poem into a reflection on the great mysteries of life, love, and art. She builds on the sexualized representation of literary production and explores the multiple contradictions and tensions she faced throughout her career. She does not, however, seek to resolve these tensions. The poems offer no easy solution to her dilemmas. On the contrary, they provide an open-ended meditation that is both unnerving and symptomatic of Agustini's rupture with the *modernista* tendency to find resolution and accord.

The first of the five poems, "Cuentas de mármol" (Marble beads) (277), fuses poet and product and thereby makes the lyric voice the object of discussion. She is "la estatua de mármol con cabeza de fuego, / Apagando mis sienes en frío y blanco . . ." (the marble statue with a head of fire, / extinguishing my temples in whiteness and cold . . .). This brilliantly visual image offers a departure from her stance in previous collections. Instead of rejecting, as she often did, the rigid lifelessness of statues and structures that are incapable of capturing the vitality of existence, here she turns herself into a marble figure and seeks to cool her temples, extinguishing the flames of desire in an icy whiteness. She turns away from heat and passion and pursues the calm chastity of the male other, who seems to embody the dispassionate perfection of art created in tranquil contemplation. She asks him to shower white lilies upon her, and she allows herself to be enveloped with him in his calming mantle.[4] Nevertheless, while she appears to accept a type of restraint that she had always spurned, what comes to the forefront is the erotic arousal she feels as she pursues his purity and invades his invulnerability. Their destinies weave together in what the lyric voice presents as her submission and exaltation:

> Yo, la estatua de mármol con cabeza de fuego,
> Apagando mis sienes en frío y blanco ruego . . .
>
> Engarzad en un gesto de palmera o de astro
> Vuestro cuerpo, esa hipnótica alhaja de alabastro
> Tallada a besos puros y bruñida en la edad;
> Sereno, tal habiendo la luna por coraza;
> Blanco, más que si fuerais la espuma de la Raza,
> Y desde el tabernáculo de vuestra castidad,
> Nevad a mí los lises hondos de vuestra alma;
> Mi sombra besará vuestro manto de calma,

> Que creciendo, creciendo me envolverá con Vos;
> Luego será mi carne en la vuestra perdida . . .
> Luego será mi alma en la vuestra diluida . . .
> Luego será la gloria . . . y seremos un dios!
> —Amor de blanco y frío,
> Amor de estatuas, lirios, astros, dioses . . .
> ¡Tú me lo des, Dios mío![5] (277)

[I, the marble statue with a head of fire, / extinguishing my temples in whiteness and cold, implore . . .

Mount in a gesture of palm tree or star / your body, that hypnotic alabaster jewel / carved by pure kisses and burnished by age; / serene, like having the moon as a breastplate; / white, more than if you were the foam of the Race, / and from the tabernacle of your chastity, / snow on me the deep lilies of your soul; / my shadow will kiss your cloak of calm, / that growing, growing will envelop me with you; / then my flesh will be lost in yours . . . / then my soul with be diluted in yours . . . / then it will be glory . . . and we will be a god! / —Love of whiteness and cold, / love of statues, lilies, stars, gods . . . / May you give it to me, dear God!]

The male other is presented in as contradictory terms as the female lyric voice. He is sexual and sexually desirable but also piously chaste. His body is like a precious piece of alabaster carved by kisses, yet it is also protected against enemy assault by the armored shield of the serene moon. He is erotic (even whiter than the foamy sperm that engenders the special "Race" of artists), and he is spiritual (able to whiten her dark, shadowy existence with the lilies of his soul). He is her lover and artistic model through whom she loses herself in order to achieve divinity, the divinity captured in the phrase "y seremos un dios!" In this way, Agustini makes new and refreshing the metaphors of sexual desire and literary production. Her final prayer, "Amor de estatuas, lirios, astros, dioses . . . / ¡Tú me lo des, Dios mío!," reveals her ongoing faith in the power of both love and art to transform and elevate. She disguises the dark side of the collection in white as she turns human fragility into marble and statuary art. She simultaneously wraps her passion in religious overtones, which, more than a reflection of traditional values, provide a preemptive move toward solace in the face of the somber threats that surface throughout this volume.

This brooding quality emerges immediately in the next poem, "Cuentas de sombra" (Beads of darkness) (278), which blends love and mortality in a poetic vision of productive passions. The white beds of earlier poems are now black and rooted in death. They are covered in sadness, sculpted by daggers, and canopied by insomnia. They capture the lyric voice's pain from years spent in nocturnal struggle with her erotic and literary longings as well as with her fears of reprisal. Yet the black beds also provide a foundation on which the future will take shape:

> Los lechos negros logran la más fuerte
> Rosa de amor; arraigan en la muerte.
> Grandes lechos tendidos de tristeza,
> Tallados a puñal y doselados
> De insomnio; las abiertas
> Cortinas dicen cabelleras muertas;
> Buenas como cabezas
> Hermanas son las hondas almohadas:
> Plintos del Sueño y del Misterio gradas. (278)

[The black beds achieve the strongest / rose of love; they take root in death. / Large beds made with sadness, / carved by a dagger and canopied / by insomnia; the open / curtains say dead heads of hair; / good as brotherly / heads are the deep pillows: / Dream's plinths and Mystery's steps.]

The windows through which inspiration had entered in earlier collections are here open curtains. The curtains announce ("dicen") the arrival of dead heads of long hair, turning the "cabelleras muertas" into text. These ghastly apparitions are, like the heads of "Mis amores" (My loves) (282–86) from later in this volume, specters of past experiences and past poems that haunt the poet's imagination. As they did in Darío's "La pesadilla de Honorio" (Honorio's nightmare) they come from all quarters, from personal and cultural experiences, from words spoken and words read, and they become a vision of the future. They will rest upon pillows that become "Dream's plinths" and "Mystery's steps," words that are associated with architecture and amphitheaters and that create an image of structures, supports, and ascent. The architectural language implies a movement toward a resolution of lasting impact. The next stanza, however, suggests a more subtle and delicate outcome:

> Si así en un lecho como flor de muerte,
> Damos llorando, como un fruto fuerte
> Maduro de pasión, en carnes y almas,
> Serán especies desoladas, bellas,
> Que besen el perfil de las estrellas
> Pisando los cabellos de las palmas!
>
> —Gloria al amor sombrío,
> Como la Muerte pudre y ennoblece
> ¡Tú me lo des, Dios mío! (278)

[If in this way in a bed like a flower of death, / we bear, crying, something like a strong fruit / ripe with passion, in flesh and souls, / they will be devastated, beautiful species, / that may kiss the contour of the stars / by treading upon the hair of the palm trees!

—Glory to dark love, / like Death it rots and ennobles / May you give it to me, dear God!]

The bedroom provides a backdrop to an encounter that produces, as has been the case before, special offspring with supernatural qualities, the "Raza" of the previous poem. Agustini compares them to a "flower of death," for they are simultaneously life affirming and rooted in a physicality that underscores the brevity of existence and the onset of decay. Perhaps for this reason the overt sexuality of her images as well as the defiance and energy with which she had faced the multiple tensions in her life seem to have receded. Her rebelliousness has been tempered by her awareness of the inflexibility of social structures, the unyielding materiality of language, and the inevitability of death.

The lovers' activities are tinged with aging and the "shadow" of mortality (the "sombra" of the title). They cry as they bear "fruit" that is already mature, old in body and soul, sorrowful and beautiful. Even though these poetic progeny may, to use Agustini's beautiful metaphors, kiss the stars and walk upon the treetops, they are the product of a gloomy love, a love defined by disappointment, death, and the uncertain result of the author's noble effort. The weight of the years and the burden of her endeavors have taken a toll that colors this poem and the entire collection, but it does not totally obscure the sensuous delight of art achieved in union with the poetic other.

In the face of the transience of life, Agustini turns to the driving energy of creativity, and in the next poem, "Cuentas de fuego" (Beads of fire) (279), she presents a set of instructions on how to "relight" the erotic dynamism of earlier works. Though the poem is built upon infinitives, leaving unclear who is being addressed, the lyric voice seems to be commanding both herself and "her love" to follow a course of action that will allow them to consummate their affair. The language is seductive and temptingly evocative of a clandestine romance. Starting in the first line Agustini signals the reassertion of erotic language, passionate discourse, and her rewriting of the images of literary paternity—all despite the general pall that hangs over the collection:

> Cerrar la puerta cómplice con rumor de caricia,
> Deshojar hacia el mal el lirio de una veste . . .
> —La seda es un pecado, el desnudo es celeste;
> Y es un cuerpo mullido un diván de delicia.—
> Abrir brazos . . . así todo ser es alado,
> O una cálida lira dulcemente rendida
> De canto y de silencio . . . más tarde, en el helado
> Más allá de un espejo como un lago inclinado,
> Ver la olímpica bestia que elabora la vida . . .
> Amor rojo, amor mío;
> Sangre de mundos y rubor de cielos . . .
> ¡Tú me lo des, Dios mío![6] (279)

[To close the accomplice door with a murmur of a caress, / to pull off toward evil the petals of the lily of a dress . . . / —Silk is a sin, nakedness is celestial; / and a soft body is a sofa of delight.— / To open arms . . . in this way all beings are winged, / or a warm lyre sweetly exhausted / by song and silence . . . later, in the frozen / beyond of a mirror like a sloping lake, / to see the Olympic beast that produces life . . . / Red love, love of mine; / blood of worlds and blush of heavens . . . / May you give it to me, dear God!]

The sexual energy is heightened with allusion to illicit behavior in the imaginative linking of "door" and "accomplice" and the creative synaesthetic phrase "murmur of a caress." The proscribed nature of the encounter is immediately reinforced in the play between evil and purity, sin and divinity, the third line inverting the traditional associations of goodness and modesty and evil and nakedness. The openness to love, life, and art promised by the nude is deemed celestial here, as it had been by Darío and other modernistas before. To be unencumbered by the trappings of prevailing values, traditions, phrases, and structures allows for insight and art. The anticipated glory of the resulting freedom is captured, as arms become wings and as the lovers' warm embrace is transmuted into the song or the silence of a lyre. Yet the warmth of the encounter literally cools as the lyric voice resurrects the brilliant metaphor of the icy depths of the mirror/lake/poem that grounded both "Nocturno" and "El cisne" from *Los cálices vacíos* (see chapter 4). While all else appears transfixed in the mirror's depth, in the frozen lake's modernista perfection the swan re-emerges as a source of vitality. The open-ended references to the ambiguous red of her love and "the blood of worlds and blush of heavens" hint at the erogenous and lyrical powers of forbidden passions as well as their ability to inflict harm. The tension between empowerment and injury was foregrounded in the red and white swans of "El cisne." This is the difficult balancing act Agustini faced throughout her career. Though she refuses to discard the hope of sexual and poetic gratification that would compensate for the pain she has endured, she does not conceal her discouragement and exhaustion.

In the next poem, "Cuentas de luz" (Beads of light) (280), her meditation on life and poetry leads Agustini to assert the lasting obligation she feels to her destiny and to the memory of her lover/mentor:

> Lejos como en la muerte
>
> Siento arder una vida vuelta siempre hacia mí,
> Fuego lento hecho de ojos insomnes, más que fuerte
> Si de su allá insondable dora todo mi aquí.
> Sobre tierras y mares su horizonte es mi ceño,
> Como un cisne sonámbulo duerme sobre mi sueño
> Y es su paso velado de distancia y reproche
> El seguimiento dulce de los perros sin dueño
> Que han roído ya el hambre, la tristeza y la noche
> Y arrastran su cadena de misterio y ensueño.
>
> Amor de luz, un río
> Que es el camino de cristal del Bien.
> ¡Tú me lo des, Dios mío! (280)

[Far away as in death

I feel a life always turned toward me burning, / a slow burning fire made of sleepless eyes, more than strong / if its unfathomable there turns my whole here golden. / On lands and seas his horizon is my frown, / like a sleep-walking swan he sleeps upon my dream / and his passage, watched over by distance and reproach, is / the sweet pursuit of ownerless dogs / that have already gnawed hunger, sadness, and the night / and drag around their chain of mystery and reverie.

Love of light, a river / that is the crystal road of Goodness. / May you give it to me, dear God!]

In this succinct, dynamic poem the burning passion ("fuego") that under-lies literary reproductive imagery and that animates the previous poem no longer rages. The cooling firewood ("fuego lento") casts an evocative mix of heat, light, and shadow. Like the memory that is invoked, the flicker-ing flames are both a presence and an absence, a past that continues to endure and an ongoing effort in the face of exhaustion. By putting the "sleepwalking" swan of modernista verse squarely in the middle of the poem Agustini emphasizes her artistic longings and her fitful encounters with her poetic aspirations, which are embodied in the sadly sweet mem-ory of the other, that is, the presence that fitfully sleeps upon her dreams. The reproach the lyric voice feels as she watches over him is hers projected onto him and, like the abandoned dogs, it follows her unfailingly through hunger, fear, sadness, and solitude. She is pursued by a gnawing sense of inadequacy, but she refuses to give up her solitary struggle to flourish. In a disturbingly surreal image, she is like these "ownerless" pets; she has broken free, but she also recognizes that she continues to drag around the chain of poetic discourse that had originally bound her. In short, the lyric voice vacillates between basking in the glow of the male other and her an-guished contemplation of her inability to achieve the level of excellence and independence that he has set for her. By the end, however, she takes solace in the fact that she has chosen to follow his illuminating love and, like the restless swan that controls her waking and sleeping, to follow his fluid and crystalline path.

All four of these "cuentas" poems end with the petition that God grant her the love that she has described ("¡Tú me lo des, Dios mío!"), even in those cases when it brings her pain and despair. "Cuentas falsas" (False beads) (281), the fifth and last "group of beads" in Agustini's erotic rosary, breaks this pattern. Resurrecting the metaphoric use of the statue to stand for all artistic production, Agustini reveals the sense of victimization that overshadows these final efforts as well as the type of subterfuge she turns to in order to protect herself, her goals, and her art. The work is attacked by black crows that hunger after "pink flesh," recalling the Promethean suffering to which she alluded in "Tu boca" (228) and "Otra estirpe" (243), from *Los cálices vacíos*. To protect her accomplishments she projects a false image of her creation in the mirror of the deceitful moon. This hard, cold, reflective surface acts to shield the human underbelly of her sculptures from the hammering attack of the crows. Despite the misdirection and their broken beaks, the crows depart satiated by the desired flesh, suggesting that, even though the lyric voice claims to be untouched behind her ironic self and language, she is not unscathed. In this context of misleading moonlight and false mirrors, the love she seeks becomes a mockery, and the cold, sculpted marble appears as something it is not:

> Amor de burla y frío
> Mármol que el tedio barnizó de fuego
> O lirio que el rubor vistió de rosa,
> Siempre lo dé, Dios mío . . . (281)

[Love of mockery and cold / marble that boredom varnished with fire / oh lily that the blush dressed in pink, / may you always give it, dear God . . .]

The ways of the world are false, and survivors protect themselves through deceptive appearances and deceitful facades.

This disjunction between reality and appearance underlies the statements of the last two stanzas, creating a type of textual wink at the reader. Agustini much prefers her "false" rosary to the one of Catholic religiosity and purity. The implication is that, despite the word "false," hers is the real rosary, for it is a fertile, living archipelago of poetry that encircles the world, and each poem is a piece of earth and not part of a starry fantasy that bears no relationship to the life she has had to carve out for herself:

> O rosario fecundo,
> Collar vivo que encierra
> La garganta del mundo.

Cadena de la tierra
Constelación caída.

O rosario imantado de serpientes,
Glisa hasta el fin entre mis dedos sabios,
Que en tu sonrisa de cincuenta dientes
Con un gran beso se prendió mi vida:
Una rosa de labios. (281)

[Oh fertile rosary, / living necklace that encloses / the neck of the world. / Chain of the earth / fallen constellation.

Oh rosary magnetized by serpents, / it glides until the end between my wise fingers, that on your smile of fifty teeth / with a great kiss my life was ignited: a rose of lips.]

Agustini favors the rosary of serpents she holds between her fingers, and she finds in its smile and kiss a life-affirming power. She exalts what has been condemned and posits a change from traditional values. By embracing the serpent that stained Eve's reputation, by overcoming the restrictions of passivity, by proclaiming movement over stasis, and by choosing creative passion over sterile purity, she grants to this "false" rosary the authority of an enabling truth.

This section of five poems, which Agustini identifies with a macabre and ironic "sonrisa de cincuenta dientes," a "smile of fifty teeth" (281), highlights life's irreconcilable tensions. Its cautionary perspective weaves its way throughout the entire final collection, which, according to Cáceres, was supposed to begin with "Mis amores" (My loves) (282–86), a lengthy poem about poetic inspiration. The first eight lines of the sixty-nine that make up "Mis amores" announce that the nocturnal hallucinations "have returned." They include the bed, the bedroom, the night, the weeping, the handkerchief, and the mourning of earlier poems, emphasizing that the "loves" of the poem's title are not human but artistic. The "heads" and "hands" of the second, third, and fourth sections are not simply the fragmented images of possible partners; they form part of an aesthetic landscape, like that of Darío's "Página blanca" (see chapter 2), one in which the scales tip in favor of silence, loss, and death.

In Agustini's personal poetic language, heads often represent sources of creativity, an identification that first appeared in *El libro blanco (Frá-*

gil) (in "El ave de luz" [152] and "El intruso" [168]) and reappeared with more menacing overtones in *Cantos de la mañana* (in "La intensa realidad de un sueño lúgubre . . ." [190], "Lo inefable" [193–94], and "Tú dormías" [204]). The surreal heads of "Mis amores" sum up the breadth of possibilities as well as the totality of her dreams and anxieties. Her responsiveness, arousal, and declaration of participation generate a nightmarish perspective on punishment and betrayal. The bombarding images come as a warning about her fate as a desirous woman and an engaged poet:

> Todas esas cabezas me duelen como llagas . . .
> Me duelen como muertos . . .
> ¡Ah! . . . y los ojos . . . los ojos me duelen más: son dobles! . . .
> Indefinidos, verdes, grises, azules, negros,
> Abrasan y fulguran,
> Son caricias, dolor, constelación, infierno.
> Sobre toda su luz, sobre todas sus llamas,
> Se iluminó mi alma y se templó mi cuerpo.
> Ellos me dieron sed de todas esas bocas . . .
> De todas estas bocas que florecen mi lecho;
> Vasos rojos o pálidos de miel o de amargura
> Con lises de armonía o rosas de silencio,
> De todos estos vasos donde bebí la vida,
> De todos estos vasos donde la muerte bebo . . .
> El jardín de sus bocas venenoso, embriagante,
> En donde respiraba sus almas y sus cuerpos,
> Embriagado en lágrimas
> Ha rodeado mi lecho . . .
>
> Y las manos, las manos colmadas de destinos
> Secretos y tendidas de anillos de misterio . . .
> Hay manos que nacieron con guantes de caricia;
> Manos que están colmadas de flores del deseo,
> Manos en que se siente un puñal nunca visto,
> Y manos en que se ve un intangible cetro;
> Pálidas o morenas, voluptuosas o fuertes,
> En todas, todas ellas, puede engarzar un sueño.[7]
> Con tristeza de alma,

Se doblegan los cuerpos
Sin velos, santamente
Vestidos de deseo.
Imanes de mis brazos
Panales de mi entraña
Como a invisible abismo se inclinan a mi lecho . . . (282–83)

[All those heads hurt me like wounds . . . / They hurt me like the dead . . . / Ah! . . . and the eyes . . . the eyes hurt me more: they are double! . . . / Indefinite, green, gray, blue, black, / they burn and shine, / they are caresses, pain, constellations, hell. / Above all their light, above all their flames, / my soul lit up and my body calmed down. / They made me thirsty for all those mouths . . . / For all these mouths that make my bed bloom; / red or pale vessels of honey or of bitterness / with lilies of harmony or roses of silence, / from all these vessels where I drank life, / from all these vessels where I drink death . . . / The poisonous, intoxicating garden of their mouths, / where I breathed their souls and their bodies, / intoxicated in tears, / has surrounded my bed . . .

And the hands, the hands filled with secret / destinies and spread with mystery rings . . . / There are hands that were born with gloves of tenderness; / hands that are filled with flowers of desire, / hands in which is felt the never-seen dagger, / and hands in which is seen an intangible scepter; / pale or dark, voluptuous or strong, / in all, all of them, a dream can be mounted. / With sadness of soul, / the bodies without veils / piously dressed in desire bend. / Magnets of my arms / honeycombs of my entrails / as over an invisible abyss they lean over my bed . . .]

Agustini again is facing the demons that arrive in her bedroom during her sleepless nights. They cause her pain by offering insights and options that entice her to cross the line, to break expectations, and to accept the burden of "secret destinies." She has, however, come to see the dangers these seducers hold in their gloved, caressing hands: "Manos en que se siente un puñal nunca visto, / Manos en que se ve un intangible cetro." She is cognizant of the invisible, oppressive arrangements that surround her as well as of the treachery of those who simultaneously lure and punish by offering dreams that lead her to the edge of the abyss.

She underscores this dilemma in the four lines from the middle of the third section that begin with "Vasos rojos." In these metaphors Agustini combines sensual pleasures with artistic achievements, poetic speech ("armonía") with silence, the fulfillment of life's possibilities with the now-dominant presence of death. In the process she comes to focus on one set of hands, one mouth, one body, and one head. She singles out as first among many the one that has traveled the farthest: "Tú has llegado el primero por venir de más lejos . . ." (You have arrived first for having come the farthest . . .") (283). He seems to parallel the knight that arrives "de lejos, vencedor de la Muerte" at the end of Darío's "Sonatina" (188); he recalls the male lyric voice who will awaken the silent princess/language to all her/its potential. The difference here is that, as Agustini makes clear, the female voice anticipates taking up the dynamic role previously reserved for him. She summons him and demands contact and answers:

> Ven a mí: mente a mente;
> Ven a mí: ¡cuerpo a cuerpo![8]
> Tú me dirás qué has hecho de mi primer suspiro,
> Tú me dirás qué has hecho del sueño de aquel beso.
> Diremos si lloramos al encontrarnos solos . . .
> Tú me dirás si has muerto,
> Mi pena enlutará la alcoba lentamente,
> Y estrecharé tu sombra hasta apagar mi cuerpo,
> Y en el silencio ahondado de tiniebla,
> Y en la tiniebla ahondada de silencio,[9]
> Nos velará llorando, llorando hasta morirse
> Nuestro hijo: el recuerdo. (284)

[Come to me: mind to mind / come to me: body to body! / You will tell me what you have made of my first sigh, / you will tell me what you have made of the dream of that kiss. / We will tell if we cry upon meeting alone . . . / You will tell me if you have died, / my sorrow will slowly dress the bedroom in mourning, / and I will embrace your shadow until I extinguish my body, / and in the deepened silence of darkness / and in the deepened darkness of silence, / our son, memory, will watch over us crying, crying until he dies.]

The hopes of the past, however, have withered just as has he. He is no longer able to conquer death, and she wonders if he has already died. The promise and power of modernista verse have faded along with the influence of its leading champion, yet she cannot imagine going on without him. She will not leave her haven for a different type of discourse, perhaps the brave new world of the avant-garde. She chooses to embrace his ghostly absence until she no longer shines, until she is extinguished. In the end her destiny is linked to his and to the world of fading memories.

Their offspring, which in earlier collections had held so much promise, is a sad, frail figure. He ("nuestro hijo") is no longer capable of waging a campaign against the forces of tradition, as in "La estatua" (101) from *El libro blanco (Frágil)*. He embodies the dying echoes of their words. The son they produce, like their union and their love, is mortal. With this symbolic shift, this poem, possibly the one with which Agustini would have chosen to start her last collection, is a sophisticated reflection not only on the impact of poetic legacies but also on the vagaries of literary history. Read within the metaphoric network Agustini had developed throughout her previous collections, "Mis amores" signals a new level of anxiety and a heightened wariness about her ability (or inability) to survive and take over from the poet/lover whom she has, virtually from the start of her career, sought to seduce and conquer. Though, as I have indicated, there can be little doubt that both biography and psychology influenced the tone and language of the poem, the injurious nocturnal visions combine social, sexual, and literary concerns that go beyond the personal.[10] They address issues of remembering and being remembered. For this reason Agustini's plight cannot be reduced, as Doris Stephens suggests, to disillusionment with life and love that has her turn "to death as a means of enhancing life as a whole and love in particular" (189).

"El arroyo" (The stream) (288), the third poem of the original *Los astros del abismo*, begins with the same backward glance of memory with which "Mis amores" ends, that is, with the poignant "¿Te acuerdas? . . ." (Do you remember? . . .). The traditional structure and rhyme scheme of this sonnet contribute to the doleful calm of its emotive images from nature, which, taken together, highlight the rhythms of life, the counterpoint of water and rock, and the alternating placidity and turbulence of streams. Yet what predominates is the awareness on the part of the lyric voice that the music of the spring that in previous collections announced promise and production here proclaims sorrow. The waters carry a sense of fatality and death, that is, the inevitable "burning corpse" of the late afternoon sun. The poem's tragic melancholy appears to result from the intimacy of two beings caught in the flow of time and in the sweep of powerful events:

> ¿Te acuerdas? . . . El arroyo fué la serpiente buena . . .
> Fluía triste y triste como un llanto de ciego,
> Cuando en las piedras grises donde arraiga la pena,
> Como un inmenso lirio, se levantó tu ruego.
>
> Mi corazón, la piedra más gris y más serena,
> Despertó en la caricia de la corriente, y luego
> Sintió cómo la tarde, con manos de agarena,
> Prendía sobre él una rosa de fuego.
>
> Y mientras la serpiente del arroyo blandía
> El veneno divino de la melancolía,
> Tocada de crepúsculo me abrumó tu cabeza,
>
> La coroné de un beso fatal; en la corriente
> Vi pasar un cadáver de fuego . . . Y locamente
> Me derrumbó en tu abrazo profundo la tristeza. (288)

[Do you remember? . . . The stream was the good serpent . . . / It flowed sad and sad like a sobbing of a blind man, / when on the gray stones where sorrow takes root, / like an immense lily, your entreaty rose up.

My heart, the grayest and most serene stone, / awoke in the caress of the current, and then / it felt how the afternoon, with Mohameddan hands, / fastened a fiery rose on to it.

And while the serpent of the stream brandished / the divine poison of melancholy, / touched by twilight your head overwhelmed me,

I crowned it with a fatal kiss; in the current / I saw a fiery corpse pass by . . . And insanely / sadness demolished me in your deep embrace.]

He (the "tú" of the poem), appropriately, fuses with the snakelike flowing water that can be heard ("se levantó tu ruego") as it encounters the bedrock of her being. She, in turn, is the stony heart, the unyielding self of line 5 that learns to feel under the influence of his caress. Though both elements come alive at the moment of contact, it is an uneasy awakening. The speaker, held in what she has come to perceive as the swiftly moving river of time, voices, and memories, finds herself contaminated by omens of death, drowning in a profound sadness. She is engulfed in the venomous embrace of melancholy, the overwhelming desolation of twilight's presence, and the plaintive entreaty of the other with whom she is emotionally involved. She "crowns" his head with a "fatal kiss," momentarily leaving uncertain whether they are linked by a common destiny or whether she, like a modern-day Judas, sends him off to face death alone. In the final line of the sonnet, however, she acknowledges that the relationship she had so hoped would lead to productivity and freedom leads to her defeat as well. They both are victims of the unrelenting forces of nature—the flow of rivers, the passage of time, and the inevitability of death—which come together in the inspired image of the blazing "reflection" of the setting sun that floats by on his serpentine body. Through this final metaphor Agustini underscores the entwining of love and death, but for her the passion is poetic as well as carnal. The poem suggests that Agustini believes the enterprise in which the two players have been engaged, that is, modernismo as a whole, may have entered its twilight years.

The preoccupation with writing is foregrounded in the title and body of the next poem, "Por tu musa" (For your muse) (289), which continues the recourse to water imagery, in this case the blue lake of modernista perfection:

> Cuando derramas en los hombros puros
> De tu musa la túnica de nieve,
> Yo concentro mis pétalos oscuros
> Y soy el lirio de alabastro leve.
>
> Para tu musa en rosa, me abro en rosa;
> Mi corazón es miel, perfume y fuego;
> Y vivo y muero de una sed gloriosa:
> Tu sangre viva debe ser mi riego.
>
> Cuando velada por un tul de luna
> Bebe calma y azur en la laguna
> Yo soy el cisne que soñando vuela;
>
> Y si en luto magnífico la vistes,
> Para vagar por los senderos tristes,
> Soy la luz o la sombra de una estela . . . (289)

[When you spill the snowy tunic / on the pure shoulders of your muse, / I gather my dark petals / and I am the lily of light alabaster.

For your muse in rose, I open myself in rose; / my heart is honey, perfume, and fire; / and I live and die of a glorious thirst: / your living blood should irrigate me.

When veiled by a lunar tulle / she drinks calm and blue on the lake / I am the swan that while dreaming flies;

And if you dress her in magnificent mourning, / to wander along the sad paths, / I am the light or the shadow of a wake . . .]

With the poem's initial reference to flowers, the lyric voice states her ability to reflect the nature of the other's muse, temporarily disguising the aggressive, erotic, and somber underpinnings of her interaction with him. She declares her talent for appearing to the world as his virginally dressed muse. She hides her dark, sexually evocative petals and presents herself as an alabaster-white lily. When his muse is adorned in pink, she blossoms in rosy pinkness. Yet the lyric voice is not interested in pretending or in playing dress up. Her concern is that these blooms need watering, and for that she demands, with vampiric implications, the other's lifeblood. As she does in so many earlier poems, she chooses to satisfy her "glorious thirst" for him, for excellence, and for poetry by drinking from the fountain of his being, taking strength from his essence, drawing life from his. Irrigated by this invigorating fluid, her flowers will grow and bear fruit.

If in the quatrains the lyric voice moves from emulation to independence, the tercets express unresolved tensions and fears. The autonomy that the lyric voice pursues in the first two stanzas reemerges in her departure from the calm, blue modernista lake in an ascent that recalls the end of "Nocturno" from *Los cálices vacíos*. She rejects the pacifying tranquility of those waters, assumes the role of the new modernista swan, and flies skyward buoyed by her dreams. Similarly, in the second tercet she proposes to turn her back on the arid bleakness of the sad paths traveled by the other's mournful muse, denying at the same time her own fears of death and dying. Yet as much as the final metaphor of the sonnet, anchored by the word "estela" (wake), moves the lyric voice from land to sea, possibly from desolation to hope, it leaves unresolved her ability to escape imitation and despair. As much as she hopes to be a lamp that will illuminate the trails of tragedy and loss, she does not discount the possibility that she will be relegated to a shadowy, secondary existence. She emphatically captures this derivativeness with the doubly dependent metaphor in which she is the shadow of a ship's wake. Being the dark imprint that follows behind Darío and other luminaries would represent for Agustini an abdication of her aspirations to create an innovative discourse, a renunciation that would be the equivalent of artistic and spiritual death.

This contradictory assessment of her achievements, evident from the start of the collection in its title, continues in the next poem, "Diario espiritual" (Spiritual diary) (290–91), which is riddled with dashed hopes and disillusionment. The poem is constructed as a type of dialogue between glorious achievements and the recognition of having lost them. While the sections assert the lyric voice's abilities by describing her soul in terms of the powerful and productive water imagery that appears throughout modernista poetry, the single line that follows each section and that changes the verb from present to past tense implies that those abilities have been lost. The opening six lines are the model for the first six stanzas:

> Es un lago mi alma;
> Lago, vaso de cielo,
> Nido de estrellas en la noche calma,
> Copa del ave y de la flor, y suelo
> De los cisnes y el alma.
>
> *
>
> *— Un lago fue mi alma . . .—* (290)

[My soul is a lake; / lake, vessel of heaven, / nest of stars in the calm night, / goblet of the bird and of the flower, and ground / of the swans and the soul.

—My soul was a lake . . .—]

In the final lines of the poem, the writer's soul leaves behind the enabling glories of lakes, springs, streams, torrents, and seas and becomes a lowly, murky mudhole. She claims that the swampy mess barely remembers its original crystalline nature and that it has forgotten the music of the mermaids and the harmony of the roses:

> *—Y mi alma fue mar . . .—*
>
> Mi alma es un fangal;
> Llanto puso el dolor y tierra puso el mal.
> Hoy apenas recuerda que ha sido de cristal;
> No sabe de sirenas, de rosas ni armonía;

Nunca engarza una gema en el oro del día . . .
Llanto y llanto el dolor, y tierra y tierra el mal! . . .

*

—*Mi alma es un fangal;*

¿Dónde encontrar el alma que en su entraña sombría
Prenda como una inmensa semilla de cristal? (291)

[—*And my soul was a sea* . . .

My soul is a mudhole; / Crying contributed the pain and earth contributed the harm. / Today it barely remembers that it has been crystalline; / it does not know about mermaids, about roses or about harmony; it never sets a jewel in the gold of the day . . . / Crying and crying pain, earth and earth evil! . . .

*

—*My soul is a mudhole;*

Where to find the soul that in its dark entrails / may take root like an immense crystal seed?]

The comparison with the "palace of pearls," "path of diamonds," and melodious fountain of previous stanzas underscores how far she feels she has fallen. The slippery filth invokes the lowest levels of life, a phenomenal descent from the nearly divine status described earlier. The search for the soul that is able to nourish its supernatural abilities within its gloomy bowels makes palpable the struggle of the lyric voice. She aspires to carry within her the crystalline seed of creation despite the physicality of existence, the materiality of language, and the base attractions of the flesh. She continues to search for the soul that can return to its original potential and that can diminish the bleak impact of events that have lead her to the brink of the abyss. Though this "spiritual diary" reveals the corrosive presence of death and failure, it pulls back from absolute despondency with the formulation of the final question.

The fall from grace is further developed in "Serpentina" (Serpentine) (294–95), a poem that confronts Christian dualism within an inventive take on the Garden of Eden. The female speaker is no longer the naive, seducible Eve but the seductive serpent that slinks into demonic control. Though she usurps male control through this most phallic of symbols, she does not relinquish her identification with female sexuality, nor does she eliminate the cognitive and intellectual side of transgression. Instead these images run together, melding male and female, body and mind, love and hate, good and evil. In the mélange of metaphors two stand out, the snake and the poet's tongue, both of which point to the appropriation of language as a key element in this oneiric self-portrait. The poem begins:

> En mis sueños de amor, ¡yo soy serpiente!
> Gliso y ondulo como una corriente;
> Dos píldoras de insomnio y de hipnotismo
> Son mis ojos; la punta del encanto
> Es mi lengua . . . ¡y atraigo como el llanto!
> Soy un pomo de abismo. (294)

[In my dreams of love, I am a serpent! / I glide and undulate like a current; / my eyes are two pills of sleeplessness / and hypnotism; the tip of enchantment / is my tongue . . . and I attract like tears! / I am a jar of abyss.]

The sleeplessness and hypnotic stare invoke her nights of writing, during which her charm is certainly her tongue, her speech, her language. She reasserts her ability to attract once again like the wail of mythical mermaids that had been silenced in "Diario espiritual" (291). She is the temptress that guides the way to the abyss and that contains within herself the erogenous power of both sexes. She is a dark, deep vial ("pomo de abismo") and a phallic snake. The third stanza clarifies this androgynous intent with the word "vaina," which exposes phonetically its origin in the Latin "vagina." The lyric voice refers to her body as the "sheath" of the bolt of lightning and affirms in this amazing image her defiant enthusiasm for erotic contact:

> Y en mis sueños de odio, ¡soy serpiente!
> Mi lengua es una venenosa fuente;
> Mi testa es la luzbélica diadema,
> Haz de la muerte, en un fatal soslayo
> Son mis pupilas; y mi cuerpo en gema
> ¡Es la vaina del rayo! (294)

[And in my dreams of hate, I am a serpent! / My tongue is a poisonous fountain; / My head is the satanic tiara, / my eyes are, in a fatal obliqueness, / a bundle of death; and my jeweled body / is the sheath of the bolt of lightning!]

She becomes a serpentine monster in her dreams of hate because of her passions, tongue, demonic head, and evocation of death. She is a monstrous snake because she rejects restrictions, seeking to think and write free of all gender-related limitations and remaining an emphatically sexual woman. The poem concludes with her assertion of self, sexuality, and poetry in the rhythmic and sensual vibrations of her being:

> Si así sueño mi carne, así es mi mente:
> Un cuerpo largo, largo de serpiente,
> Vibrando eterna, ¡voluptuosamente! (295)

> [If I dream of my flesh in this way, this is the way that my mind is: / A long, long body of a serpent, / vibrating eternally, voluptuously!]

The deadliness of this daring unconventionality takes center stage in the next poem.

In "Sobre una tumba cándida" (Over a white grave) (296) Agustini addresses a woman, most certainly a poet, possibly herself. This modified sonnet opens with the information that "she" has died. The lyric voice responds that she does not understand, capturing the sense of irreality that often overcomes real-life recipients of bad news: "«Ha muerto . . . ha muerto» . . . dicen tan claro que no entiendo. . . ." ("She has died . . . she has died," they say so clearly that I do not understand . . .). This numb, imprecise response continues into the exclamation of the second line with its open-ended use of the infinitive and with the undefined "gentle liquor" and "container": "¡Verter licor tan suave en vaso tan tremendo! . . ." (To pour such a delicate liquor into such an enormous vessel! . . .). Is Agustini lamenting that the deceased's sweet soul pours out of her mortal body into the vast container of the universe? Is her reference more specifically poetic? Does the tender liquid of her soul flow toward transcendence in the same way it had into her art? This delicate ambiguity introduces the interplay of death, salvation, divinity, and art, a deliberate melding developed in the remaining lines. The focus of the poem passes from the "I" of the first line to the deceased female "you," who repeats the behavior and gestures of the lyric voice from earlier poems. These echoes suggest that the woman who has died is actually the speaker's alter ego:

> Tal vez fue un mal extraño tu mirar por divino,
> Tu alma por celeste, o tu perfil por fino . . .

Tal vez fueron tus brazos dos capullos de alas . . .
Eran cielo a tu paso los jardines, las salas,
Y te asomaste al mundo dulce como una muerta!
Acaso tu ventana quedó una noche abierta,
—¡Oh, tentación de alas una ventana abierta!—

¡Y te sedujo un ángel por la estrella más pura . . .
Y tus alas abrieron, y cortaron la altura
En un tijereteo de luz y de candor!

Y en la alcoba que tu alma tapizaba de armiño,
Donde ardían los vasos de rosas de cariño,
La Soledad llamaba en silencio al Horror . . . (296)

[Perhaps it was a strange malady your watching for what is divine / your soul for what is celestial, or your profile for what is fine . . .

Perhaps your arms were two buds of wings . . . / the gardens, the rooms, were heaven along your way, / and you showed up at the world sweet, like a dead woman! / Perhaps your window remained open one night, / —Oh, temptation of wings, an open window!—

And an angel seduced you by the purest star . . . / and your wings opened, and cut the height / in a scissoring action of light and purity!

And in the bedroom that your soul upholstered in ermine, / where the vessels of roses of affection were burning, / loneliness was calling to Horror in silence . . .]

Images of previous poems reappear in the other's elaborately decorated bedroom, the window that opens to the night sky, her wings and ascent, and, ultimately, her loneliness, silence, horror, and death. The seductive "angel" of the tenth line is a variation on the many spiritual/poetic guides and mentors of early works. It also provides an illuminating contrast with the diabolic snake of the previous poem. If the lyric voice in "Serpentina" is tainted by evil because of her break with acceptability, her alter ego can be eulogized now that she is dead. Stepping back from the defiant anger and erotic energy that characterize "Serpentina," Agustini presents the fatal attraction of unconventional behavior as a search for transcendence: "Tal vez fue un mal extraño tu mirar por divino" (l. 3). The seductive angel/lover/mentor/poet of the ninth line allows her soul to take flight, a process that is captured in the spectacular metaphor in which her ascent shortens the heights of heaven as her beating wings, in a scissorlike action of light and innocence, move upward. Her ascent, however, is choppy, a "tijereteo," or a clumsy cutting with scissors, and her bedroom is covered in white like the frozen figures of the aged lovers of earlier collections. The earthbound materiality, loneliness, silence, and horror of the last line are the ultimate reality of the poem. Her mortality is emotional, spiritual, and poetic; it is a silencing of her aspirations on all these levels. Thus, in the context of sublime intentions Agustini pulls the reader back to the stifling limitations imposed by conventionality and daily life.

These tensions between inclusion and exclusion and between the glories of success and the agonies of creative endeavors seldom disappear. They are, however, particularly salient in the next poem, "Mi plinto" (My plinth) (297–98), which draws upon architectural imagery to describe the process of building a literary career. As abstract as the references appear to be, the possessive adjective of the title and the assertion of the first person singular in the final phrase make this poem all about the aspirations of the lyric voice:

> Es creciente, diríase
> Que tiene una infinita raíz ultraterrena . . .
> Lábranlo muchas manos
> Retorcidas y negras,
> Con muchas piedras vivas . . .
> Muchas oscuras piedras
> Crecientes como larvas.
>
> Como al impulso de una omnipotente araña
> Las piedras crecen, crecen;
> Las manos labran, labran,
>
> > —Labrad, labrad, ¡oh manos!
> > Creced, creced, ¡oh piedras!
> > Ya me embriaga un glorioso
> > Aliento de palmeras.
>
> Ocultas entre el pliegue más negro de la noche,
> Debajo del rosal más florido del alba,
> Tras el bucle más rubio de la tarde,
> Las tenebrosas larvas
> De piedra, crecen, crecen,

Las manos labran, labran,
Como capullos negros
De infernales arañas.

   —Labrad, labrad, ¡oh manos!
   Creced, creced, ¡oh, piedras!
   Ya me abrazan los brazos
   De viento de la sierra.

Van entrando los soles en la alcoba nocturna,
Van abriendo las lunas el silencio de nácar . . .

   Tenaces como ebrias
   De un veneno de araña
   Las piedras crecen, crecen,
   Las manos labran, labran.

   —Labrad, labrad, ¡oh, manos!
   Creced, creced, ¡oh, piedras!
   ¡Ya siento una celeste
   Serenidad de estrella! (297–98)

[It is growing, one would say / that it has an infinite, unearthly root . . . / Many hands, twisted and black, build it / with many living stones . . . / Many dark stones / growing like larvae.

As if upon the urge of an omnipotent spider / the stones grow, grow; / the hands build, build,

—Build, build, oh hands! / Grow, grow, oh stones! / a glorious breath of palm trees / is already making me drunk.

Hidden within the blackest fold of the night, / beneath the floweriest rose-bush of the dawn, / behind the blondest ringlet of the afternoon, / the gloomy larvae / of stone, grow, grow, / the hands build, build, / like black cocoons / of infernal spiders.

—Build, build oh hands! / Grow, grow, oh stones! / The arms of the mountain wind / already embrace me.

The suns are entering the nocturnal bedroom, / the moons are opening the pearly silence . . .

Tenacious as if drunk / with a spider's poison / the stones grow, grow, / the hands build, build.

—Build, build, oh hands! / Grow, grow, oh stones! / I already feel a star's celestial serenity!]

Word by word, poem by poem, book by book, Agustini's artistic edifice grows from its "infinita raíz ultraterrena." While its base may be other-worldly, even divine, the construction is carried out by black, twisted hands overshadowed by dark, nightmarish elements. These images pull the poem and the poet's work between fear and hope, between horror and delight, between damnation and salvation. Though the poem ends with a metaphoric breakthrough of light, calm, and achievement, the terrify-ing nature of each of the figurative building blocks dominates. The fears are the same as those that have appeared throughout previous collections. She works under the imposing presence of an "omnipotent spider." This all-powerful and menacing weaver (of words?) stands in for the maddening drive to create in spite of the intractability of language and the standards of excellence pursued. Under its influence she demands that the stones accu-mulate. In return she asserts her faith in her future glory. Notwithstanding the upward thrust of the living stones, the restless discomfort of being a poet remains as vibrant as the final consolation of vision and insight.

These contradictions continue in "En el camino" (On the road) (300). More significant, in "En el camino" Agustini offers her final reflection on the male other who has been central to her erotic and artistic self. She presents a poem in which Darío as mentor, amorous partner, and poetic model reemerges as the dominant force in her pursuit of literary aspira-tions. She rewrites Darío's "Melancolía" (286), a metapoetic tour de force, from *Cantos de vida y esperanza* (1905).[11] She builds upon his images of illumi-nation and darkness, religious brotherhood, medieval vestments, and the uncertain path toward artistic insight. She repeats his sense of inadequacy as he faces the burden of poetic responsibility. But more than anything she emphasizes the frustration she feels at living in his shadow:

> Yo iba sola al Misterio bajo un sol de locura,
> Y tú me derramaste tu sombra, peregrino;
> Tu mirada fue buena como una senda oscura,
> Como una senda húmeda que vendara el camino.
>
> Me fue pródiga y fértil tu alforja de ternura:
> Tuve el candor del pan, y la llama del vino;

Mas tu alma en un pliegue de su astral vestidura,
Abrojo de oro y sombra se llevó mi destino.

Mis manos, que tus manos abrigaron, ya nunca
Se enfriarán, y guardando la dulce malla trunca
De tus caricias ¡nunca podrán acariciar! . . .

En mi cuerpo, una torre de recuerdo y espera
Que se siente de mármol y se sueña de cera,
Tu Sombra logra rosas de fuego en el hogar;
Y en mi alma, un castillo desolado y sonoro
Con pátinas de tedio y humedades de lloro,
¡Tu Sombra logra rosas de nieve en el hogar! (300)

[I was going alone to Mystery beneath a sun of madness, / and you spilled your shadow on me, pilgrim; / your gaze was good like a dark path, / like a humid path that would bandage the road.

Your saddlebag of tenderness was, to me, generous and fruitful: / I received the purity of the bread, and the flame of the wine; / but your soul in the fold of its astral vestment, / thistle of gold and shadow took away my destiny.

My hands, that your hands kept warm, will no longer / get cold, and keeping the sweet truncated mesh / of your caresses they will never be able to caress! . . .

In my body, a tower of memory and waiting / felt to be of marble and dreamed to be of wax, / your Shadow achieves fiery roses in its hearth; / and in my soul, a desolate and resonant castle / with patinas of boredom and moistness of crying, / your Shadow achieves snowy roses in its hearth!]

Here, the lyric voice pursues the "Mystery" of the divine mission that defines her existence. She sets out toward it, on her own, beneath a "burning sun of insanity," that is, the blinding passion of her inner calling. She struggles to find her way and to achieve her destiny, but her encounter with her fellow pilgrim alters her fate. At first he appears to come to her aid, but his actions are equivocal. He shades her from the unforgiving light of the sun, but he also covers her in a shadow that darkens her path. His "tender" generosity provides support and facilitates her growth and creativity. He offers her the sacrament of bread and wine that would sustain and consecrate their common task, but ultimately he robs her of what she had hoped to achieve. She recognizes in the astral garment of his soul the divinity she sought for herself, but he stops her from attaining her life goals, robbing her of her destined greatness.

Despite his apparent cruelty she seeks an ongoing amorous exchange. Even their caress is riddled with ambivalence. His hands keep hers warm, but his touch becomes a tightly woven metal mesh, which stops her from receiving all future caresses. Worse still, the waxy malleability with which she dreamed of addressing her memories and desires becomes hardened, the type of inflexible structure Agustini's lyric voice would reject throughout her work. The speaker's soul holds a dark, dank, gloomy castle, like the tower from which she sought to escape in "¡Oh tú!" (229–30) from *Los cálices vacíos*. His influence and the authority of his vision take over, casting a shadow that prevents her from finding her way. Agustini sets out to follow her aspirations and to find a mentor in the supreme poet of the day, initially viewing his work as a guiding light. She finds at this moment, however, that she cannot strike out on her own. Instead, she succumbs to a sense of weakness and defeat, ironically turning once again to the language of passion and the images of love to define this loss. The roses of fire cool and become roses of snow.

How much of this weariness is tied to the painful end of Agustini's relationship with Reyes will remain unknown, but there can be no doubt that "En el camino" and *Los astros del abismo* as a whole offer a review of the hard choices she made. Rather than affirming a reconciliation with the difficulties she opted to meet head on, Agustini presents one disturbing vision after another. She examines the implications of challenging convention and seeking participation in the exclusive men's club of sexual privilege and poetic self-expression. Neither love nor art offers unfailing joy and peace. Moreover, a careful reading of this final volume reveals how the trajectory that began in earnest in *El libro blanco (Frágil)* finds its conclusion. It is a conclusion colored by her awareness of the entrenched resistance to social, linguistic, and cultural change as well as by the sense that all artistic innovation, regardless of quality or worth, is a Sisyphean task in which those on the top wind up on the bottom as others strive to supersede earlier breakthroughs. The weariness and resignation in these texts reflect the accumulated fatigue she felt as she continued to face personal and artistic frustrations and disappointments. Death creeps into these poems as a result of this exhaustion and the ever-increasing awareness that all memories fade and all models recede. At the same time, however, Agustini continues to express a poignant longing for something greater than herself, a desire that was one of the defining features of modernismo and its faith in the transcendence of art. In this endeavor she does nothing less than take on the master of modern Hispanic verse and one of his central conceits. The erotic other is the substance of art that must be lured into becoming the perfect creative partner.

By failing to recognize in Agustini's writings the language of poetic desire and productivity, critics have misread her dramatic statements about art and artistic responsibility and have diminished her complex, powerful, intelligent work. They have ignored her revolutionary engagement with the dominant male discourse and its standard bearer, Darío. By claiming her poetry to be the unexpected confession of a proper young woman they have denied it the seriousness that similar statements of desire by male writers are accorded. Barbara Johnson, in an article on Baudelaire and Marceline Desbordes-Valmore, elucidates a parallel situation: "When men employ the rhetoric of self-torture, it is *read* as rhetoric. When women employ it, it is confession. Men are read rhetorically; women literally. Yet within the poetic tradition, it is the rhetorical, not the literal, that is taken seriously" (123). She goes on to clarify: "Rhetoric, in other words, is a way of shifting the domain of a poem's meaning to a higher, less referential, more abstract and theoretical level. And this is done by universalizing, that is, by denying the presence of the sexual difference out of which the poem springs" (124).

I have read Agustini rhetorically without ignoring that her sex and sexuality inform all her poetic decisions. To reclaim the metaphorical dimension of Agustini's poetry is to recognize her participation in the community of modernista writers and how she cleverly takes full advantage of every opportunity that comes her way. She responds to modernismo's embrace of the irrational, the spiritual, the beautiful, and the antiutilitarian. She finds favorable options via the inroads made by progressive ideas that operated in opposition to the conservative, hegemonic, and patriarchal premises that continued to dominate Spanish America well into the twentieth century. She exploits to great artistic advantage the sexual language as well as the sexual tensions of her day. Yet her greatest accomplishment is her relationship with Darío and his texts. She turns what might have been a paralyzing presence into a source of originality and poetic power. This book reveals the majesty of her verse and provides insight into the process of poetic influence, the development of literary movements, and the way in which writers align themselves with and struggle against dominant linguistic patterns.

Agustini's poetry became a model for women who followed her. Her successors were drawn to her writing because Agustini breaks with what would normally be expected of women writers; she does not hold back. Agustini does not alter her vision to conform to conventional society. Yet there is something at work that is much like what Johnson indicates with regard to Desbordes-Valmore. Though on many levels Agustini does not try to fit into the preconceived notion of proper femininity, her most public persona is that of "la nena," the typical, infantilized female. Whereas Desbordes-Valmore rewrites her life to present a more palatable version of herself to her male contemporaries (112), Agustini is willing to risk disapproval by rejecting the sociocultural and literary restrictions against women writers. She does not marginalize or censor her poetic persona. These bold options were made possible by the unusual personal and social circumstances in which she found herself in turn-of-the-century Montevideo, as I showed in chapter 1. Her risk taking turned her into a celebrated figure at the time and afterward, saving her from the fate of more conservative writers whose work has remained buried in libraries and newspaper archives. Nevertheless, her end leaves no doubt that her choices, which inevitably joined her personal and professional goals in an inextricable tangle of hopes and expectations, were fraught with danger.

Besides the type of critical prejudice outlined by Johnson, there were other factors that made Agustini's creative daring take a backseat to more literal readings of her erotic and sadomasochistic images and her poetic reflections on pain and death. Though she participated in the literary circles of the day, her lack of critical statements about her own writing and about the authors she was reading created the impression that she was a natural, intuitive, spontaneous poet. Her acceptance of the mantle of childlike innocence, found even in her personal correspondence with Enrique Job Reyes, supported this perspective, one that fit nicely into the patriarchal view of women as the unformed, raw material of artistic production and of men as the forgers of serious accomplishments and culture. Her premature death allowed others to take even greater control over the way in which her words would be interpreted. They softened her dynamic confrontation with established discursive modes and hid the power of her reconfiguration of the sense that she, like others of her generation, lived in the wake of an incomparable artist. Yet now, one hundred years after her death, Agustini's verse is read no longer as a curiosity but for its linguistic and conceptual richness. Readers can now recognize the inspired models for self-empowerment and self-reflection in her startlingly dramatic images. She ties the poet's struggles with a commanding predecessor to the language of sexual seduction and vampiric conquest and imagines the fading of traditions in terms of the ebb and flow of erotic desire and the natural passage of time. The issues that reside at the core of her inventiveness are not limited to women writers, but her gender and the sexual conceits with which she chose to rebel against personal and professional restrictions have converted her into a type of founding matriarch.

The legacy that is recognized by younger women poets is the direct and assertive confrontation with and challenge to the language that had defined women for centuries as being incapable of intelligent, active engagement in artistic endeavors. These poetic possibilities were further reinforced by sociopolitical developments. As Vicky Unruh acknowledges in the introduction to her insightful *Performing Women and Modern Literary Culture in Latin America,* by the 1920s women were active and acknowledged participants in cultural change. They had come to view themselves

> as part of the action and their writing as an assertive intervention in public cultural life. Many undertook a critical dialogue with modern male writers or embraced a vanguard conception of artistic work as a dynamic cultural engagement. But as these women imagined themselves as instigators for change rather than its muses, they unleashed penetrating critiques of projects for social or artistic modernization, including—but by no means exclusively—their casting of women. (2-3)

This changing context led to changes in language, style, and strategies for inclusion in the society of artists. While the poetry of the twentieth century has been characterized by ever-greater defiance and the struggle for participation by all previously invisible and silenced groups, not all engagement was openly aggressive. An early figure like Gabriela Mistral adopted a tentative approach. Mistral chose not to assail the status quo directly, hiding many key elements of her life, including her homosexuality. She opted instead for a conservative stance, a language that is saturated with religiosity and a tone that is often solemn and didactic. Her rebellion against the oppression that has restricted the purview and power of women and minorities drew strength from conventional views of women. Her exaltation of maternity as a noble, visionary, and dynamic enterprise—tied to the earth and issues of national significance—reworked traditional images to redress inequities. Mistral's activism on behalf of children and education went hand in hand with her warm and embracing verse. At the same time, however, the destructive implications of unjust sociocultural conventions surface in the violence scattered throughout her writing and in the doubly potent figure of the Mater Dolorosa.[12] As Margaret Bruzelius shows, Mistral links motherhood and suffering in the figure of the Virgin Mary "to address female experience and summon to her side a cultural authority that allowed her to speak as a woman" (281). Her success was reflected in the worldwide attention and acclaim she received, acclaim that culminated in her being awarded the Nobel Prize in Literature in 1945.

The younger Alfonsina Storni, like Agustini, declared her awareness that feminine independence and rebellion are perceived to be "monstrous," and she too wrote openly about her sexuality and erotic desires. The language she used, however, is different. Moving away from modernista flourishes, her verse drew upon everyday, conversational speech and parody. She cultivated an angry, defiant poetry that rejected the roles women had been forced to accept and the damage that those roles inflicted upon them. In countless poems she attacked sexual inequalities, criticized women's dependence on men, ridiculed the double standard of patriarchal society, and denounced the hypocrisy that surrounded her. In articles she publicly promoted women's rights and attacked the gender injustices that continued despite sociopolitical advances in her native Argentina. Both her prose and her poetry directly and emphatically asserted her impatience with patriarchal rules and expectations that resisted the forces of modernization. In the words of María Rosa Olivera-Williams, Storni's work revealed her assault on "the unfairness of phallic power" (160). Her rejection of convention extended, toward the end of her life, to the form and structure of poetry, an aspect of her work evident in her creation of dense, fourteen-line unrhymed poems which she called antisonnets.[13]

Mistral and Storni are just two of the poets who, while influenced by Agustini, took her legacy in different directions. Well into the twentieth century, as changing expectations, patterns, and laws chipped away at inequality and injustice, women writers continued to turn to Agustini as a model of defiant creativity in the ongoing struggle against patriarchal arrangements and linguistic conventions. Both Olga Orozco (b. 1920) and Alejandra Pizarnik (b. 1936), for example, take up Agustini's concerns about participation in a literary world that remains dominated by men and male discourse. A related area of interest for both poets, as it was for Agustini, is the poet's relationship with tradition. Even younger writers such as Irene Gruss (b. 1950), Tamara Kamenszain (b. 1947), Diana Bellessi (b. 1946), María del Carmen Colombo (b. 1950), and Mirta Rosenberg (b. 1951) acknowledge the impact of Agustini's verse.

While her poetry is a model for women writers, it also highlights one of the fundamental reasons for modernismo's pivotal place in Spanish American literature. The modernistas were the first generation of Spanish Americans to confront the radical changes wrought by the arrival of modern life. To a great degree their anxieties continue to undergird contemporary concerns. They struggled with the alterations brought on by the ever-greater incorporation of their nations into the world economy and world capitalism, by the erosion of traditional values (spiritual, aesthetic, social, and so on), and shifting political structures within their own nations and across the globe. They were also the first generation to appreciate the intractability and uncertainty of language. They suffered from a sense of belatedness as they acknowledged the great models they sought to emulate. At the same time, they rushed to assert their originality, their modernity, and their unique vision as Spanish Americans.

Agustini was sensitive to all of these issues, but the ones she felt on an intimate, virtually somatic level were those related to the place and role of women. The visceral intensity of her response made it easy to read her work as the consequence of unobscured passion. In comparison, Darío's erotically charged poetry appears coolly distant, filtered through the language and images of ancient myths and sophisticated museums. Agustini's engagement with Darío and the embedded patriarchal perspective of his verse is, as a result, the product of an ambitious, inventive poet who was also aware that modernization required a reevaluation of gender-related expectations as much as it necessitated other readjustments. Modernismo's contestatory stance opened the door to Agustini's complex exploration of life, language, desire, and poetic legacy. The incomparable brilliance of Darío's poetry guided Agustini as she created a new way to be a modernista poet.

NOTES

Chapter One. Agustini and Her World

1. All translations are mine, unless otherwise noted.

2. This aspect of her work has not gone totally unnoticed. Jorge Luis Castillo, for example, focuses on what he calls Agustini's "subversive *modernismo*," while many of the pieces in Escaja's *Delmira Agustini y el Modernismo: Nuevas propuestas de género* tackle Agustini's confrontational dialogue with both social and literary traditions. Of particular note in this regard are the articles by Lasarte, Bosteels, Kirkpatrick, and Ehrick.

3. The full quotation in Spanish is "Delmira Agustini es, sin duda, la figura más problemática de la literatura uruguaya; y probablemente de la poesía hispanoamericana. No en cuanto a los valores de su poesía misma, ya reconocidos unánimemente por la crítica, entre los más altos de la lírica de nuestra lengua, sino en cuanto a la personalidad de la poetisa" (Silva, *Pasión*, 7).

4. The various masks worn by Agustini have been studied as a function of both her life choices and her poetic discourse. See Varas's *Las máscaras del Delmira Agustini* and Girón Alvarado's *Voz poética y máscaras femeninas en la obra de Delmira Agustini*. Taking a different tack, Eleonora Cróquer Pedrón has presented an exploration of the way Agustini allowed herself to be represented in the press. She sees in these images "una doble mecánica de exhibición y control" (191). More recently, in her insightful study *Performing Women and Modern Literary Culture in Latin America: Intervening Acts*, Vicky Unruh turns to the concept of performance to examine how the next generation of women authors negotiated their literary

personae and their writing projects. Unruh explores how the women writing in the 1920s and 1930s, not unlike Agustini before them, had to negotiate competing perspectives about literature, politics, and gender and how, despite their creativity and independence, they could not fully escape the cultural scripts they inherited (8).

The creative works that have focused on Agustini are the novels *Una mujer inmolada* by Vicente Salaverri (1914), *Un amor imprudente* by Pedro Orgambide (1994), *Fiera de amor: La otra muerte de Delmira Agustini* by Guillermo Giucci (1995), *Delmira* by Omar Prego Gadea (1996), and *Tan extraña, tan querida* by Raquel Minoli (2000). A play by Milton Schinca, *Delmira y otras rupturas*, was published in 1977. In addition, there is Carlos Martínez Moreno's *La otra mitad*, which links the fate of one his characters with that of the murdered poet (see, in particular, 156–212).

5. Carlos Real de Azúa points to a complex of philosophic currents as background to the development of the doctrine of free love, which was endorsed by a number of contemporaneous writers. He states, "Un complejo de corrientes, en verdad ya muy mencionadas en estas páginas: el determinismo materialista, el escepticismo, el nihilismo ético, el amoralismo nietzscheano, el esteticismo, la concepción decimonánica de la libertad, suscitó hacia fin de siglo—con abundante ilustración en la literatura—cierta divinización del impulso erótico y genésico sin trabas, muy diverso, sin embargo, de la trascendente pasión romántica encarnada en las grandes figuras de 1820 y 1830. Lo que le peculiarizó entonces, en la doctrina del *amor libre*, fué un sesgo político-social de protesta contra la regla burguesa y de desafío a las convenciones de la generalidad" (33).

6. The original Spanish reads as follows: "Para este grupo la experiencia fundamental fué el *Modernismo*. El cambio en la sensibilidad vital . . . estaba indicado explícitamente por el contenido de *Prosas profanas* y *Los raros* (ambos de 1896). Los jóvenes del 900 captaron ese cambio y apuraron en sus primeras obras su ansia de nuevas fórmulas, de nuevas rutas, de nuevos maestros" (48–49).

7. The original Spanish reads as follows: "En sentido absoluto no hay ningún caudillo en el grupo, lo que por otra parte, está de perfecto acuerdo con el culto de la propia personalidad, con el individualismo acrático, del *Modernismo*. Hay, en cambio, un modelo o paradigma, ante quien oscilaron los escritores del grupo entre la aceptación plena y el desvío consciente: Rubén Darío" (52). Also under "Generational Language," Rodríguez Monegal underscores the consistency derived from *Modernismo*. "Beyond the variety of styles, the unity of *style* is evident. The language is that of *Modernismo*, with all that that word implies about renovation of the modes of expression, about linguistic transformation, and about verbal imagery" (53). The original Spanish of this section is, "Por encima de la variedad de estilos, se acusa la unidad de *estilo*. Su lenguaje es el del *Modernismo*, con lo que la voz implica de renovación de los medios expresivos, de transformación idiomática, de imaginería verbal" (53).

8. In this literary evolution Agustini's poetry shows a remarkable coincidence with the work of Rachilde (Rachilde is the nom de plume of the French author Marguerite Vallette-Eymery [1860–1953]), most notably *La marquise de Sade*, which was published in 1887. As

Rita Felski, in her now-classic study *The Gender of Modernity*, indicates, this novel contains an interplay of female pleasure and power with the deliberate infliction of suffering. More important, the structuring principle is seduction. Seduction provides women with the power to subjugate and destroy men and is "intimately linked to, rather than severed from, hierarchical dynamics of power and the articulation of sadistic desire" (186–90). This coincidence highlights, as I will note throughout this study, how consistently Spanish American modernismo paralleled European literary responses to modernity and modernization. In this case, it further highlights the often unwitting similarity between the ways women writers on both sides of the Atlantic confronted gendered social roles and literary conceptions during the period of the *fin de siècle*. See Bruzelius's insightful article on this coincidence.

9. For biographical information I am indebted to a number of sources. The chapter on Agustini included in *Mujeres uruguayas: El lado femenino de nuestra historia* written by Ana Inés Larre Borges summarizes the major events of her life, linking her publications with her personal experiences and activities. María-Elena Barreiro de Armstrong in *Puente de luz: Eros, eje de la estructura pendular en "Los cálices vacíos" de Delmira Agustini* makes the case that in order to understand the myth that has developed around Agustini it is necessary to understand her life, works, and context. The following sources provide additional details: Tina Escaja's *Salomé decapitada*, Magdalena García Pinto's introduction to her edition of Agustini's *Poesías completas*, Clara Silva's two studies, *Pasión y gloria de Delmira Agustini* and *Genio y figura de Delmira Agustini*, Renée Scott's "Delmira Agustini: Portraits and Reflections," Patricia Varas's *Las máscaras de Delmira Agustini*, and Prego Gadea's novel *Delmira*, which focuses on the tragedy of her death.

10. The various studies by Aníbal Barrios Pintos on the development of Montevideo document the push toward a modern, European way of life and the creation of wide avenues and impressive public buildings, theaters, plazas, parks, and monuments.

11. The contrast between the manuscripts in Agustini's own hand and those recopied by her father is startling. Thanks to Alejandro Cáceres I have been able to examine these manuscripts in detail. Agustini's are barely legible, and her father's appear to be the work of a calligrapher.

12. Clara Silva states, "Delmira no concurre de niña, a ningún colegio público ni privado. Su única maestra es su propia madre de quien recibe toda la instrucción primaria de la época. Hacia 1902, estudia el francés con Mlle. Madelaine Casey (de enero a abril) y prosigue sus estudios con el profesor Willems, francés, hasta el año 1905. . . . En 1903 comienza a estudiar el piano con Mme. Bemporat y luego prosigue con el profesor Martín López, hasta completar el sexto año. Estudia también pintura con el profesor Domingo Laporte. En el estudio de este pintor conoce a André Giot De Badet, joven como ella, más tarde escritor franco-uruguayo, vinculado a Delmira hasta su muerte" (*Pasión* 10).

13. The original Spanish reads as follows: "Un rasgo sumamente característico de este grupo es que (con la excepción de Vaz Ferreira) sus integrantes no fueron universitarios. En otra oportunidad he señalado este divorcio, indicando que las vinculaciones de sus componentes con la Universidad fueron tenues y azarosas. En efecto, la mayoría de ellos, no

logró títulos universitarios. . . . Frente a la cultura universitaria floreció a fines del siglo la cultura adquirida paciente o penosamente en el libro, con entusiasmo y distracción en la mesa de café y en el exaltado ambiente de los cenáculos. Los escritores del 900 fueron en realidad autodidactos" (45).

Carlos Real de Azúa concludes his impressive analysis of the diverse influences that came to form the "spiritual atmosphere of the Generation of 1900" with the following assertion regarding the generation's self-instruction: "La Universidad iberoamericana se halló en esos años relativamente ausente del proceso creador de la cultura. Asumieron los autodidactos el papel protagónico de la renovación intelectual; tuvieron en la peña del café—completada a veces con la mal provista biblioteca—el natural sucedáneo de la clase, del foro y del desaparecido salón." He goes on to comment, "En realidad, en países como los nuestros, faltos de una tradición cultural cabal, con sus zonas forzosamente esotéricas o simplemente difíciles, la autodidaccia o la formación universitaria no presentan la misma diferencia que asumen en otras partes" (36).

14. Scott mentions an engagement to Amancio D. Solliers, whom she describes as a journalist and literary dandy from the state of Minas, in 1906. According to her, this relationship lasted only one year (262).

15. The original Spanish reads as follows: "Lo más próximo que tiene Delmira como modelo de un auténtico y exótico príncipe de la poesía. Su imaginación teje pronto en torno a él una trama de pasiones" (60).

16. The original letter reads as follows: "Perdón si le molesto una vez más. Hoy he logrado un momento de calma en mi eterna exaltación dolorosa. Y éstas son mis horas más tristes. En ellas llego a la conciencia de mi inconsciencia. Y no sé si su neurastenia ha alcanzado nunca el grado de la mía. Yo no sé si usted ha mirado alguna vez la locura cara a cara y ha luchado con ella en la soledad angustiosa de un espíritu hermético. No hay, no puede haber sensación más horrible. Y el ansia, el ansia inmensa de pedir socorro contra todo—contra el mismo Yo, sobre todo—a otro espíritu mártir del mismo martirio. Acaso su voluntad, más fuerte necesariamente que la mía, no le dejará comprender jamás el sufrimiento de mi debilidad en lucha con tanto horror. Y en tal caso, si viviera usted cien años, la vida debía resultarle corta para reir [*sic*] de mi [*sic*]—si es que Darío puede reir [*sic*] de nadie—. Pero si por alguna afinidad mórbida llega usted a percibir mi espíritu, en el torbellino de mi locura, me tendrá usted la más profunda, la más afectuosa compasión que pueda sentir jamás.

"Piense usted que ni aún me queda la esperanza de la muerte, porque la imagino llena de horribles vidas. Y el derecho del sueño se me ha negado casi desde el nacimiento. Y la primera vez que desborda mi locura es ante usted. ¿Por qué? Nadie debió resultar más imponente a mi timidez. ¿Cómo hacerle crer [*sic*] en ella a usted, que sólo conoce la valentía de mi inconsciencia? Tal vez porque le reconocí más esencia divina que a todos los humanos tratados hasta ahora. Y por lo tanto más indulgencia. A veces me asusta mi osadía; a veces, ¿a qué negarlo?, me reprocho el desastre de mi orgullo. Me parece una bella estatua despedazada a sus pies. Sé que tal homenaje nada vale para usted, pero yo no puedo hacerlo más grande. A mediados de octubre pienso internar mi neurosis en un sanatorio, de dónde, bien o mal, saldré en noviembre o diciembre para casarme. He resuelto arrojarme al abismo medroso de casamiento. No sé: tal vez en el fondo me espera la felicidad. ¡La vida es tan rara! ¿Quiere usted dejar caer en un alma que acaso se aleja para siempre, una sola palabra paternal? ¿Quiere usted escribirme una vez más, aunque sea la última, para decirme solamente que no me desprecia?"

17. The original text reads as follows: "Cuando alguna señorita por inconstancia rechaza al novio (lo que sucede muy rara vez) alegando que no lo quiere, la mamá con ayuda de las casadas de la familia, se reúnen para persuadirla de que lo debe aceptar. En tono de firmísima convicción se le dice: 'Tú no tienes experiencias; tú no sabes; el cariño viene después. . . .' La cachondez en este punto no anda desorientada. Las señoritas son agradecidas. . . . Cuando prueban de ese dulce idolatran al esposo: 'A nosotros,' le dicen, 'que te aconsejamos, nos ha pasado lo que a ti; recién casadas hemos sabido lo que es amor. ¡Cásate, cásate; cuanto antes, hija mía!'" (138).

18. The original Spanish states, "De todas cuantas mujeres hoy escriben en verso ninguna ha impresionado mi ánimo como Delmira Agustini, por su alma sin velos y su corazón de flor" (qtd. in Agustini, *Poesías completas*, 223).

19. Alejandro Cáceres, in his "Doña María Murfeldt Triaca de Agustini: Hipótesis de un secreto," draws many interesting conclusions regarding the relationship between Enrique Job Reyes and Delmira based on the letter he wrote to her after their separation. Cáceres finds Reyes old-fashioned and sexually conservative, especially in comparison with Agustini, who, as stated in the letter, had begged to have sexual relations with him before marriage. More important, Cáceres emphasizes that part of the letter in which Reyes alludes to Delmira's mother's wish that she remain childless, concluding that his future mother-in-law requested on the day of the wedding that Reyes use some form of contraception. Whether Reyes found the request or the actual practice offensive is unclear, but he calls the entire conversation with Delmira's mother "monstrous revelations of impurity and dishonor" (revelaciones monstruosas de impureza y deshonor) (33). Cáceres further rejects the assumption that Delmira abandoned Reyes because of sexual dissatisfaction. He believes that her displeasure (the "vulgarity" she complained about) had something to do with Reyes's treatment of Delmira's mother or with Delmira's resentment of domestic chores.

20. The recent "Nation Building, International Travel, and the Construction of the Nineteenth-Century Pan-Hispanic Women's Network" by Leona S. Martin underscores the influence of women intellectuals in diverse areas of Latin America, their international network, which was supported by international travel, and their contribution to the nation-building project of the nineteenth century.

21. While women writers across the centuries responded to the restrictive roles they were supposed to assume, academic criticism, traditionally dominated by male scholars, was slower to expand its vision to include feminist perspectives. Just a few years ago the fundamentals of patriarchal tenets and discourse that today are so recognized came under scrutiny and formed the basis of critical innovation. The insights that began with the

breakthrough studies by Gilbert and Gubar (1979) have engendered countless works that have contributed to a fuller appreciation of the complexity of the achievements of women writers. For Spanish American modernismo, the most pertinent studies, in addition to the already mentioned contributions by Felski and Unruh, are the early essays by Sarah Castro-Klarén, Sylvia Molloy, and Beatriz Sarlo in their anthology *Women's Writing in Latin America* (1991), Debra Castillo's *Talking Back: Toward a Latin American Feminist Literary Criticism* (1992), Francine Masiello's *Between Civilization and Barbarism: Women, Nation, and Literary Culture in Modern Argentina* (1992), Doris Meyer's critical collection *Reinterpreting the Spanish American Essay: Women Writers of the 19th and 20th Centuries* (1995), and Jill Kuhnheim's *Gender, Politics, and Poetry in Twentieth-Century Argentina* (1996). Other studies that have influenced my thinking include Alicia Ostriker's *Stealing the Language: The Emergence of Women's Poetry in America* (1986), her *Writing like a Woman* (1983), and Kelly Oliver's *Subjectivity without Subjects: From Abject Fathers to Desiring Mothers* (1998).

22. In this regard, Felski explores how women were represented both as commodity and consumer, often becoming associated with the worst aspects of social change (61–90).

23. In 1996 Robert Jay Glickman, drawing upon a lifetime of research on modernismo, published a collection of these articles, first in a volume entitled *Vestales del Templo Azul: Notas sobre el feminismo hispanoamericano en la época modernista* and later in *Fin del siglo: Retrato de Hispanoamérica en la época modernista*. The breadth of these articles is impressive, and as a group they illustrate the points I have been making.

24. "Admitiendo, como admitimos nosotros, la igualdad de los sexos, no podemos negar a la mujer el mismo sentir del hombre. Sentada esta premisa, para nosotros importante, me pregunto: ¿podemos negar nosotros la misma libertad a la mujer de multiplicar sus sensaciones sexuales cohabitando con dos o más hombres? ¿Hoy nosotros, los emancipados, no nos sentimos aguijoneados por la necesidad de poseer dos o más mujeres? Pues bien, si admitimos esto, aceptemos también como lógico del deseo idéntico que pueda sentir la mujer.

"Contradecir este razonamiento significa que el sujeto que discute está todavía embebido en la vieja doctrina de la superioridad del macho sobre la desgraciada hembra" (originally published as "Del amor libre en la sociedad futura," in *Germen* in Buenos Aires, February 1908, reprinted in Glickman, *Fin del siglo*, 332).

25. "El puente levadizo, que cerraba la entrada de la mujer al palacio encantado del saber, del trabajo y de la fortuna, ha caído derribado para siempre por las exigencias de la época y la protección de los hombres" ("Las obreras . . . ," reprinted in Glickman, *Vestales*, 111).

26. "El día en que el varón se convenza de que la mujer ilustrada, lejos de ser inútil para el hogar, no sólo lo realza sino que su beneficio se hace extensivo hasta los que la rodean, tendremos leyes que nos protejan como las de los Estados Unidos de Norteamérica" ("La emancipación . . . ," reprinted in Glickman, *Vestales*, 106).

27. "La virilidad de una mujer está en dominar el sentimiento por la razón, y dar a la voluntad el señorío que le pertenece. Impresionabilidad e imaginación excesivas, y junto

con una sensibilidad demasiado desarrollada, inferioridad relativa de las facultades mentales, es la condición de la mujer. Conviene, por tanto, ejercitarla mucho en moderar el exceso y corregir el defecto" (262–63, qtd. in Caetano 266).

28. "Examine si cuida bien de su familia. Si trata al marido con cariño y humildad. Si ama a sus hijos con cariño excesivo, dejándolos vivir según sus caprichos, excúsandolos y defendiéndolos cuando el padre quiere castigarlos justamente. . . . Si ha resistido injustamente al marido y porfiado con él. Si ha malgastado el dinero en vanidades, galas y antojos. . . . Si en el traje, modo de hablar y proceder ha guardado el recato y la modestia convenientes. Si ha perdido el tiempo en visitas, conversaciones frívolas y murmuraciones" (*El Reparador de la Pasión*, 68, qtd. in Caetano 227).

29. "El 'desorden', la esencia del pecado para los católicos, era, en sustancia, la desobediencia al Padre, a Dios y sus reglas; la 'barbarie', la esencia del mal uruguayo para los liberales anticlericales, era, también en sustancia, una desobediencia, la del 'salvaje' a los dictados de la 'civilización'. Iglesia y Burguesía estuvieron de acuerdo en imponer a todos, incluyendo a sus propios integrantes, el disciplinamiento de las pulsiones, en otras palabras, en crear un tipo determinado de cultura y ese tipo concluyó enlazado de alguna manera con el modo de producción y el sector social dominante, por lo cual la impronta burguesa fue más definitoria que la eclesial" (23).

30. As Michael Aronna has shown, the language used to discuss these issues develops during the Enlightenment in thinkers like Immanuel Kant through their recourse to models drawn from the biological sciences. The metaphors of growth and maturation, through various intermediate steps and influences, are turned first into their inverse, the central trope of decay, degeneration, and decadence, and then into the broader one of disease (11–33). The policies and programs based on this way of thinking "permeated," as Aronna points out, "the private and public spheres, rigidifying and antagonizing relations between the sexes, social classes and ethnic groups" (11).

31. Though Masiello's study focuses on Argentina, the same tensions emerged, *mutatis mutandis*, throughout Spanish America.

32. This situation parallels what was happening in Europe. Felski, relying on Patricia Mills's *Dialectic of Enlightenment*, states, "An association of the feminine with the non-rational and the asymbolic does not allow for any independent conception of female identity, agency, or desire. Woman is reduced to the libidinal, inexpressible, or aesthetic, the repressed Other of patriarchal reason" (6–7).

33. In the first chapter of her *Las máscaras de Delmira Agustini,* Varas presents a number of theories that address the "changing and contradictory values" of the *fin de siglo* period. She also links the widely uneven development of Latin America to Agustini's personal and literary development (7–39).

34. Javier Lasarte Valcárcel is one of only a few critics to highlight the centrality of this ambivalence. He summarizes the situation as follows: "Sus búsquedas exhibirán un carácter fundamentalmente diversificado —y no pocas veces contradictorio, oscilante, ambiguo—. . . Será entonces el modernismo el lugar donde podrán leerse tanto los intentos

modernos de constituir una tradición y el auge de los nacionalismos literarios, como las críticas o reformulaciones de las viejas ideologías, las defensas culturalistas, los cosmopolitismos, las reivindicaciones del egoísmo y el del placer, o el nacimiento de la literatura social—de base con no poca frecuencia anarquista—. . . ; la incorporación, en fin, de otros actores" (38).

35. In this regard, the modernistas followed the lead of the English romantics, who imagined the prophetic powers of the poet in terms of the holy marriage of the mind (male) with the external universe (female), a union by which a vision of paradise is attained. "This 'great consummation' will nevertheless suffice to create the restored paradise predicted in the Apocalypse" (Abrams, *Natural Supernaturalism*, 28, 56).

36. "El otro, percibido como una amenaza al poder hegemónico, debe ser necesariamente controlado, anulado. Con tal fin son creados a partir de la segunda mitad del siglo XIX, con el auxilio de la ciencia y la religión, modelos culturales de mujer y ciudadano. . . . El conjunto de estas identidades marginales [la mujer, el inmigrante, el homosexual] contribuyó a desvigorizar la supremacía masculina en el aparato de poder y la virilidad como una de las causas esenciales de su dominio. La institución estatal de los 'tiempos modernos' no estaba dispuesta a dejar lugar para otro deseo que no fuera el masculino.

"El modernismo, en cambio, desde una postura que se expresa en contra del filisteísmo burgués encaramado en el poder, vuelve visible al otro, le ofrece, aunque condicionado, un espacio. . . . Asimismo, el carácter sexualizado que presenta la escritura modernista, especialmente en Uruguay, invita a todos por igual a mirar y participar en los tan atrayentes márgenes. Contra la corriente de prejuicios existentes en una sociedad que niega la sexualidad, surge una escritura de intenso contenido erótico que abre una vía de expresión artística a la mujer y al homosexual, dos 'sexualidades periféricas'" (260).

37. This work from 1979 brought the issue of gendered speech and imagery to the attention of the North American academic community and opened this productive line of inquiry.

38. "Las metáforas sexuales que configuran la poética de la novela realista contienen todos los elementos precisos para la comisión de un incesto: el autor es visto bajo la figura de un padre autoritario y todopoderoso; el personaje aparece como un hijo de carne y hueso; la virilidad es concebida como una de las virtudes esenciales en el desempeño de la autoría; la escritura es equiparada a un coito; finalmente, el personaje, hombre o mujer, es indefectiblemente feminizado" (55).

39. In a very brief article on Agustini, Darío, and the "gender-linked privileges of poetic creation," Patrick O'Connell also turns to Gubar's "'The Blank Page'" to help explicate the different perspectives adopted by these two modernista poets.

40. "Como cada palabra tiene un alma, hay en cada verso, además de la harmonía verbal, una melodía ideal. La música es sólo de la idea, muchas veces" (180). All quotes from Darío's collections of verse refer to the Ayacucho edition unless otherwise noted.

41. In "Mientras tenéis, oh negros corazones . . ." (258) the concluding apocalyptic vision

consoles the suffering poet, who is converted into a Christ-like figure. He leads his readers out of the imperfect present into an ideal future on the back of Pegasus.

42. Much of the critical attention directed toward "Sonatina" as well as "Era un aire suave . . ." has focused on the musicality referred to in their titles. Nevertheless, the role of music as a central poetic ideal linked to a transcendent, pure, unvarnished vision of the universe has tended to be overlooked. See Anderson Imbert, 78–81. O'Brien tends to trivialize the entire endeavor by continuing to read "Sonatina" as a manifesto of escapist poetry.

43. "Cada libro de poesía moderna, cada poema moderno, formula una poética propia, precisamente porque la Modernidad ha abandonado la poética como categoría autónoma que demarca un lenguaje y dicta sus reglas" ("Martí," 27).

44. While these observations will be developed more fully with regard to specific poems, it is worth noting at this point that feminist theory has continued to find mirror imagery a productive way to discuss women's interaction with the outside world. Julia Kristeva holds that seeing the self leads to self-awareness and self-consciousness. Kelly Oliver refines Kristeva's position by adding that it is through representation of that outside self that self-recognition takes place. She further states, "Because we can never adequately or completely represent ourselves, we keep trying, we keep talking" (97). Taking this perspective as a point of departure, W. Michael Mudrovic has made catoptric imagery the focus of his recent *Mirror, Mirror on the Page: Identity and Subjectivity in Spanish Women's Poetry (1975–2000)*.

45. One of the many uncanny metaphoric coincidences is the appearance of the "swan-like supernatural white life" in Elizabeth Barrett Browning's *Aurora Leigh* (Gilbert and Gubar, 18).

46. The story of Lot is told in the Old Testament (Genesis 11–14, 19). He was the son of Haran, who was the brother of Abraham, the progenitor of the Hebrew people. After years of neighborly relations, Lot and Abraham separated and staked out individual grazing lands. As a resident of the sinful city of Sodom, Lot was visited by two angels who warned him to flee that city in the face of its impending destruction. The townspeople demanded that Lot give up these two visitors. Believing such actions to be against the law of God, he offered his two daughters instead. The townspeople were angered by the suggestion of such an exchange, prompting God to punish the city by unleashing a rain of fire that destroys the entire city. Although warned not to look back as they leave, "Lot's wife behind him looked back, and she became a pillar of salt" (Genesis 19:26). Surrounded by ruin, Lot and his two daughters fled to a cave in the mountains. Believing that they were the sole survivors of the human race, the daughters were determined to save humanity. On successive evenings they got their father drunk and mated with him, producing Moab, the father of the Moabites, and Ben-am'mi, the father of the children of Ammon.

47. Felski also discusses seduction as a mechanism used by women to overcome powerlessness and to subjugate and destroy men (189–93).

48. King Shahryar, in reprisal for his first wife's betrayal, would marry, possess, and execute a new wife every day. This pattern continued until three thousand women had been

killed and until he was stopped by Scheherazade's storytelling. Despite her father's desires and the threat of death, Scheherazade asked to spend the night with the king. Under the pretense of saying good-bye to her sister, she recounted a story with such grace that the king stayed awake, spellbound by what he was hearing. At dawn he asked for another story, but Scheherazade said he would have to wait until the following evening. As a result, the king kept Scheherazade alive night after night, until three sons had been born, one thousand and one stories had been told, and the king had been educated by Scheherazade, who became his queen. Eliana S. Rivero, in "Scheherazade Liberated: *Eva Luna* and Women Storytellers," emphasizes the importance of this figure as a type of model for women writers.

49. Insistently masculine in his perspective, Freud rejected Jung's label in favor of "feminine Oedipal complex." Under either category, the complex privileges the male. "At its most basic level, the Electra complex refers to the phenomenon of the little girl's attraction to her father and hostility to her mother, whom she now sees as her rival. The girl's desire to possess her father is linked to her desire to possess the penis, and the Electra complex is often described as penis envy" (Scott, *Electra after Freud*, 8).

50. In addition, in pragmatic terms Agustini's struggle to find her voice in the tight-knit literary community of early twentieth-century Montevideo is consistent with the conflicts that Polhemus outlines for "Lot's daughters": "If ambitious daughters were successfully to push for more education, look for a broader scope of action, seek fulfillment through new vocational opportunities, want higher cultural status and greater autonomy, they would have to become both closer to men and more independent from them. To open up the world they would need to attract the favor and mentoring good will from men, but then also they would have to find ways to control and distance them" (25).

Agustini confronted these tensions during a telling episode in September of 1911 that is recalled by Varas. The incident centers on a literary debate that arose between Agustini and Alejandro Sux in *La Razón* over the originality of her work (98–103). Sux set out to defend Agustini against those who saw her work as derivative of Darío, Nervo, and Lugones. His language, nevertheless, reflected the predominant patriarchal and paternalistic perspective. More important, his praise of her uniqueness set her apart and isolated her from the modernista tradition. Agustini's response reflected her simultaneous acceptance and rejection of the "influence" that the three male authors had on her work, or, as Varas states, "Con un golpe magistral Agustini reclama el modernismo como su tradición, a los modernistas como sus colegas e iguales, y le da a su obra autoridad y originalidad al mismo tiempo" (101). In other words, Agustini sets out to preserve the word/seed of her father(s) at the same time that she asserts her independence, restricting the degree of control she allows them to exert. To take hold of the future, she must seduce and dominate the patriarchs of modernismo, and to do so she turns to transgressive sexual language.

51. The full quote from Gilbert and Gubar emphasizes the difference in the "anxiety of influence" as it is perceived by women and men writers. They point out that "the son of

many fathers, today's male writer feels hopelessly belated; the daughter of too few mothers, today's female writer feels that she is helping to create a viable tradition which is at last definitively emerging" (50).

52. For Agustini's impact on Orozco, see Jill S. Kuhnheim, *Gender, Politics, and Poetry in Twentieth-Century Argentina*, 20–24. For her impact on the women poets of the generation of 1980s in Argentina, see Alicia Genovese, *La doble voz: Poetas argentinas contemporáneos*, 18–40.

53. An example of the open and openly sexual attitudes that permeated the literary circles at the time Agustini was beginning to write appears in *El pudor. La cachondez* by Julio Herrera y Reissig. These two pieces, which remained unpublished until 1992, were written between 1901 and 1902 and were originally to be part of a larger work entitled *Los nuevos charrúas*, referring to the native Americans of Uruguay. They contain explicit, outrageous, ironic commentaries on the hypocritical social and sexual behavior of both men and women, and, as the editors of the 1992 edition make clear, reflect "un particular impulso erótico que briosamente recorrió el ambiente cultural del novecientos montevideano" (14–15). I quote from the section entitled "La cachondez," in which Herrera y Reissig describes with gusto the unconventional pleasures in which certain of his female contemporaries indulged: "Por lo que se refiere a la cachondez y a lo que con ella reza, . . . las mujeres se dividen en histéricas-masturbadoras (que despedazan velas), en consolatrices (que usan consoladores comprados en los de Miller), en homífogas (que se comen a los maridos), en uterinas (que connubian con los sirvientes, con los cocheros y con los niños), en canidóla-tras (que viven con perritos amaestrados), en tortilleras (que cohabitan con hermanas de clitoris desarrollados, amigas marimachos), en buscadoras (que van a las amuebladas), y en prostitutas (las de la calle Santa Teresa)" (124–25). Herrera y Reissig ends this short section with a typically ironic note: "Libertinos no hay más que tres; uno se halla en Buenos Aires. Amantes, no alcanzan a media docena. Concubinas abundan en todas las clases" (125).

54. Other critics have only glimpsed aspects of this crucial feature. As María José Bruña Bragado in her extensive review of the critical literature observes, Agustini's contact with her contemporaries has not been seriously explored (15, n. 5). More problematic was the tendency that reigned for decades for critics to oscillate between psychosexual and mystical perspectives (30–33). As might be expected, attitudes toward Agustini's work changed considerably with the emergence of feminist ideas and women's studies. Those who opened the way for further exploration of the depth and complexity of Agustini's work are Uruguay Cortazzo, Gwen Kirkpatrick, Sylvia Molloy, and Margaret Bruzelius. Nevertheless, Agustini's textual relationship with Darío has remained in the shadows. Even though Girón Alvarado recognizes the importance of the "dialogue" between Darío's texts and Agustini's work (8), the relationship appears only sporadically in her study.

In her *Salomé decapitada: Delmira Agustini y estética finisecular de la fragmentación*, the revision of her dissertation of 1993 entitled "La lengua en la rosa: Dialéctica del deseo en la obra de Delmira Agustini," Tina Escaja presents one of the best overall explorations of Agustini's poetry to date. Even so, she only occasionally includes references to Darío's work. In her study Escaja traces the development of Agustini's poetry through a series of overarching metaphors. She links her early period, that of *Libro blanco (Frágil)*, to weakness, fragility, and death and defines it in terms of the image of Ophelia. Escaja defines fragmentation as the dominant trope of *Los cálices vacíos* and contends that the dismembered Orpheus is its central figure. Within these contexts, she proposes that Agustini wishes to join with the "tú" of poetry, her "superhuman lover," in order to achieve an ideal, which she links to François Lyotard's vision of the postmodern.

Nydia Ileana Renfrew, in her *La imaginación en la obra de Delmira Agustini* (1987), originally written as a doctoral dissertation at Michigan State University in 1985, shows that the focus of Agustini's poetry is the nature of art and the creative imagination, for which Eros is the central metaphor. For Renfrew, Agustini's "lovers" are not separate entities but two poles through which imagination is revealed.

María-Elena Barreiro de Armstrong's *Puente de luz: Eros, eje de la estructura pendular en "Los cálices vacíos" de Delmira Agustini*, which she first wrote as a doctoral dissertation in 1996, and published two years later in Germany with the same title, presents a similar thesis. She holds that the central metaphor of Agustini's *Los cálices vacíos* is Eros, which is simultaneously the "tú" of her poetry, the object of her quest, and the transcendence achieved through a union with the other. In addition, she shows how the pendular structure within and between specific poems enhances the reconciliation between poetic polarities.

Before Renfrew, Armstrong, and Escaja, Clara Silva understood that Agustini's eroticism was more than a reflection of physical desire and, as a result, labeled it heroic: "Porque se ha comprendido que todo erotismo es en ella un evasión hacia un más allá heroico, casi sobrehumano, de la carne y de los sentidos, aunque se valga de la realidad carnal humana, en su vivencia subjetiva, para alzarse en una transfiguración ardiente y dolorosamente idealizada de la materia" (*Genio*, 140).

María Rosa Olivera-Williams, in her short article on the figure of the muse in the poetry of both Darío and Agustini, asserts that, though the "male other-lover" is the source of her writing, he is a product of her own creation (159). Even more assertive is Jorge Luis Castillo's reassessment of Agustini's poetry as a type of subversive modernismo, that is, a rewriting of modernista images and discourse from a woman's point of view. Still others, like Renée Scott, Arcea Fabiola Zapata de Aston, and Inmaculada Sánz-Mateos continue to interpret Agustini's poems in terms of biography and emotions, most notably love. Scott modifies this perspective somewhat by indicating that the "poet addresses an ideal lover who will liberate her from a world in which she feels imprisoned" (261).

Carla Giaudrone's dissertation of 2003 and its later published version, *La degeneración del 900: Modelos estético-sexuales de la cultura en el Uruguay del Novecientos*, develop points already found in her earlier works and focus on the Uruguayan generation that includes Agustini, Roberto de las Carreras, Julio Herrera y Reissig, and José Enrique Rodó. She shows how they sexualized language and exalted the erotic, thus challenging the pressures to conform to the hegemonic goals of modernization.

Other noteworthy studies on Agustini include Barbara Ware's dissertation (2002), which rethinks the writing of *posmodernista* women from a Jungian perspective, Linda Kay Davis East's "The Imaginary Voyage: Evolution of the Poetry of Delmira Agustini" (Stanford University, 1981), Doris Thomason Stephens's "Delmira Agustini and the Quest for Transcendence" (University of Tennessee, 1974), Jeanette Yvonne Deguzman Valenti's "Delmira Agustini: A Re-interpretation of Her Poetry" (Cornell University, 1971), Laura Teixeira Tarquinio's "La poesía de Delmira Agustini" (Stanford University, 1968), Sidonia Carmen Rosenbaum's now-classic *Modern Woman Poets of Spanish America: The Precursors, Delmira Agustini, Gabriela Mistral, Alfonsina Storni, Juana De Ibarbourou*, as well as an excellent article by Aida Beaupied.

55. For more on the figure of the vampire, see chapter 3.

56. All quotes of Agustini's verse refer to the Cátedra edition unless otherwise noted.

57. The response to patriarchy is key to many of these studies. For example, in her article "Tradition and Women's Writing," Adriana Méndez Rodenas makes the point that in women's writing "the stroke of the pen inscribes the image of the female body but it also evokes the return of the repressed. A mobile and ambivalent text would reverse the 'phallologocentric' notion of the text as a monument or book of stone" (47). These are the very images Agustini draws upon to create her own modernista discourse. Some of the principal critics working in this area, in addition to those already mentioned, are Alicia Ostriker, Sara Castro-Klarén, Sylvia Molloy, and Beatriz Sarlo.

Chapter Two. The Dialogue Begins

1. Agustini organized and ordered the poems of the first edition of *El libro blanco (Frágil)*. Her family published a posthumous edition of her poetry in 1924 in which they altered the placement and order she had given them. García Pinto's edition of Agustini's *Poesías completas* (2000), which I use throughout this study unless otherwise indicated, is consistent with Agustini's initial wishes.

2. This pattern of development is consistent with but modifies the three stages outlined by Elaine Showalter: "First there is a prolonged phase of *imitation* of the prevailing modes of the dominant tradition, and *internalization* of its standards of art and its views on social roles. Second, there is a phase of *protest* against these standards and values, and *advocacy* of minority rights and values, including a demand for autonomy. Finally, there is a phase of *self-discovery*, a turning inward freed from some of the dependency of opposition, a search for identity" (13). The greatest departure by Agustini from this generalized picture is in the degree of creativity and self-assertion manifested throughout the three stages. Despite this inventiveness, chapters 2 and 3 of Girón Alvarado's *Voz poética y máscaras femeninas en la obra de Delmira Agustini* reveal the extent to which Agustini had, in *El libro blanco (Frágil)*, adopted the dominant tradition that tied authorial authority to the male creator, leaving the role of inspirational muse to the female.

3. Tina Escaja, in *Salomé decapitada*, indicates that the title shift first appears in Zum Felde's edition of Agustini's poetry (38). Patricia Varas recognizes "El poeta leva el ancla"

as "un arte poética" (91). Gwen Kirkpatrick, in "Prodigios," explores the full richness of that metaphor of sea travel with regard to "La barca milagrosa."

4. In her book Escaja points out the connection between the symbolism of "El poeta leva el ancla" and "la página en blanco" but does not indicate any link to Darío's poem (38). In the dissertation, however, she does allude to certain echoes between the two pieces (160).

5. I refer to sections 5 and 6 of "La página blanca":

> Los tardos camellos
> —como las figuras en un panorama—,
> cual si fuese un desierto de hielo,
> atraviesan la página blanca.
>
> Éste lleva
> una carga
> de dolores y angustias antiguas,
> angustias de pueblos, dolores de razas;
> ¡dolores y angustias que sufren los Cristos
> que vienen al mundo de víctimas trágicas! (214)

6. Emilio Oribe's understanding of the end of this poem and the reference to "los Cristos" is a perfect example of how Agustini's poetry has been interpreted through the details of her life. He states, "Puede encerrar la clave del destino de la mujer que lo escribió. Leyendo este poema muchas veces he pensado que entonces la poetisa apareció ya con el privilegio maravilloso y trágico a la vez de aquella Casandra de Esquilo, que poseía el don de la adivinación y que, aunque el amor la conmovía, al mismo tiempo iba leyendo su destino, por anticipado, bebiéndolo como un vino amargo, antes de vivirlo, mientras él tendía a realizarse, a pesar de todo lo que hiciera ella por impedirlo. Como Casandra en la proa de su nave, Delmira adivina lo que le preparan Eros y la muerte" (quoted in Machado de Benvenuto 178).

7. I refer to the first two sections:

> Mis ojos miraban en horas de ensueños
> la página blanca.
>
> Y vino el desfile de ensueños y sombras.
> Y fueron mujeres de rostros de estatua,
> mujeres de rostros de estatuas de mármol,
> ¡tan tristes, tan dulces, tan suaves, tan pálidas! (213)

8. Like the Parnassians, the modernistas sought to pattern their verse upon the elaborate and harmonious perfection of the graphic arts (as in the Parnassian "enamel" and "cameo" poems). However, the modernistas, virtually from the beginning, joined ranks with the symbolists, aspiring to capture, along with formal perfection, vitality, movement, and spirit.

9. It is this struggle between the perfection of form and the representation of life and passion that Trambaioli puts at the center of her excellent article on the statue in Agustini's poetry. She associates this division with the Apollonian and the Dionysian and explores their diverse manifestations in the figure of the statue throughout Agustini's poetry. Puentes de Oyenard finds a similar struggle between "flesh and marble" in the poem "Fiera de amor" from *Los cálices vacíos*. In contrast, by reading Agustini's poetry through the filter of amorous desire, Ricardo Dino Taralli offers a skewed interpretation of "La estatua," overlooking clear indications of broader concerns. In *El amor en la poesía de Delmira Agustini: Referencias especiales*, he writes, "En 'La estatua' (soneto), comienzan sus visiones metafísicas, aunque siempre el amor ocupa el primer plano: 'Miradla así, sobre el follaje oscuro / recortar la silueta soberana . . . / No parece el retoño prematuro / de una gran raza que será mañana?' Por eso implora: 'Dios! . . . Moved ese cuerpo, dadle un alma!'" (6).

10. Here I am using "campañas" from Alejandro Cáceres's edition of Agustini's *Poesías completas* (143) instead of the "compañas" from the García Pinto edition of *Poesías completas* (101).

11. The "estirpe sobrehumana" first appears in the third poem of *El libro blanco (Frágil)*, "Noche de Reyes" (97) in a reference that maintains strongly religious associations. This sonnet, which is missing the first half of the first quatrain, begins with the following six lines. They only hint at Agustini's later, more secular take on divinity and salvation, one that nevertheless maintains the link between the poet and Christ-like abilities:

> «Tenía en las pupilas un brillo nunca visto,
> Era rubio, muy dulce y se llamaba Cristo! . . .»
>
> —¡Ah, sigue! —el mago erguía la frente soberana—
> —«Mi copa es del Oriente, es sagrado este vino—
> »Allá en Betlheem, un día legendario y divino
> »Yo vi nacer al niño de estirpe sobrehumana. (97)

12. Agustini states, "Ved la grandeza que en su forma duerme . . . ," seemingly to follow Darío's lead in "Coloquio de los centauros": "Amo el granito duro que el arquitecto labra / y el mármol en que duermen la línea y la palabra . . ." (205). (For a detailed analysis of "Coloquio de los centauros," see my *Rubén Darío*, 27–45.) In "Yo soy aquel . . . ," Darío achieves what Agustini proposes. His statue lives; marble becomes flesh: "En mi jardín se vio una estatua bella; / se juzgó mármol y era carne viva" (245).

13. Both Escaja (96–97) and Burt (115–24) have explored Agustini's recourse to the statue-centered myth of Pygmalion. I discuss Agustini's reworkings of these figures with regard to "A una cruz" (191–92) from *Cantos de la mañana* (see chapter 3) and with regard to "Tres pétalos a tu perfil" (234), "Visión" (236–37), "Fiera de amor" (248), "Plegaria" (258–59) from *Los cálices vacíos* (see chapter 4).

14. The following are the parts of "Coloquio de los centauros" that resonate most clearly in "Por campos de ensueño." The introductory section describes the centaurs and their aggressive movement across the land:

> Son los Centauros. Unos enormes, rudos; otros
> alegres y saltantes como jóvenes potros;
> unos con largas barbas como los padres-ríos;
> otros imberbes, ágiles y de piafantes bríos,
> y de robustos músculos, brazos y lomos aptos
> para portar las ninfas rosadas en los raptos.
>
> Van en galope rítmico. Junto a un fresco boscaje,
> frente al gran Oceano, se paran. El paisaje
> recibe de la urna matinal luz sagrada
> que el vasto azul suaviza con límpida mirada.
> Y oyen seres terrestres y habitantes marinos
> la voz de los crinados cuadrúpedos divinos. (200)

15. I discuss this poem more completely in *Modernismo, Modernity, and the Development of Spanish American Literature* (83).

16. Underlying many of these images of artistic aspiration is, as noted by M. H. Abrams in *Natural Supernaturalism*, "a long series of footnotes to Plotinus" (146). Both the fountain/ overflowing spring and the soul as lover seeking to return to "the One" as beloved find their distant origin in Plotinus's radical monism, which came to modernismo by way of the English and German romantics and the French symbolists. In contrast to my presentation, Zapata de Aston interprets "La sed," as she does virtually all the poems she discusses, as "una evocación del amor pleno, real, directo, sin máscaras. Es el placer y el goce en acción" (120).

17. The artistic ideal of purity as represented by the shining brilliance of a star appears in Darío's poetry in poems like "Pegaso" (*Cantos de vida y esperanza* 254–55):

> Cuando iba yo a montar ese caballo rudo
> y tembloroso, dije: "La vida es pura y bella",
> entre sus cejas vivas vi brillar una estrella.
> El cielo estaba azul y yo estaba desnudo. (254)

18. It is for this diversity of elements offered as a source of inspiration that Girón Alvarado sees "El poeta y la diosa" as "una imitación y corrección del poema de Rubén Darío titulado 'Autumnal'" (71–72).

19. "¿Y la cuestión métrica? ¿Y el ritmo? Como cada palabra tiene un alma, hay en cada verso, además de la harmonía verbal, una melodía ideal. La música es sólo de la idea, muchas veces" (180).

20. With this Agustini anticipates the "orthopedic molds" of Darío's "Dilucidaciones," which was published in *El canto errante* the same year as *El libro blanco (Frágil)*. The phrase to which I am referring highlights the coincidence between their poetics. "No gusto de *moldes* nuevos ni viejos. . . . Mi verso ha nacido siempre con su cuerpo y su alma, y no le he aplicado nunguna clase de ortopedia. He, sí, cantado aires antiguos; y he querido ir hacia el

porvenir, siempre bajo el divino imperio de la música—música de las ideas, música del verbo" (304).

21. Agustini presents a less dichotomous view of art and nature in the untitled "Mi musa tomó un día la placentera ruta . . ." (123). Perhaps because of the male perspective she adopts, she even appears to soften her attack against middle-class aspirations to upper-class respectability. While this sonnet continues to signal the primacy of all that is natural, naked, and unencumbered, the lyric voice speaks of dressing her muse in Parisian high fashion. The artistic compromise is stated in the final two lines: "Y ella hoy grave pasea por mis brillantes salas / Un gran aire salvaje y un perfume de espliego." Recognizing the inevitable imposition of form and structure, the poet insists upon maintaining the essence and spirit of her inspiration.

22. In her book Stephens presents the "pains and pleasures of creativity" as part of Agustini's quest for transcendence (95–104), yet she fails to recognize that most of the examples of "sadism" she finds in Agustini's poetry are actually part and parcel of the search for artistic excellence (184–89).

23. "Los versos son su mayor placer, pero también son su tormento. A veces, su tensión nerviosa es tanta que preferiría que no los hiciera, aunque comprendo que son para ella una necesidad" (quoted in Silva, *Genio* 36).

24. One is reminded of Pablo Neruda's famous "Walking around" in which he longs for a disruption of his meaningless routine:

> Sin embargo sería delicioso
> asustar a un notario con un lirio cortado
> o dar muerte a una monja con un golpe de oreja.
> Sería bello
> ir por las calles con un cuchillo verde
> y dando gritos hasta morir de frío.

25. Agustini further elaborates on the complexity of the vision she seeks to present in "La musa gris" (114–16). Recalling Darío's synesthetic masterpiece "Sinfonía en gris mayor" (216), a poem he is believed to have modeled on Théophile Gautier's "Symphonie en Blanc Majeur," Agustini embraces the doubts, despair, and dangers revealed by her gray muse. Her female guide embodies the sadness of those who do not close their eyes to unpleasant realities and who struggle to write about them.

26. In addition to being in "¡Torres de Dios! ¡Poetas! . . ." Darío's well-known complaints about insensitive, uninformed readers are evident in his "El rey burgués" and in "Palabras liminares" from *Prosas profanas*. In this introductory text he attacks both the general public and those who should know better as being incapable of understanding his goals and aspirations: "Por la absoluta falta de elevación mental de la mayoría pensante de nuestro continente, en la cual impera el universal personaje clasificado por Remy de Gourmont con el nombre de *Celui-qui-ne-comprend-pas*. *Celui-qui-ne-comprend-pas* es entre nosotros profesor,

académico correspondiente de la Real Academia Española, periodista, abogado, poeta, *rastaquouère*" (179).

27. "El *yo* afirma de manera tajante 'Sueño una estatua de mujer muy fea', oponiéndola a la Afrodita clásica, que le parece un 'helado resplandor de escama'" (59).

28. "Bulbul" also appears in "Iniciación" (155).

29. I am referring to the final two sections of "El reino interior":

> Ella no me responde.
> Pensativa se aleja de la obscura ventana
> —pensativa y risueña,
> de la Bella-durmiente-del-bosque tierna hermana—,
> y se adormece en donde
> hace treinta años sueña.
>
> *
>
> Y en sueño dice: "¡Oh dulces delicias de los cielos!
> ¡Oh tierra sonrosada que acarició mis ojos!
> —¡Princesas, envolvedme con vuestros blancos velos!
> —¡Príncipes, estrechadme con vuestros brazos rojos!" (227)

30. This type of inclusion stands in sharp contrast to the exclusion represented in "La loba" by Alfonsina Storni. In "La loba" the female figure is excluded from both male and female society, and the poem expresses its sense of injustice and outrage. The image of the lyre reappears in *Cantos de la mañana* in "Primavera" (205–6). There the lyric voice enthusiastically, almost erotically, embraces the symbol of poetic accomplishment (see chapter 3).

31. As Chemris has shown in her article, while Darío does not hesitate to join forces with the sexually aggressive Zeus, especially in "Los cisnes" III (264), he also joins the ranks of the victimized. Chemris links this victimization with the trauma of imperialist domination in her exploration of "Los cisnes" I.

32. "Ave de luz" reads as follows:

> Existe un ave extraña de vuelo inconcebible,
> De regias esbelteces, de olímpica actitud;
> Sus alas al batirse desflecan resplandores
> Sus ojos insondables son piélagos de luz!
>
> Es toda luz, su sangre es un licor de fuego;
> De briznas de fulgores su rica plumazón;
> Su pico al entreabrirse desgrana sartas de astros;
> Como ella es toda lumbre, de lumbre es su canción!
>
> Su vuelo inconcebible ignora los obstáculos!
> Abarca lo infinito en toda su extensión,
> Arranca negras sombras del fondo del abismo,
> Collares de destellos a veces trae el sol!

> Con filamentos de astros y polvos de diamantes,
> Labro bello su nido: lucífero joyel!
> Lo teje en los cerebros más claros: allí encuentra
> La esencia de la lumbre que es savia de su ser!
>
> Postraos ante el hombre que lleva en su cerebro
> Esa ave misteriosa ¡manojo de fulgor!
> Que mata, que enloquece, que crea y que ilumina
> ¡Aquel en quien anida, es émulo de Dios!
>
> . . . .
>
> ¡Oh Genio! ¡extraña ave de vuelo inconcebible!
> De regias esbelteces, de olímpica actitud;
> Escucha: yo te brindo mis frescas ilusiones,
> Mis mágicos ensueños, mi rica juventud,
> ¡A cambio de un instante de vida en mi cerebro!
> ¡A cambio de un arpegio de tu canción de luz! (152–53)

33. Both Linda East (75) and Tina Escaja (42–44) stress the poem's visual images and its emphasis on light. They therefore move the discussion away from the human pursuit of transcendence through poetry to a more abstract search for the sublime. Escaja in particular, invoking Lyotard, declares, "La finalidad de la poeta es la de aproximarse al Ideal por intercambio carnal con el ave divina" (43).

34. Escaja in particular focuses on the fragmentation in Agustini's appropriation of the myth of Orpheus. In this regard, she states, "La tradición del mito de Orfeo ejemplifica entonces diversos grados de misoginia canónica que tanto la obra como la persona de Delmira Agustini cuestionan" (101).

35. Of "Orla rosa" Girón Alvarado writes, "Es la verdadera iniciación de Agustini como poeta original y diferente en el mundo literario hispanoamericano. No porque por fin use una voz femenina ni tampoco porque sus temas fuesen el erotismo o la pasión amorosa; sino porque por primera vez una mujer poeta usa una voz femenina para hablar sobre sus deseos, pasiones y experiencias haciendo uso de un lenguaje sensual y explícitamente erótico" (90). Anticipating this position years earlier, Visca focused on "Orla rosa" as the moment when Agustini's poetry changed and became more erotic (11).

36. Zapata de Aston, who provides many insights into Agustini's work, narrows the scope of her interpretations by insisting on a more literal reading of the poems. She states, "Su poesía para nosotros obedece a objetivos simples, y a la vez trascendentales: la expresión del sentir. Pero un sentir que logró romper las barreras de lo prohibido en la sociedad de la época, y que fue más allá de lo bueno y 'aceptado' en la sociedad rioplatense de las primeras décadas del siglo XX" (104). Girón Alvarado sees love as the focus of Agustini's poetry but holds her creative breakthrough to be her recourse to the language of mysticism (95). Armstrong's position is more nuanced. Though she places Eros at the center of her discussion of Agustini's works, she understands that the tension between the "tú" and the

"yo" of her poetry is somehow tied to poetic creation. She writes, "El tú puede ser, a veces, una proyección del yo, otras un reflejo del yo o el yo mismo, así como un tú *per se*. El yo es siempre una 'voz femenina'; el tú, el objeto, el interlocutor es el ser 'masculino.' El yo pasa de amada a amante, de yo empírico a onírico y de onírico a empírico. Esto mismo ocurre en el tú. El tú no tiene un nombre fijo y no habla sino actúa. Actúa en la mente-cuerpo del yo, o su 'actuar' se refleja en la acción-experiencias del yo mente-cuerpo, enunciadas por el yo. El tú pasa de amado a amante y de amante a amado." (44) She goes on to clarify, "El vacío existencial del yo lírico se convierte en sublime existencia sobrehumana, sin limitaciones. El resultado es la creación poética: fruto de una unión. Creación que expresa la experiencia, las emociones y los sentimientos en forma directa y audaz, por medio de un yo lírico femenino sincretizado en el binomio con un tú masculino" (46). Escaja identifies the "tú," that is, Agustini's "superhuman lover," with the sublime and the divine, which she links to the nature of the modern and postmodern as defined by Lyotard (16, 20). For Renfrew, Agustini's "lovers" are not separate entities but two poles through which imagination is revealed. Regardless of the discrepancies in our points of view, both Escaja and Renfrew come closest to the line of argumentation I pursue here.

37. As Clara Silva points out, the innovative nature of Agustini's verse was immediately recognized. She notes, "La poesía de Delmira Agustini, fue en su hora, el primer cuarto de este siglo, una revelación sorprendente, que llenó de admiración a toda la crítica hispanoamericana" (Silva, *Pasión*, 95).

38. These images appear in "Pegaso" (254–55) and very clearly in his statement in "Yo soy aquel que ayer no más decía . . .": "La torre de marfil tentó mi anhelo; / quise encerrarme dentro de mí mismo, / y tuve hambre de espacio y sed de cielo / desde las sombras de mi propio abismo" (245).

39. "Blasón" follows "Sonatina" in *Prosas profanas* and presents the swan in exactly the way that it appears throughout *El libro blanco (Frágil)*, that is, as emblematic of modernismo.

40. Escaja also sees in "Íntima" a realignment in traditional assumptions about control and domination: "Sin embargo, la relación especular de la que la poeta es eje resulta intercambiable, con lo que se subvierte la imagen tradicional de los roles femenino (pasivoreflejante), y masculino (activo-reflejado). . . . La intercambiabilidad entre el tú reflejado y el yo reflejante permite igualar las dos esferas abisales que se proyectan recíprocamente y que conjugan su dialéctica en el yo del poema" (55). Similarly, Armstrong recognizes the balancing between the "tú" and "yo," but her interpretation of their meanings is much more abstract. She sees the spacial and temporal "before" as the abyss and the existential emptiness tied to death and the "after" or "beyond" as the flowering of happiness and life (55).

41. Among the poems by Darío that most directly address the issues alluded to in "Misterio, ven" are "Ama tu ritmo . . ." (236–37), "Palabras de la satiresa" (235–36), "Alma mía" (240–41), and "Helios" (258–60).

42. "Da voz a un erotismo femenino que en Darío se pierde, se deperdicia, por carecer

de palabra. . . . El erotismo en Agustini necesita decirse, inscribirse, no como queja de vencida que se pierde en el viento sino como triunfante—y temible—placer" (66).

43. Perhaps for this reason Girón Alvarado insists, with what I believe is flawed logic, that Agustini's only theme is love (105).

44. "La exaltación apasionada de la voz femenina, que narra con erotismo la relación hombre-mujer" (52). Despite her overriding emphasis on a philosophic interpretation of Agustini's poetry, one in which the dialectic between the "tú" and the "yo" represents the struggle between existential despair and spiritual hopefulness, Armstrong acknowledges the erotic physicality of this "key," especially when read in union with "the eyes" of line 5 and "the head" of line 7. Armstrong agrees, while continuing to emphasize the metaphysical displacement toward the sublime, that "El intruso" also reflects a highly sexualized move from male to female (50–52).

Chapter Three. Drinking from the Fountain of the Other

1. The studies by Uruguay Cortazzo explain these critical maneuvers and focus on the innovative quality of Agustini's work. Such obfuscation and redirection were the mechanisms with which mainstream critics dealt with all marginal groups whose sexuality made them uncomfortable. See the groundbreaking works by Sylvia Molloy and Oscar Montero regarding the traditional reading of homosexual authors.

2. Sylvia Molloy comments on the importance of this exclusion: "It is not without irony that the literary movement so often acclaimed as the first concerted reflection on Latin American cultural identity—I speak of turn-of-the-century *modernismo*— should have excluded women. *Modernismo* sees woman exclusively as subject matter: it focuses on her as the passive recipient of its multiple desires, as a commodity that is alternately (or at times simultaneously) worshiped in the spirit and coveted in the flesh. A movement that prizes the crafting and collecting of precious objects, *modernismo* makes woman the most valuable piece in its museum" ("Introduction," 109).

3. Escaja foregrounds dismemberment in her study. Molloy also provides key insights into the issues of fragmentation ("Introduction," 116–20).

4. Twenty of the twenty-two poems initially published in 1910 were incorporated in the 1913 publication of *Los cálices vacíos*. Some revisions, mostly minor, were made during the three-year period between the two collections. The poems that appear here are the revised versions found in the García Pinto edition of Agustini's *Poesías completas*. Cáceres presents the original versions in his edition with notes indicating the later changes.

5. "Yo no encuentro entre las poetisas autóctonas de América una sola comparable a ella por su originalidad de buena cepa y por la arrogancia viril de sus cantos" (178).

6. Though she does not use the word, Girón Alvarado's entire thesis is predicated on the shift that Agustini makes from a masculine to a feminine voice. Escaja uses the term at least twice (33, 46). See also note 3 in chapter 1.

7. "En este siglo las literatas y poetisas han sido un ejército, a punto de que cierto autor

ha publicado un tomo con el catálogo de ellas—¡y no las nombra a todas!—. Entre todo el inútil y espeso follaje, los grandes árboles se levantan: la Coronado, la Pardo Bazán, Concepción Arenal. Estas dos últimas, particularmente, cerebros viriles, honran a su patria. En cuanto a la mayoría innumerable de Corinas cursis y Safos de hojaldre, entran a formar parte de la abominable *sisterhood* internacional a que tanto ha contribuído la Gran Bretaña con sus miles de *authoresse* [*sic*]. Para ir hacia el palacio de la mentenda Eva futura, las [*sic*] falta a éstas cambiar el pegaso por la bicicleta" (*Obras completas*, 3: 361–62).

8. This interpretation of "Fragmentos" differs sharply from the one offered by Escaja, who focuses on the images of physical and spiritual fragmentation and on Agustini's postmodern search for the sublime. I believe instead that "Fragmentos" offers Agustini what Escaja recognizes in other poems, namely, a way to "autolegitimarse como escritora" (73).

9. In chapter 1 I draw the parallel with the recourse to the language of cannibalism by the Brazilian modernist Oswald de Andrade to counter European cultural hegemony in Brazil. As explained there, the Brazilian modernists turned to the central metaphor of devouring assimilation to create the new body of "native originality." As a result, they were able to present themselves as resourcefully aggressive creators rather than weak, dependent imitators.

10. Though in her book Stephens acknowledges the pain of creativity Agustini felt throughout her career, she fails to see this pain in "El vampiro." Instead, she restricts its meaning by focusing on the fusion of love and death through a unique form of sadism (188).

11. Stephens focuses on Agustini's "quest for transcendence," by which she seems to mean the search for ways to surpass everyday existence. Only in the last chapter of her book does she address the relationship between death and transcendence, but even there she does not discuss Agustini's take on immortality.

12. I have placed the prose translations at the end of each numbered stanza:

Supremo idilio

En el balcón romántico de un castillo adormido	I
Que los ojos suspensos de la noche adiamantan,	
Una figura blanca hasta la luz . . . Erguido	
Bajo el balcón romántico del castillo adormido,	
Un cuerpo tenebroso . . . Alternándose cantan.	

[On the romantic balcony of a sleeping castle / that the night's suspended eyes sparkle with diamonds, / a figure so white as to become light . . . Standing erect / beneath the romantic balcony of the sleeping castle, / a dark body . . . They take turns singing.]

—¡Oh tú, flor augural de una estirpe suprema	II
Que duplica los pétalos sensitivos del alma,	
Nata de azules sangres, aurisolar diadema	
Florecida en la sienes de la Raza! . . . Suprema-	
Mente pulso en la noche tu corazón en calma!	

[—Oh, you, portentous flower of a supreme lineage / that doubles the sensitive petals of the soul, / finest essence of blue bloods, golden lit crown / abloom on the temples of the Race! . . . / Supremely I strum your calm heart during the night!]

> —¡Oh tú que surges pálido de un gran fondo de enigma,   III
> Como el retrato incógnito de una tela remota! . . .
> Tu sello puede ser un blasón o un estigma;
> En la aguas cambiantes de tus ojos de enigma
> Un corazón herido—y acaso muerto—flota!

[—Oh, you, who emerges pale from a great enigmatic depth, / like the unknown portrait of a distant canvas! . . . / Your seal can be a coat of arms or a stigma; / In the changing waters of your enigmatic eyes / an injured—and perhaps dead—heart floats!]

> —Los ojos son la Carne y son el Alma: mira!   IV
> Yo soy la Aristocracia lívida del Dolor
> Que forja los puñales, las cruces y las liras,
> Que en las llagas sonríe y en los labios suspira . . .
> Satán pudiera ser mi semilla o mi flor!

[—Eyes are the Flesh and they are the Soul: look! / I am the livid Aristocracy of the Pain / that forges the daggers, the crosses, and the lyres, / that, within the wounds, smiles and on the lips sighs . . . / Satan could be my seed or my flower!]

> Soy fruto de aspereza y maldición: yo amargo   V
> Y mancho mortalmente el labio que me toca;
> Mi beso es flor sombría de un Otoño muy largo . . .
> Exprimido en tus labios dará un sabor amargo,
> Y todo el Mal del Mundo florecerá en tu boca!

[I am the fruit of roughness and cursedness; I embitter / and fatally stain the lip that touches me; / my kiss is the dark flower of a very long Autumn . . . / squeezed on your lips, it will give a bitter flavor, / and all the Evil of the World will bloom in your mouth!]

> Bajo la aurora fúlgida de tu ilusión, mi vida   VI
> Extenderá las ruinas de una apagado Averno;
> Vengo como el vampiro de una noche aterida
> A embriagarme en tu sangre nueva: llego a tu vida
> Derramada en capullos, como un ceñudo Invierno!

[Beneath the resplendent dawn of your dreams, my life / will extend the ruins of an extinguished Hell; / I come like the vampire of a freezing night / to get drunk on your new blood: I come to your life, / drenched in buds, like a frowning Winter!]

   —Como en pétalos flojos yo desmayo a tu hechizo! . . .   VII
   Traga siniestro buitre mi pobre corazón!
   En tus manos mi espíritu es dúctil como un rizo . . .
   El corazón me lleva a tu siniestro hechizo
   Como el barco inconsciente el ala del timón!

[—As in loose petals I faint under your spell! . . . / A sinister vulture swallows my poor heart! / In your hands my spirit is yielding like a curl . . . / My heart carries me to your sinister spell / like the fin of the rudder does the unconscious ship!]

   Comulga con mi cuerpo devoradora sima!   VIII
   Mi alma clavo en tu alma con una estrella de oro;
   Florecerá tu frente como una tierra opima,
   Cuando en tu almohada trágica y honda como una sima,
   Mis rizos se derramen como una fuente de oro!

[Devouring chasm, take the sacrament of my body! / I nail my soul on your soul like a golden star; / your forehead will bloom like an abundant land, / when on your tragic pillow, deep like a chasm, my curls spill like a golden spring!]

   —Mi älma es negra tumba, fría como la Nieve . . .   IX
   —Buscaré una rendija para filtrarme en luz!
   —Albo lirio! . . . A tocarte ni mi sombra se atreve . . .
   —Te abro; ¡oh mancha de lodo! mi gran cáliz de nieve
   Y tiendo a ti eucarísticos mis brazos, negra cruz!

[—My soul is a black tomb, cold like the Snow . . . / —I will seek a crack to be filtered in light! / —White lily! . . . Not even my shadow dares to touch you . . . / —I open for you; oh muddy stain! my great chalice of snow / and I extend to you, black cross, my Eucharistic arms!]

   Enróscate; ¡oh serpiente caída de mi Estrella   X
   Sombría a mi ardoroso tronco primaveral! . . .
   Yo apagaré tu Noche o me incrustaré en ella:
   Seré en tus cielos negros el fanal de una estrella
   Seré en tus mares turbios la estrella de un fanal!

[Coil up; oh serpent fallen from my dark Star / around my ardent Springtime tree trunk! . . . / I will extinguish your Night or I will embed myself in it: / in your dark heavens I will be the star's lantern; / on your turbid seas I will be the lantern's star!]

   Sé mi bien o mi mal, yo viviré en tu vida!   XI
   Yo enlazo a tus espinas mi hiedra de ilusión . . .
   Seré en ti una paloma que en una ruina anida;
   Soy blanca, y dulce, y leve; llévame por la Vida
   Prendida como un lirio sobre tu corazón!

[Be my good or my ill; I will live in your life! / I bind my ivy of hope to your thorns . . . / I will be in you a dove that nests in a ruin; / I am white and sweet and light; carry me throughout your Life / fastened like a lily on your heart!]

—¡Oh dulce, dulce lirio! . . . Llave de las alburas! XII
Tú has abierto la sala blanca en mi alma sombría,
La sala en que silentes las ilusiones puras
En dorados sitiales, tejen mallas de alburas! . . .
—Tu alma se vuelve blanca, porque va siendo mía!

[—Oh sweet, sweet lily! . . . Key to all whiteness! / You have opened the white room in my dark soul, / the room in which pure hopes / silently weave meshes of whiteness on golden seats of honor! . . . / —Your soul becomes white, because it is becoming mine!]

—¡Oh leyes del Milagro! . . . yo, hijo de la sombra XIII
Morder tu carne; ¡oh fruto de los soles!
—Soy tuya fatalmente: mi silencio te nombra,
Y si la tocas tiembla como un alma mi sombra!—,
¡Oh maga flor del Oro brotada en mis crisoles!

[—Oh laws of the Miracle! . . . I, son of darkness / to bite your flesh; oh fruit of the suns! / —I am fatally yours: my silence names you, / and if you touch it my shadow trembles like a soul!—, / Oh magical flower of Gold that sprouted in my crucibles!]

—Los surcos azurados del Ensueño sembremos XIV
De alguna palpitante simiente inconcebida
Que arda en florecimientos imprevistos y extremos;
Y al amparo inefable de los cielos sembremos
De besos extrahumanos las cumbres de la Vida!

[—Let us sow the blue-hued furrows of Dream / with some unimagined throbbing seed / that it may blaze within unexpected and extreme flowerings; / and with the ineffable protection of the heavens let us sow / the peaks of Life with extrahuman kisses!]

Amor es milagroso, invencible y eterno; XV
La vida formidable florece entre sus labios . . .
Raíz nutrida de la entraña del Cielo y del Averno,
Viene a dar a la tierra el fuerte fruto eterno
Cuyo sangriento zumo se bebe a cuatro labios!

[Love is miraculous, invincible, and eternal; / life, which is formidable, flourishes between its lips . . . / The root that is nourished by the bowels of Heaven and Hell, / comes to give the land the strong eternal fruit / whose bloody juice is drunk by four lips!]

Amor es todo el Bien y todo el mal, el Cielo   XVI
Todo es la arcada ardiente de sus alas cernidas . . .
Bajar de un plinto vano es remontar el vuelo . . .
Y Él te impulsa a mis brazos abiertos como el Cielo
¡Oh suma flor con alma, a deshojar en vidas! . . .

[Love is all the Good and all the evil, the whole of Heaven / is the burning arch of its purified wings . . . / To descend from a vane plinth is to soar . . . / and He propels you toward my open arms like Heaven. / Oh supreme flower with a soul, to shed your petals in lives! . . .]

En el balcón romántico de un castillo adormido   XVII
Que los ojos suspensos en la Noche adiamantan,
El Silencio y la Sombra se acarician sin ruido . . .
Bajo el balcón romántico del castillo adormido
Un fuerte claro-oscuro y dos voces que cantan . . .

[On the romantic balcony of a sleeping castle / that the night's suspended eyes sparkle with diamonds, / Silence and Darkness caress each other without a noise . . . / Beneath the romantic balcony of the sleeping castle / a strong chiaroscuro and two voices that sing . . .]

13. "Las partes implicadas del debate amoroso acaban, por lo tanto, en un intercambio mimético, especular, invirtiéndose los papeles respectivos hasta convertirse los oponentes en dobles de sí mismos. Esta derivación sintoniza con la teoría de René Girard sobre la violencia y lo sagrado, según la cual los opuestos en un conflicto o debate por la adquisición de un objeto deseado acaban por parecerse" (79).

14. Armstrong's reading of "Supremo idilio" places the emphasis on love (60–62).

15. The footnote by García Pinto reinforces this point. She writes, "Este poema sin título fue omitido de la primera edición de *Cantos de la mañana* y del índice de la edición de *Los cálices vacíos*, en el que se lo incluyó, que es la versión que transcribimos. Es un poema diferente del anterior, «Supremo idilio», con el cual parece haber sido confundido" (190).

16. See the informative and wide-ranging dissertation by Petra Dierkes-Thrun on the Salome theme in modern literature and film. She includes in this study the following authors of the fin de siècle: Heinrich Heine, Gustave Flaubert, Joris-Karl Huysmans, Jules Laforgue, and Stéphane Mallarmé. The graphic artists most taken with Salome include Gustave Moreau, Gustave Klimt, and Aubrey Beardsley, all of whom influenced the development of modernismo.

17. Nassaar and Shaheen explore the link between Wilde's representation of Salome and the image of the vampire. They write, "The vampiric associations are made clear at the opening of the play, when the young Syrian notes how pale Salome is and the page of Herodias says of her, 'She is like a woman rising from a tomb. She is like a dead woman' (583). Symbolically she is dead and in search of a human to satisfy her raging desire for blood,

like any vampire. She chooses Jokanaan, but his continuous rejection of her creates a tense and expectant atmosphere. Salome claims Jokanaan's head, and in a moment of darkness, she kisses and bites the severed head, her ultimate coupling with the dead prophet" (133).

18. The three features of Bécquer's works that have had the greatest impact on modernismo are (1) the assertion of the ineffable nature of existence, (2) the representation of the desired object as the passive feminine other, and (3) the identification of love as one of the overriding passions of life, which are ultimately unattainable. See, for example, the works by the critics Angel Esteban, Cristóbal Cuevas García and Enrique Baena, and Stephen Gilman. These three elements are clearly present in Bécquer's famous "Rima I":

> Yo sé un himno gigante y extraño
> que anuncia en la noche del alma una aurora,
> y estas páginas son de ese himno,
> cadencias que el aire dilata en las sombras.
>
> Yo quisiera escribirlo, del hombre
> domando el rebelde, mezquino idioma,
> con palabras que fuesen a un tiempo
> suspiros y risas, colores y notas.
>
> Pero en vano es luchar; que no hay cifra
> capaz de encerrarlo, y apenas, ¡oh hermosa!,
> si, teniendo en mis manos las tuyas,
> pudiera al oído cantártelo a solas. (3)

According to Trambaioli, Bécquer is also a source of the worms, larvae, and creative insomnia that appear in Agustini's poetry (62–65).

19. "He expresado lo expresable de mi alma y he querido penetrar en el alma de los demás, y hundirme en la vasta alma universal. . . . y he visto con desinterés lo que a mi yo parece extraño, para convencerme de que nada es extraño a mi yo. He cantado, en mis diferentes modos, el espectáculo multiforme de la Naturaleza y su inmenso misterio" (304).

20. For ease of reference, I include Darío's "Sonatina" here:

> La princesa está triste . . . ¿qué tendrá la princesa?
> Los suspiros se escapan de su boca de fresa,
> que ha perdido la risa, que ha perdido el color.
> La princesa está pálida en su silla de oro,
> está mudo el teclado de su clave sonoro;
> y en un vaso olvidada se desmaya una flor.
>
> El jardín puebla el triunfo de los pavos-reales.
> Parlanchina, la dueña dice cosas banales,
> y, vestido de rojo, piruetea el bufón.

La princesa no ríe, la princesa no siente;
la princesa persigue por el cielo de Oriente
la libélula vaga de una vaga ilusión.

¿Piensa acaso en el príncipe de Golconda o de China,
o en el que ha detenido su carroza argentina
para ver de sus ojos la dulzura de luz?
¿O en el rey de las Islas de las Rosas fragantes,
o en el que es soberano de los claros diamantes,
o en el dueño orgulloso de las perlas de Ormuz?

¡Ay! La pobre princesa de la boca de rosa
quiere ser golondrina, quiere ser mariposa,
tener alas ligeras, bajo el cielo volar,
ir al sol por la escala luminosa de un rayo,
saludar a los lirios con los versos de mayo,
o perderse en el viento sobre el trueno del mar.

Ya no quiere el palacio, ni la rueca de plata,
ni el halcón encantado, ni el bufón escarlata,
ni los cisnes unánimes en el lago de azur.
Y están tristes las flores por la flor de la corte;
los jazmines de Oriente, los nelumbos del Norte,
de Occidente las dalias y las rosas del Sur.

¡Pobrecita princesa de los ojos azules!
Está presa en sus oros, está presa en sus tules,
en la jaula de mármol del palacio real,
el palacio soberbio que vigilan los guardas,
que custodian cien negros con sus cien alabardas,
un lebrel que no duerme y un dragón colosal.

¡Oh, quién fuera hipsipila que dejó la crisálida!
(La princesa está triste. La princesa está pálida)
¡Oh visión adorada de oro, rosa y marfil!
¡Quién volara a la tierra donde un príncipe existe
(La princesa está pálida. La princesa está triste)
más brillante que el alba, más hermoso que abril!

—¡Calla, calla, princesa —dice el hada madrina—,
en caballo con alas, hacia acá se encamina,
en el cinto la espada y en la mano el azor,
el feliz caballero que te adora sin verte,
y que llega de lejos, vencedor de la Muerte,
a encenderte los labios con su beso de amor! (187–88)

21. Since the age of romanticism poets have been visionaries who imagine worlds and who are harbingers of the future. See Calinescu's discussion of these features, 105–6.

Chapter Four. Turning Loss into Empowerment

1. The following Spanish translation is by Alejandro Cáceres:

> De pie, sobre mi orgullo, quiero mostrar, ¡oh noche!
> El revés de mi manto de luto por tu encanto,
> Su pañuelo tan negro, infinito pañuelo,
> Tan suave, gota a gota, llenaré con mi llanto.
>
> Pondrá sus blancos lirios en mis rosas de llama
> Y vendajes de calma en mi sien delirante . . .
> ¡Será una noche hermosa! . . . Tendrá para mí el alma
> Clara y la profundidad del cuerpo de un magnífico amante. (96)

Camille Sutton has rendered the French into English:

> Standing on my pride I want to show the night
> The inside of my cloak that mourns your charms,
> Its infinite handkerchief, its black and black handkerchief
> Drop by drop, tenderly, will drink up all my tears.
>
> The night lays white lilies upon my flaming roses
> And calming bandages upon my delirious brow . . .
> How good the night will be . . . Having for me the pure
> Soul and the profound body of a magnificent lover.

2. A nocturne is primarily a musical composition linked to the night. Like its predecessor, the serenata, the nocturne is usually a lyrical work written for a solo instrument, often intended for intimate settings. The modern variation began to flourish during the romantic period and continued to develop throughout the nineteenth and twentieth centuries. In the hands of Frédéric Chopin and Claude Debussy the nocturne came to possess great evocative power and for this reason came to serve as a model for French symbolist and, later, Spanish American modernista poetry, lending its title to many poems of different lengths and intensity. Agustini includes two "Nocturnos" in *Los cálices vacíos*. Darío wrote three famous "Nocturnos," which were studied as a group by Ycaza Tigerino.

3. Throughout his psychological biography of Agustini, William James focuses on the dependence/independence dichotomy, which he links primarily to her relationship with her strong-willed mother.

4. While García Pinto's edition has the plural "tienen," Cáceres has the verb in the singular, consistent with the singular "-es" of the next line along with the singular "vívida" and "cálida," referring to "una gruta de oro y gemas raras" (278).

5. While Escaja recognizes in Agustini's poem the assertion of poetic authority, her in-

terpretive emphasis is on the fragmentation and reification of woman in the text (73). I believe, however, that the arm and hand that appear in "Ofrendando el libro" do not invoke simply the struggle between dismembered lovers. They allude instead to the act of writing and the access to reconciliation and reintegration through art and passion.

6. Comparing the final line of "Ofrendando el libro" with Darío's "celeste carne de la mujer," Jorge Luis Castillo finds that Agustini resists the paradox of the oxymoron (74) and that she refuses to alter the nature of the categories of the sacred and the profane by melding the two. Cortazzo, on the other hand, sees a vindication of sexuality, that is, a recuperation of its ancient sanctity through which humanity can once again be reconciled with nature, time, and death (204).

7. It appears in the section entitled "Del chorro de la fuente" in the 1952 edition of *Poesías completas* by Aguilar (1035):

> En las constelaciones Pitágoras leía,
> yo en las constelaciones pitagórgicas leo;
> pero se han confundido dentro del alma mía
> el alma de Pitágoras con el alma de Orfeo.
>
> Sé que soy, desde el tiempo del Paraíso, reo;
> sé que he robado el fuego y robé la armonía;
> que es abismo mi alma y huracán mi deseo;
> que sorbo el infinito y quiero todavía . . .
>
> Pero ¿qué voy a hacer, si estoy atado al potro
> en que, ganado el premio, siempre quiero ser otro,
> y en que, dos en mí mismo triunfa uno de los dos?
>
> En la arena me enseña la tortuga de oro
> hacia dónde conduce de las musas el coro
> y en dónde triunfa, augusta, la voluntad de Dios.

8. Escaja draws another parallel between "Tu boca" and "Las alas" by suggesting that the plunge at the end of "Tu boca," like that of the earlier poem, evokes the fall of Icarus (83). While there are some similarities with the myth of Icarus, the differences are more significant. The labors of the lyric voice are performed on rocky soil, not in the creation of wings or in flight. In addition, as the word "pride" in the second line indicates, her undoing results from the effect of her interaction with the poetic other. There is much more of a sense of having been toppled or vanquished than of having simply fallen.

9. Whether Agustini actually wanted to enter into the debate that swirled around the swan and the owl cannot be known. She does, however, draw upon the same avian comparisons. González Martínez's beautifully executed "Tuércele el cuello al cisne . . ." (116) attracted considerable attention from the moment it was published in 1911 because it proposed replacing the modernista swan with the *posmodernista* owl. Whereas the swan's natural, fluid grace embodied for Darío and other modernistas the seamless elegance and har-

mony of the universe, González Martínez sees in it only the hollow and insincere echoes found in the hackneyed, imitative "modernista" poetry that had become common at the time that he was writing. It is this counterfeit, insensitive, and undiscerning swan of deceitfully alluring plumage that he seeks to supplant, for it fails to "hear the soul of things and the voice of the landscape." Though the owl does not have the swan's splendor, it does have the ability to see in the dark and to perceive what others cannot (see my *Modernismo, Modernity*, esp. 95–99).

10. "Si Darío es para el mundo el rey de los poetas, para mi [*sic*] es Dios en el Arte" (*Correspondencia íntima* 46).

11. As noted earlier, Kelly Oliver's redefinition of the Lacanian concept of the mirror state of psychological development coincides with the way in which Agustini's reflective surfaces serve to empower her. Building on Julia Kristeva's position that the individual should embrace otherness as an essential if paradoxical feature of self-consciousness, Oliver holds that it is through representation, talking, and, by extension, writing that self-recognition takes place (96). By writing about the image of herself that she finds in others and their texts Agustini gains increased control over her vision of herself.

Escaja, referring to two poems ("Desde lejos" and "Íntima") from *El libro blanco (Frágil)*, discusses this metaphorical move toward empowerment: "La relación especular de la que la poeta es eje resulta intercambiable, con lo que se subvierte la imagen tradicional de los roles femenino (pasivo-reflejante), y masculino (activo-reflejado). . . . La intercambiabilidad entre el tú reflejado y el yo reflejante permite igualar las dos esferas abisales que se proyectan recíprocamente y que conjugan su dialéctica en el yo del poema" (55). As noted above in chap. 2, n. 40, Escaja acknowledges reflection to be an element in Agustini's empowerment.

The continuing centrality of reflection for women poets has been explored in a recent study by W. Michael Mudrovic. In *Mirror, Mirror on the Page*, he examines how many Spanish women poets of the post-Franco era turn to catoptric imagery in general and to the page as mirror in particular to deal with issues of identity and subjectivity.

12. García Pinto's edition has this line ending with "Con alma," whereas Cáceres's edition, coinciding with the O. M. Bertani edition of 1913, has the line ending with the more logical "Con calma" (287).

13. It is not, as suggested by Castillo, that the face is not hers (77–78). On the contrary, she perceives in the water the tensions of her life.

14. In nineteenth-century poetry and graphic arts the sphinx was one of the great female icons. Linked both to the mysteries of life and to death, it tended to reinforce patriarchal beliefs about the fundamental inscrutability and fatal powers of women. Two examples of Darío's recourse to the sphinx are "Alma mía" (240) from "Las ánforas de Epicuro" in *Prosas profanas* and "Ay, triste del que un día" (284) from *Cantos de vida y esperanza*.

15. Another example of how earlier modernistas addressed similar concerns appears in "Mi verso" by Amado Nervo. In this, the second poem of *Los jardines interiores* (1905), Nervo presents an *ars poetica* in which he sets out to forge verses equal in value and worth to the great artistic achievements of the past. For the Mexican poet the goal is not simply to con-

vert the mundane into the sublime but also to have his verse effectively compete with gold for status and esteem in the materialistic context of the day:

> Querría que mi verso, de guijarro,
> en gema se trocase y en joyero;
> que fuera entre mis manos como el barro
> en la mano genial del alfarero.
>
> Que lo mismo que el barro, que a los fines
> del artífice pliega sus arcillas,
> fuese cáliz de amor en los festines
> y lámpara de aceite en las capillas.
>
> Que, dócil a mi afán, tomase todas
> las formas que mi numen ha soñado,
> siendo alianza en el rito de las bodas,
> pastoral en el índex del prelado;
>
> .   .   .   .
>
> Yo trabajo, mi fe no se mitiga,
> y, troquelando estrofas con mi sello,
> un verso acuñaré del que se diga:
> Tu verso es como el oro sin la liga:
> radiante, dúctil, poliforme y bello. (2: 1533-34)

16. While others have examined this poem in considerable detail, only Escaja has observed what for me is the crucial element of the poem, what she defines as the allegorization of poetic construction (89). Armstrong (77–83) examines the binomial structure and dialectic between the "you" and the "I" of the poem. She focuses in particular on the phrase "el profundo espejo del deseo" and the ultimate return to "la sombra y la soledad del vacío existencial" (83). Zapata begins with the snake and other animals that appear in the fifth section and insists that "se nos hace muy difícil considerar su erotismo como trascendental y místico, ya que en esencia sentimos la presencia de la fuerza instintiva y feroz del animal, lo que ella a su vez quiere equiparar con la voluptuosidad" (108–18). Castillo finds a feminization of traditional Western dichotomies (75–76). Bruzelius studies "Visión" as one Agustini's "vampiric" poems. Though I believe that this focus is misleading, her conclusions correctly underscore Agustini's struggle to reconfigure dominant images of women. She writes, "But in her conflation of the image of the dark lover who is associated with bats and night with the story of the god/swan of Leda, Agustini has written the female answer to the swan written by Darío and the French symbolists and given a parodic twist to the image of the fatal woman" (62).

17. Olivera-Williams finds in this undermining of the image of passivity the key both to her interpretation of "Visión" and to Agustini's poetics. She states, "Agustini succeeds in recreating ironically the passive image of woman in order to subvert it and transform it into

the woman creator of her own muse. The male other-lover is the source of her poetry, the impulse of her writing, but he is created by her. Here, in my opinion, lies the main difference between the 'female muse' of the male poet, let's say Darío, and Agustini's male muse. For Darío the female muse corresponds to the primary signified, the mother, in the symbolic order of language. She exists as the seed of language, although she is mute and she only germinates through union with the male poet. She germinates and language is born in him, the bearer of language. Agustini's muse does not preexist her language. Agustini creates the muse as 'other' in the moment that she speaks/writes, liberating herself from the symbolic order that constrains the male poet" (159–60).

18. The conversion of the lover into a source of salvation (holy bread, Eucharist, sacred wine) is not uncommon among male writers as well. The most famous example in Darío's work is found in "¡Carne, celeste carne de la mujer! . . ." (280–81).

19. In an unrelated but interesting coincidence, Mary Wollstonecraft used a similar biological metaphor, which Gordon finds to be essential to the earlier crusader's perspective on new rights and new roles for women. In 1787 she wrote in a letter to her sister Everina "I am . . . going to be the first of a new genus—I tremble at the attempt" (quoted in *Mary Wollstonecraft: A New Genus* by Lyndall Gordon, v).

20. Because of the unequivocal nature of these images, both Armstrong (87–88) and Escaja (97, 111) acknowledge that Agustini is writing about the creative process in this poem.

21. M. H. Abrams explains: "Plotinus' solution to this problem [multiplicity and evil] follows from the concept traditionally named 'emanation'—perhaps the most seminal of the radical metaphors of metaphysical thinking. The categories of emanation are derived from analogy with the spring which overflows, or the fire which radiates heat and light, or (in Shelley's fusion of both of Plotinus' figures) the 'burning fountain' from which everything flows and which is 'the fire for which all thirst.' According to Plotinus, the undifferentiated One, by virtue of the very fullness of its perfection, overflows (without diminution of itself) into an other, and so on into all existing things, through a series of states, or 'hypostases'— first, mind (including the totality of the fixed Platonic forms), then soul (including all levels of individual souls), and at the farthest possible limit, the material universe" (*Natural Supernaturalism* 147).

22. Seeing the fusion of creator and creation as an end in itself, Armstrong contends that both the poem and the fountain are "closed" (sealed) by the feat that is achieved (88).

23. Despite the fact that Armstrong recognizes the centrality of poetic aspirations in "El surtidor de oro," she returns to the theme of love when discussing this poem. Specifically in reference to line 15, "Y desde entonces muerdo soñando un corazón," she states, "Por lo tanto, mira hacia el más allá, que para este yo es el de la imposibilidad de ser correspondido. O sea, metafóricamente, debe participar de la frigidez del tú y mirar hacia la muerte misma" (89–90). Escaja also reverts to a sexual interpretation (109). Surprisingly, Zapata, who consistently stresses Agustini's declarations of erotic independence, finds in "Fiera de amor" suggestions of the literary vocation that, according to her, the poet turns to in the face of the loneliness imposed by her unique position (114).

24. This substance reappears in the very short "Ceguera" (249), the next poem in the collection, as a star that both protects and blinds. The light that watches over the lyric voice also erases the world, eradicating the banalities and trivialities of life that are not associated with her "astral" mission.

25. "Rompen con Darío usando su texto, no desechándolo, vaciando signos para cargarlos según otras pulsiones. No en vano pertenecen estos dos poemas a *Los cálices vacíos*, título que ya anuncia, al recordar los cálices 'llenos' de Darío—*Las ánforas de Epicuro*, por ejemplo—, el propósito divergente inquisidor de los textos que encabeza" (64).

26. While Castillo and I agree on this particular point, I disagree strongly with his conclusion that the flight of the bleeding swan represents a departure from writing (80).

27. This interpretation coincides with Molloy's. She suggests that one read "Nocturno" "como respuesta, violenta e iconoclasta, a un maestro de cuya poesía se separaba" (69).

28. In a very different interpretation, Peters does not see any relationships in this poem. Instead she believes that the two swans are two aspects of Agustini's own self or, in other words, that they represent the body/soul divide that is conquered by what Peters holds to be Agustini's unique type of mystical transcendence (165).

29. Molloy acknowledges this aspect of the poem. She writes, "La lectura del cisne que propone Agustini es tan sacrílega como el célebre soneto de González Martínez, publicado tres años antes" (63). I believe that Agustini's reading is much more sacrilegious. González Martínez reaffirms modernismo's fundamental tenets, criticizing those who have been tempted by the allure of false beauty. Agustini fights against male hegemony embedded in modernista tenets and for the truth as she perceives it.

30. M. H. Abrams, in his comprehensive study of romantic literary theory *The Mirror and the Lamp*, uses these metaphors to discuss the transformation in concepts regarding the role of the mind in literary production. He writes, "The change from imitation to expression, and from the mirror to the fountain, the lamp, and related analogues, was not an isolated phenomenon. It was an integral part of a corresponding change in popular epistemology—that is, in the concept of the role played by the mind in perception which was current among romantic poets and critics. And the movement from eighteenth- to early nineteenth-century schemes of the mind and its place in nature is indicated by a mutation of metaphors almost exactly parallel to that in contemporary discussions of the nature of art" (57).

31. Trambaioli points instead to Darío's short poem "Plegaria" as a point of comparison. Though the images of hardness are similar to those in Agustini's poem, the issues are quite different. As the poem indicates, Darío's primary concern is with death. Echoing the vision contained in "Lo fatal," he prefers the hardness of the rock because it is less aware of and less responsible for its fate. "Plegaria" appears among the uncollected poems from "Del chorro de la fuente" (1106) that Alfonso Méndez Plancarte included in his edition, poems that were not included in the Ayacucho edition. Trambaioli is correct, however, in asserting that in her "Plegaria" Agustini indicates that her inspiration comes not from "el

depurado mundo de la belleza helénica sino en la existencia en sus aspectos más concretos, el erotismo en primer lugar" (60).

32. Jill S. Kuhnheim, in tracing the influence Agustini had on the poetry of Olga Orozco, stresses the many levels on which these metaphors work. Kuhnheim focuses on how both poets struggle with what they find to be the empty, stale, and sepulchral qualities of established concepts of formal beauty and how both seek to revitalize from a woman's perspective the inherited forms of patriarchal tradition. Following the example set by Agustini, Orozco alters the constructs of her "fathers" and engages in a "paradoxical positioning," the term Kuhnheim uses to refer to the process by which she situates herself as both outcast from and participant in a predominantly male-defined poetic heritage (24).

33. Armstrong phrases this conclusion a bit differently, limiting its implications to sexual behavior. She writes, "En 'Plegaria' Delmira expone las limitaciones y las restricciones impuestas a la mujer por el decoro imperante de la época" (95). Cortazzo also sees only one dimension to this complex poem: "Este poema, más allá de su alta densidad simbólica, puede leerse como un auténtico manifiesto de liberación sexual. El orar de Delmira Agustini no está orientado a lograr la comunicación con el mundo ultraterreno, sino que es una petición para que se desencadenen las fuerzas eróticas contra aquellos que se resisten a comulgar sexualmente: calma, pureza, espiritualidad, moral, castidad, eternidad, son esos los valores de la torre en que el varón ha aprisionado a la sociedad toda y que aquí aparece como el 'mirador enhiesto del orgullo'" (203–4).

Chapter Five. Aspirations and Abiding Disappointments

1. I agree with Alejandro Cáceres that this is the appropriate title for Agustini's final collection. Cáceres's conclusion is supported by extensive archival research: "Mi investigación de tantos años ya, en la obra de la poeta, me induce a pensar que *El rosario de Eros* no es el título de su obra póstuma sino un subtítulo dentro de un libro de poemas titulado *Los astros del abismo*. Recordemos que Delmira Agustini ya había incluido secciones con subtítulos en su primer y tercer libro: *Orla rosa,* y *Lis púrpura* y *De fuego, de sangre y de sombra* respectivamente. En mi opinión considero que Agustini, al morir, estaba preparando un nuevo libro de poesía llamado *Los astros del abismo*—ya anunciado en dos oportunidades, en 1910 y en 1913—consistente en un grupo de varios poemas, más una sección final que, bajo el subtítulo *El rosario de Eros*, contenía cinco poemas, cada uno escrito sobre uno de los cinco misterios del rosario" ("Notas del editor," 6).

2. Magdalena García Pinto, who follows the traditional use of the title *El rosario de Eros* to refer to Agustini's fourth volume of verse, explains how "Los astros de abismo" became *El rosario de Eros:* "En 1924, diez años después de la muerte de la poeta, su familia autorizó a Maximino García, editor, la publicación de *Obras Completas* de Delmira Agustini. Tomo I. *El rosario de Eros;* tomo II. *Los astros del abismo.* La edición fue dirigida por el escritor Vicente Salaverry. . . . La edición de 1924 . . . es importante porque, además de la obra ya publicada de Agustini, se incluye por primera vez los poemas inéditos que abren el tomo I bajo

el título «El rosario de Eros» con diecisiete poemas. Con esta edición revisada por Santiago Agustini, el padre, y Antonio Agustini, su hermano, quedan publicados casi todos los textos de la poeta uruguaya" (45–46). Both the edition by Cáceres and the one by García Pinto follow the same order of presentation. The only difference is that Cáceres places the five poems based on the mysteries of the rosary at the end and García Pinto has them come first.

3. "Yo he dicho, en la misa rosa de mi juventud, mis antífonas, mis secuencias, mis profanas prosas. . . . Tocad, campanas de oro, campanas de plata; tocad todos los días, llamándome a la fiesta en que brillan los ojos de fuego, y las rosas de las bocas sangran delicias únicas" (*Poesía*, 180).

4. The García Pinto edition of Agustini's poetry has the line "Nevad a mí los lises hondos de vuestra alma" (277). Cáceres has "Elevad" as the first word of that line (373).

5. Cáceres's edition separates the last three lines of verse into a separate stanza, a pattern followed by the next three poems. I use here both his formatting and his final line, which differs from the one published by García Pinto, "¡Tú me los des, Dios mío!" (373).

6. I follow here the stanzaic structure that appears in Cáceres's edition (375).

7. I use here the verse that appears in Cáceres's edition (346), a verse that is more grammatically consistent than the one in the García Pinto edition, "En todas, ellas puede engarzar un sueño."

8. Again with this line I use the punctuation from the Cáceres edition (347), which in the García Pinto edition is missing altogether.

9. The comma that appears in the Cáceres edition (348) appears to be more appropriate than the period of the García Pinto edition.

10. See also Visca's prologue to Agustini's *Correspondencia íntima*, 14.

11. Darío's sonnet is as follows:

> Hermano, tú que tienes la luz, dime la mía.
> Soy como un ciego. Voy sin rumbo y ando a tientas.
> Voy bajo tempestades y tormentas,
> ciego de ensueño y loco de armonía.
>
> Ese es mi mal. Soñar. La poesía
> es la camisa férrea de mil puntas cruentas
> que llevo sobre el alma. Las espinas sangrientas
> dejan caer las gotas de mi melancolía.
>
> Y así voy, ciego y loco, por este mundo amargo;
> a veces me parece que el camino es muy largo,
> y a veces que es muy corto . . .
>
> Y en este titubeo de aliento y agonía,
> cargo lleno de penas lo que apenas soporto.
> ¿No oyes caer las gotas de mi melancolía? (286)

12. See, for example, Karen Peña, "Violence and Difference in Gabriela Mistral's Short Stories (1904–1911)."

13. George Yúdice compares Storni's poetry with Neruda's in an approach reminiscent of Johnson's, showing how different criteria are applied to men and women. His conclusion, while similar to Johnson's, highlights the critical predisposition to give male writers greater latitude. He states, "En el caso de los hombres que han hecho poesía a partir de su particular dilema sexual, la crítica no ha considerado necesario abandonar el critero autonomista para apreciar su poeticidad" (187).

WORKS CITED

Abrams, Meyer Howard. *The Mirror and the Lamp: Romantic Theory and the Critical Tradition*. London: Oxford University Press, 1971.

———. *Natural Supernaturalism: Tradition and Revolution in Romantic Literature*. New York: Norton, 1971.

Agustini, Delmira. *Correspondencia íntima*. Edited by Arturo Sergio Visca. Montevideo, Biblioteca Nacional, 1969.

———. *Poesías completas*. Edited by Alejandro Cáceres. Montevideo: Ediciones de la Plaza, 1999.

———. *Poesías completas*. Edited by Magdalena García Pinto. Madrid: Ediciones Cátedra, 2000.

———. *Selected Poetry of Delmira Agustini: Poetics of Eros*. Edited and translated by Alejandro Cáceres. Foreword by Willis Barnstone. Carbondale: Southern Illinois University Press, 2003.

Armstrong, Maria-Elena Barreiro de. "Puente de luz: Eros, eje de la estructura pendular en 'Los cálices vacíos' de Delmira Agustini." Ph.D. diss., Middlebury College, 1996. Ann Arbor: UMI, 1997. AAT 9701020.

———. *Puente de luz: Eros, eje de la estructura pendular en "Los cálices vacíos" de Delmira Agustini*. Kassel, Germany: Edition Reichenberger, 1998.

Aronna, Michael. *"Pueblos Enfermos": The Discourse of Illness in the Turn-of-the-Century*

Spanish and Latin American Essay. Chapel Hill: North Carolina Studies in the Romance Languages and Literatures, 1999.

Barrán, José Pedro. *El disciplinamiento (1860-1920)*. Vol. 2 of *Historia de la sensibilidad en el Uruguay*. 2 vols. Montevideo: Ediciones de la Banda Oriental, 1991.

Barrán, José Pedro, Gerardo Caetano, and Teresa Porzecanski, eds. *Historias de la vida privada en el Uruguay: El nacimiento de la intimidad, 1870-1920*. Vol. 2. Montevideo: Ediciones Santillana, 1996.

Barrios Pintos, Aníbal. *La Ciudad Nueva: El Centro de Montevideo*. Montevideo: Intendencia Municipal de Montevideo, 2001.

———. *Montevideo: Los barrios*. 2 vols. Montevideo: Editorial Nuestra Tierra, 1971.

Beaupied, Aída. "Otra lectura de 'El cisne' de Delmira Agustini." *Letras femeninas* 22.1-2 (1996): 131-42.

Bécquer, Gustavo Adolfo. *Rimas, leyendas y narraciones*. Mexico City: Editorial Porrúa, 1968.

Bloom, Harold. *The Anxiety of Influence: A Theory of Poetry*. New York: Oxford University Press, 1973.

Bosteels, Bruno. "Más allá de Ariel y Calibán: Notas para una crítica de la razón cultural." In *Delmira Agustini y el Modernismo: Nuevas propuestas de género*, ed. Tina Escaja, 78-106. Rosario, Argentina: Beatriz Viterbo Editora, 2000.

Bruña Bragado, María José. *Cómo leer a Delmira Agustini: Algunas claves críticas*. Madrid: Editorial Verbum, 2008.

Bruzelius, Margaret. "'En el profundo espejo del deseo': Delmira Agustini, Rachilde, and the Vampire." *Revista Hispánica Moderna* 46.1 (June 1993): 51-64.

———. "Mother's Pain, Mother's Voice: Gabriela Mistral, Julia Kristeva, and the Mater Dolorosa." *Tulsa Studies in Women's Literature* 18.2 (Autumn, 1999): 215-33.

Burt, John R. "Agustini's Muse." *Chasqui* 17.1 (1988): 61-65.

———. "The Personalization of Classical Myth in Delmira Agustini." *Crítica Hispánica* 9.1-2 (1987): 115-24.

Cáceres, Alejandro. "Doña María Murfeldt Triaca de Agustini: Hipótesis de un secreto." In *Delmira Agustini: Nuevas penetraciones críticas*, ed. Uruguay Cartazzo, 13-47. Montevideo: Vintén Editor, 1996.

———, ed. and trans. *Selected Poetry of Delmira Agustini: Poetics of Eros*. Foreword by Willis Barnstone. Carbondale: Southern Illinois University Press, 2003.

Cáceres, Zoila Aurora. "La emancipación de la mujer." *Búcaro americano*, May 1896. In *Vestales del templo azul: Notas sobre el feminismo hispanoamericano en la época modernista*, introd. Ivan A. Schulman, 104-7. Toronto: Canadian Academy of the Arts, 1996.

Caetano, Gerardo, and Roger Geymonat. *La secularización uruguaya (1859-1919)*.

Vol. 1: *Catolicismo y privatización de lo religioso*. Montevideo: Ediciones Santillana, 1997.

Calinescu, Matei. *Five Faces of Modernity: Modernism, Avant-Garde, Decadence, Kitsch, Postmodernism*. Durham: Duke University Press, 1987.

Casal, Julián del. *The Poetry of Julián del Casal: A Critical Edition*. Edited by Robert Jay Glickman. 2 vols. Gainesville: University Presses of Florida, 1976–78.

Castillo, Debra A. *Talking Back: Toward a Latin American Feminist Literary Criticism*. Ithaca: Cornell University Press, 1992.

Castillo, Jorge Luis. "Delmira Agustini o el modernismo subversivo." *Chasqui* 27.2 (1998): 70–84.

Castro-Klarén, Sara. "Introduction to Part 1, Women, Self, and Writing," In *Women's Writing in Latin America: An Anthology*, 3–26. Boulder: Westview Press, 1991.

Castro-Klarén, Sara, Sylvia Molloy, and Beatriz Sarlo, eds. *Women's Writing in Latin America: An Anthology*. Boulder: Westview Press, 1991.

Chemris, Crystal. "Continuities of Góngora in Darío's Swan Poems: On the Poetics of Rape, Colonialism and Modernity." *Calíope* 16.2 (2010): 75–94.

Cortazzo, Uruguay. "Delmira Agustini: Hacia una visión sexo-política." In *Delmira Agustini y el Modernismo: Nuevas propuesta de género*, ed. Tina Escaja, 195–204. Rosario, Argentina: Beatriz Viterbo Editora, 2000.

———. "¿Dónde está la concha de Delmira Agustini?" *La oreja cortada* 2 (Montevideo 1988): 25–27.

———. "Una hermenéutica machista: Delmira Agustini en la crítica de Alberto Zum Felde." In *Delmira Agustini: Nuevas penetraciones críticas*, ed. Uruguay Cartazzo, 48–71. Montevideo: Vintén Editor, 1996.

Cróquer Pedrón, Eleonora. "Una 'esfinge de color de rosa': Delmira Agustini, esta advenediza . . . ese resto." *Revista canadiense de estudios hispánicos* 28.1 (Fall 2003): 191–213.

Cuevas García, Cristóbal, and Enrique Baena, eds. *Bécquer: Origen y estética de la modernidad. Actas del VII Congreso de Literatura Española Contemporánea*. Málaga: Publicaciones del Congreso de Literatura Española Contemporánea, 1995.

Darío, Rubén. "La mujer española." In *España contemporánea. Obras completas*, 3: 355–65. Madrid: Afrodisio Aguado, 1950.

———. "El pájaro azul." *Cuentos completos*. Edited and annotated by Ernesto Mejía Sánchez. Introduction by Raimundo Lida. Mexico: Fondo de Cultura Económica, 1950.

———. *Poesía*. Caracas: Biblioteca Ayacucho, 1977.

———. *Poesías completas*. Edited by Alfonso Méndez Plancarte. Augmented by Antonio Oliver Belmás. Madrid: Aguilar, 1968.

Dierkes-Thrun, Petra. "The Salomé Theme in the Wake of Oscar Wilde: Transformative Aesthetics of Sexuality in Modernity." 2003. Ann Arbor: UMI. AAT 3117761.

Dijkstra, Bram. *Evil Sisters: The Threat of Female Sexuality and the Cult of Manhood.* New York: Alfred A. Knopf, 1996.

East, Linda Kay Davis. "The Imaginary Voyage: Evolution of the Poetry of Delmira Agustini." Ph.D. diss., Stanford University, 1981. Ann Arbor: UMI, 1981. AAT 8108918.

Ehrick, Christine. "De Delmira a Paulina: Erotismo, racionalidad y emancipación femenina en el Uruguay, 1890–1930." In *Delmira Agustini y el Modernismo: Nuevas propuestas de género,* ed. Tina Escaja, 228–43. Rosario, Argentina: Beatriz Viterbo Editora, 2000.

Escaja, Tina Fernandez. "La lengua en la rosa: Dialéctica del deseo en la obra de Delmira Agustini." Ph.D. diss., University of Pennsylvania, 1993. Ann Arbor: UMI, 1993. AAT 9331772.

———. *Salomé decapitada: Delmira Agustini y estética finisecular de la fragmentación.* Amsterdam: Rodopi, 2001.

Esteban, Angel. *Bécquer en Martí y en otros poetas hispanoamericanos finiseculares.* Madrid: Editorial Verbum, 2003.

Felski, Rita. *The Gender of Modernity.* Cambridge: Harvard University Press, 1995.

Fitzgibbon, Russell H. *Uruguay: Portrait of a Democracy.* New York: Russell and Russell, 1966.

Frederick, Bonnie. *Wily Modesty: Argentine Women Writers, 1860–1910.* Tempe: Arizona State University, 1998.

García Pinto, Magdalena. "Introduction." *Poesías completas* by Delmira Agustini. Madrid: Ediciones Cátedra, 2000.

Genovese, Alicia. *La doble voz: Poetas argentinas contemporáneos.* Buenos Aires: Biblos, 1998.

Giaudrone, Carla Elena. *La degeneración del 900: Modelos estético-sexuales de la cultura en el Uruguay del Novecientos.* Montevideo: Ediciones Trilce, 2004.

———. "Deseo y modernización: El modernismo canónico esteticista en el fin de siglo uruguayo." In *Uruguay: Imaginarios culturales: Desde las huellas indígenas a la modernidad,* ed. Hugo Achugar and Mabel Moraña, 259–92. Pittsburgh: Instituto Internacional de Literatura Iberoamericana, 2000.

———. "Modernismo y modelos estético-sexuales de la cultura: La degeneración del Novecientos." Ph.D. diss., New York University, 2003. Ann Arbor: UMI, 2003. AAT 3075499.

Gilbert, Sandra M., and Susan Gubar. *The Madwoman in the Attic: The Woman*

Writer and the Nineteenth-Century Literary Imagination. New Haven: Yale University Press, 1979.

Gilman, Stephen. "El *Proemio* de *La voz a ti debida*." *Asomante* 19.3 (1963): 7–15.

Girón Alvarado, Jacqueline. "Voz poética y máscaras femeninas en la obra de Delmira Agustini." Ph.D. diss., Pennsylvania State University, 1993. Ann Arbor: UMI, 1994. AAT 9334741.

———. *Voz poética y máscaras femeninas en la obra de Delmira Agustini*. New York: Peter Lang, 1995.

Giucci, Guillermo. *Fiera de amor: La otra muerte de Delmira Agustini*. Montevideo: Vintén Editor, 1995.

Glickman, Robert Jay. *Fin del siglo: Retrato de Hispanoamérica en la época modernista*. Toronto: Canadian Academy of the Arts, 1999.

———. *Vestales del templo azul: Notas sobre el feminismo hispanoamericano en la época modernista*. Introduction by Ivan A. Schulman. Toronto: Canadian Academy of the Arts, 1996.

González Echevarría, Roberto. "Martí y su 'Amor de ciudad grande': Notas hacia la poética de *Versos libres*." In *Isla a su vuelo fugitiva: Ensayos críticos sobre literatura hispanoamericana*, 27–42. Madrid: José Porrúa Turanzas, 1983.

———. "Oye mi son: El canon cubano." *Encuentro de la Cultura Cubana* 33 (Summer 2004): 5–18.

González Martínez, Enrique. *Obras completas*. Edited and annotated with a prologue by Antonio Castro de Leal. Mexico City: Colegio Nacional, 1971.

Gordon, Lyndall. *Mary Wollstonecraft: A New Genus*. London: Little Brown, 2005.

Gubar, Susan. "'The Blank Page' and the Issues of Female Creativity." In *Writing and Sexual Difference*, ed. Elizabeth Abel, 73–93. Chicago: University of Chicago Press, 1982.

Gutiérrez Nájera, Manuel. *Obras: Estudios y antología general*. Edited by José Luis Martínez. Mexico City: Fondo de Cultura Económica, 2003.

Herrera y Reissig, Julio. *El pudor. La cachondez*. Edited by Carla Giaudrone and Nilo Berriel. Montevideo: ARCA Editorial, 1992.

James, William. *Dependence, Independence, and Death: Toward a Psychobiography of Delmira Agustini*. New York: Peter Lang, 2009.

Jrade, Cathy L. *Modernismo, Modernity, and the Development of Spanish American Literature*. Austin: University of Texas Press, 1998.

———. *Rubén Darío and the Romantic Search for Unity: The Modernist Recourse to Esoteric Tradition*. Austin: University of Texas Press, 1983.

Johnson, Barbara. "Gender and Poetry: Charles Baudelaire and Marceline Desbordes-Valmore." In *The Feminist Difference: Literature, Psychoanalysis, Race, and Gender*, 101–28. Cambridge: Harvard University Press, 1998.

Kirkpatrick, Gwen. "The Limits of Modernismo: Delmira Agustini and Julio Herrera y Reissig." *Romance Quarterly* 36.3 (1989): 307–14.

———. "Delmira Agustini y el 'Reino interior' de Rodó y Darío." In *¿Qué es el modernismo?: Nueva encuesta, nuevas lecturas*, ed. Richard A. Cardwell and Bernard McGuirk, 295–306. Boulder: Society of Spanish and Spanish-American Studies, 1993.

———. "'Prodigios de almas y de cuerpos': Delmira Agustini y la Conjuración del Mundo." In *Delmira Agustini y el Modernismo: Nuevas propuestas de género*, ed. Tina Escaja, 228–43. Rosario, Argentina: Beatriz Viterbo Editora, 2000.

Kristeva, Julia. *The Kristeva Reader*. Edited by Toril Moi. New York: Columbia University Press, 1986.

Kuhnheim, Jill S. *Gender, Politics, and Poetry in Twentieth-Century Argentina*. Gainesville: University Press of Florida, 1996.

Larre Borges, Ana Inés. "Delmira Agustini." In *Mujeres uruguayas: El lado femenino de nuestra historia*, ed. Blanca Rodríguez, 15–41. Montevideo: Ediciones Santillana, 1997.

Lasarte Valcárcel, Javier. "Pueblo y mujer: Figuraciones dispares del intelectual modernista. (Martí y González Prada)." In *Delmira Agustini y el Modernismo: Nuevas propuestas de género*, ed. Tina Escaja, 38–54. Rosario, Argentina: Beatriz Viterbo, 2000.

Lerner, Gerda. *The Creation of Patriarchy*. New York: Oxford University Press, 1986.

Lugones, Leopoldo. *Los crepúsculos del jardín*. Buenos Aires: Arnaldo Moen y Hermanos, 1905.

Luisi, Luisa. *A través de libros y de autores*. Buenos Aires: Ediciones de "Nuestra América," 1925.

Machado de Benvenuto, Ofelia. *Delmira Agustini*. Montevideo: Editorial Ceibo, 1944.

Martin, Leona S. "Nation Building, International Travel, and the Construction of the Nineteenth-Century Pan-Hispanic Women's Network." *Hispania* 87.3 (2004): 439–46.

Martínez Moreno, Carlos. *La otra mitad*. Mexico: Joaquín Mortiz, 1966.

Masiello, Francine. *Between Civilization and Barbarism: Women, Nation, and Literary Culture in Modern Argentina*. Lincoln: University of Nebraska Press, 1992.

———, ed. *Dreams and Realities: Selected Fiction of Juana Manuela Gorriti*. Introduction by Fancine Masiello. Oxford: Oxford University Press, 2003.

Matto de Turner, Clorinda. "Las obreras del pensamiento en la América del Sur," *Búcaro americano*, February 1896. In *Vestales del templo azul: Notas sobre el feminismo hispanoamericano en la época modernista*, introd. Ivan A. Schulman, 108–12. Toronto: Canadian Academy of the Arts, 1996.

Méndez Rodenas, Adriana. "Tradition and Women's Writing." In *Engendering the Word*, ed. Temma F. Berg, 29–50. Urbana: University of Illinois Press, 1989.

Merrim, Stephanie. *Early Modern Women's Writing and Sor Juana Inés de la Cruz.* Liverpool: Vanderbilt University Press and Liverpool University Press, 1999.

Meyer, Doris. *Reinterpreting the Spanish American Essay: Women Writers of the 19th and 20th Centuries.* Austin: University of Texas Press, 1995.

Minoli, Raquel. *Tan extraña, tan querida.* Montevideo: Quijote Editores. 2000.

Mistral, Gabriela. *Desolación. Tenura. Tala. Lagar.* Mexico City: Editorial Porrúa, 1998.

Molloy, Sylvia. "Dos lecturas del cisne: Rubén Darío y Delmira Agustini." In *La sartén por el mango*, ed. Patricia Elena González and Eliana Ortega, 57–70. Río Piedras, Puerto Rico: Ediciones Huracán, 1984.

———. "Introduction to Part 2, Female Textual Identities: The Strategies of Self-Figuration." In *Women's Writing in Latin America: An Anthology*, 107–24. Boulder: Westview Press, 1991.

———. "The Politics of Posing." In *Hispanisms and Homosexualities*, ed. Sylvia Molloy and Robert McKee Irwin, 141–60. Durham: Duke University Press, 1998.

———. "Too Wilde for Comfort: Desire and Ideology in Fin-de-Siècle Spanish America." *Social Text* 31–32 (1992): 187–201.

Montero, Oscar. *Erotismo y representación en Julián del Casal.* Amsterdam: Rodopi, 1993.

———. "Modernismo and Homophobia: Darío and Rodó." In *Sex and Sexuality in Latin America*, ed. Daniel Balderston and Donna J. Guy, 101–17. New York: New York University Press, 1997.

Mudrovic, W. Michael. *Mirror, Mirror on the Page: Identity and Subjectivity in Spanish Women's Poetry (1975-2000).* Bethlehem, Penn.: Lehigh University Press, 2008.

Nassaar, Christopher S., and Nataly Shaheen. "Wilde's *Salomé.*" *The Explicator* 59.3 (Spring 2001): 132–34.

Nervo, Amado. *Obras completas.* Edited by Francisco González Guerrero and Alfonso Méndez Plancarte. 2 vols. Madrid: Aguilar, 1956.

O'Connell, Patrick. "Delmira Agustini, Rubén Darío y la 'Tabula Rasa': Sangre, cisne, y creatividad femenina." *Explicación de textos literarios* 26.1 (1997): 72–79.

Oliver, Kelly. *Subjectivity without Subjects: From Abject Fathers to Desiring Mothers.* Lanham, Md.: Rowman and Littlefield, 1998.

Olivera-Williams, María Rosa. "Feminine Voices in Exile." In *Engendering the Word: Feminist Essays in Psychosexual Poetics*, ed. Temma F. Berg, 151–66. Urbana: University of Illinois Press, 1989.

Orgambide, Pedro. *Un amor imprudente.* Bogotá: Editorial Norma, 1994.

Ostriker, Alicia Suskin. *Stealing the Language: The Emergence of Women's Poetry in America*. Boston: Beacon Press, 1986.

————. *Writing Like a Woman*. Ann Arbor: University of Michigan Press, 1983.

Paz, Octavio. *Children of the Mire: Modern Poetry from Romanticism to the Avant-Garde*. Translated by Rachel Phillips. Cambridge: Harvard University Press, 1974.

————. *Los hijos del limo: Del romanticismo a la vanguardia*. Barcelona: Seix Barral, 1974.

Peña, Karen. "Violence and Difference in Gabriela Mistral's Short Stories (1904–1911)." *Latin American Research Review* 40.3 (2005): 68–96.

Peters, Kate. "*Fin de Siglo* Mysticism: Body, Mind, and Transcendence in the Poetry of Amado Nervo and Delmira Agustini." *Indiana Journal of Hispanic Literatures* 8 (1996): 159–76.

Polhemus, Robert M. *Lot's Daughters: Sex, Redemption, and Women's Quest for Authority*. Stanford: Stanford University Press, 2005.

Prego Gadea, Omar. *Delmira*. Madrid: Alfaguara, 1998.

Puentes de Oyenard, Sylvia. "Sicocrítica de 'Fiera de amor' de Delmira Agustini." *Letras Femeninas* 15.1–2 (Spring–Fall 1989): 105–18.

Real de Azúa, Carlos. "Ambiente espiritual del 900." *Número* 2.6–8 (January–June 1950): 15–36.

Renfrew, Nydia Ileana. "La imaginación en la obra de Delmira Agustini." Ph.D. diss., Michigan State University, 1985. Ann Arbor: UMI, 1986. AAT 8603475.

————. *La imaginación en la obra de Delmira Agustini*. Montevideo: Letras Femeninas, 1987.

Rivero, Eliana S. "Scheherazade Liberated: *Eva Luna* and Women Storytellers." In *Splintering Darkness: Latin American Women Writers in Search of Themselves*, ed. and introd. Lucía Guerra Cunningham, 143–56. Pittsburgh: Latin American Literary Review Press, 1990.

Rocca, Pablo. "Mujer y privacidad en la literatura uruguaya (1890–1920)." In *Historias de la vida privada en el Uruguay: El nacimiento de la intimidad, 1870-1920*, vol. 2, ed. José Pedro Barrán, Gerardo Caetano, and Teresa Porzecanski, 147–73. 2 vols. Montevideo: Ediciones Santillana, 1996.

Rodríguez Monegal, Emir. "La Generación del 900." *Número* 2.6–8 (January–June 1950): 37–61.

————. *Sexo y poesía en el 900: Los extraños destinos de Roberto y Delmira*. Montevideo: Editorial Alfa, 1969.

Rosenbaum, Sidonia Carmen. "Modern Woman Poets of Spanish America: The Precursors, Delmira Agustini, Gabriela Mistral, Alfonsina Storni, Juana De Ibarbourou." Ph.D. diss., Columbia University, 1946.

————. *Modern Woman Poets of Spanish America: The Precursors, Delmira Agustini,*

Gabriela Mistral, Alfonsina Storni, Juana De Ibarbourou. Westport, Conn.: Greenwood Press, 1978.

Salaverri, Vicente. *Una mujer inmolada.* Montevideo: Cooperativa Editorial Pegaso, 1914.

Sánz-Mateos, Inmaculada. "En el profundo espejo del deseo: El exilio interior en la poesía de Delmira Agustini." *Exilios femeninos* (2000): 227–34.

Sarlo, Beatriz. "Introduction to Part 3, Women, History, and Ideology." In *Women's Writing in Latin America: An Anthology,* 231–48. Boulder: Westview Press, 1991.

Schinca, Milton. *Delmira y otras rupturas: Teatro.* Montevideo: Ediciones de la Banda Oriental, 1977.

Scott, Jill. *Electra after Freud: Myth and Culture.* Ithaca: Cornell University Press, 2005.

Scott, Renée. "Delmira Agustini: Portraits and Reflections." In *A Dream of Light and Shadow,* ed. by Marjorie Agosín, 253–69. Albuquerque: University of New Mexico Press, 1995.

Selcke, Gretchen. "Delmira Agustini: *Los cálices vacíos* and the Poetic Body." Paper read at conference "Rubén Darío: 90 Years Later." Hofstra University. 24 October 2006.

Showalter, Elaine. *A Literature of Their Own: British Women Novelists from Brontë to Lessing.* Princeton: Princeton University Press, 1999.

Silva, Clara. *Genio y figura de Delmira Agustini.* Buenos Aires: Editorial Universitaria de Buenos Aires, 1968.

———. *Pasión y gloria de Delmira Agustini.* Buenos Aires: Losada, 1972.

Spooner, David. *The Poem and the Insect: Aspects of Twentieth Century Hispanic Culture.* San Francisco: International Scholars Publication, 1999.

Stephens, Doris Thomason. "Delmira Agustini and the Quest for Transcendence." Ph.D. diss., University of Tennessee, 1974. Ann Arbor: UMI, 1974. AAT 7417737.

———. *Delmira Agustini and the Quest for Transcendence.* Montevideo: Ediciones Geminis, 1975.

Storni, Alfonsina. *Antología mayor.* Edited by Jesús Munárriz. Madrid: Ediciones Hiperión, 1997.

Swanson, Philip. "Civilization and Barbarism." In *The Companion to Latin American Studies,* ed. Philip Swanson, 69–85. London: Arnold, 2003.

Tablada, José Juan. *Poesía.* Vol. 1 of *Obras.* Edited by Héctor Valdés. Mexico City: UNAM, 1971.

Taralli, Ricardo Dino. *El amor en la poesía de Delmira Agustini: Referencias especiales.* La Banda, Argentina: Ediciones María Adela Agudo, 1966.

Tarquinio, Laura Teixeira. "La poesía de Delmira Agustini." Ph.D. diss., Stanford University, 1968. Ann Arbor: UMI, 1968. AAT 6908278.

Tiffany, Daniel. *Toy Medium: Materialism and Modern Lyric.* Berkeley: University of California Press, 2000.

Trambaioli, Marcella. "La estatua y el ensueño: Dos claves para la poesía de Delmira Agustini." *Revista Hispánica Moderna* 50.1 (June 1997): 57–66.

Unruh, Vicky. *Performing Women and Modern Literary Culture in Latin America: Intervening Acts.* Austin: University of Texas Press, 2006.

Valenti, Jeanette Yvonne Deguzman. "Delmira Agustini: A Re-interpretation of Her Poetry." Ph.D. diss., Cornell University, 1971. Ann Arbor: UMI, 1971. AAT 7118917.

Varas, Patricia. *Las máscaras de Delmira Agustini.* Montevideo: Vintén Editor, 2002.

Visca, Arturo Sergio, Amanda Berenguer, and José Pedro Díaz. *La poesía de Delmira Agustini.* Montevideo: Fundación de Cultura Universitaria, 1968.

Ware, Barbara Blithe. "Transforming the Gaze: Feminine Validation in Postmodernista Poetry, A Jungian Perspective." Ph.D. diss., Temple University, 2002. Ann Arbor: UMI, 2002. AAT 3057120.

Ycaza Tigerino, Julio. *Los nocturnos de Rubén Darío y otros ensayos.* Madrid: Ediciones Cultura Hispánica, 1964.

Yúdice, George. "La vanguardia a partir de sus exclusiones." In *Carnal Knowledge: Essays on the Flesh, Sex and Sexuality in Hispanic Letters and Film*, ed. Pamela Bacarisse, 183–97. Pittsburgh: Ediciones Tres Ríos, 1991.

Zamora Juárez, Andrés. *El doble silencio del Eunuco: Poéticas sexuales de la novela realista según Clarín.* Madrid: Editorial Fudamentos, 1998.

Zapata de Aston, Arcea Fabiola. "Fuerza erótica y liberación: Un nuevo sujeto femenino en la poesía de Delmira Agustini, Juana de Ibarbourou y Alfonsina Storni." Ph.D. diss., University of Iowa, 2002. Ann Arbor: UMI, 2002. AAT 3052486.

INDEX

Abrams, M. H., 129, 206*n*35, 214*n*16, 231*n*21, 232*n*30

Abyss: of artistic aspiration, 122, 128–30; chalice as, 162; in Darío's poetry, 47, 108, 130; dizziness of, 70; dreams leading to, 176; of light, 108; of marriage, 7; reflection of, 152–53; and search for the soul, 183; "sima" for, 153; spacial and temporal "before" of, 218*n*40; temptress leading to, 184; and title of "Los astros del abismo" (The stars of the abyss), 8, 35, 164–65, 233–34*nn*1–2; of unattainable "Venus," 160, 165; vampire compared with, 161

Agamemnon, 28

Agustini, Delmira: biographical information on, 4–10; birth and childhood of, 4–5; as contributor to *La Alborada* (Daybreak), 5; correspondence by, with Darío, 6–8, 37, 53–54, 134; Darío's endorsement of, 85; divorce by, 8, 9, 191, 203*n*19; education of, 5; engagement of, to Solliers, 202*n*14; family of, 4–5, 9, 29, 54, 201*n*11, 203*n*19, 227*n*3; femininity of, as public persona, 1–2, 5, 7, 8, 193; friendships of, 5–7; and Generation of *1900*, 3; international perspective of, 10, 11; marriage of, 7, 9, 31, 163, 164; masks of personae of, 2, 30, 52, 55, 84, 199–200*n*4; murder of, 1, 9–10, 31, 193–94; novels and plays on, 200, 201*n*9; Reyes as lover of, following their divorce, 1, 8, 9–10; and Ugarte, 5–6, 9, 31–32

Agustini, Delmira, poetic process of: achievements of, x, 1, 37, 193–94; architectural images for building literary career, 187–89; and artistic and spiritual death, 181–83; autonomy and self-confidence as poet, 63, 67–73, 76–78, 82–83, 85–88, 92, 105, 116–17, 123, 140–43, 152, 162–64, 181; and cosmic